Earning a living

Memories of Work in and around Sheffield

A collection of stories and anecdotes of working life from Sheffield, and the changes at work we have all seen over the last 50 years

Volume II

**by
The Memories of Work group**

Earning a Living - Volume II

The Sheffield Branch of the WEA
(Workers' Educational Association) is very
pleased to endorse this publication; surely
none of us who live in Sheffield can fail to
find pleasure and fascination in reading it.
The dedication and enthusiasm of the
"Memories of Work Group" is an example
to all of us who aim to enrich lives through
learning in communities.

John Wills
Chairman, Sheffield Branch

ISBN: 9780900823879

© Memories of Work Group, 2009

Workers' Educational Association
Yorkshire & Humber Region
3 Vicarage Road, Attercliffe, Sheffield S9 3RH
Tel: 0114 242 3609
www.wea.org.uk/yh

The Workers' Educational Association (WEA) is a charity registered in England and Wales
(number 1112775) and in Scotland (number SC039239) and a company limited by guarantee registered in
England and Wales (number 2806910).

"This book does not claim to be anything so dignified as history. It is only a gathering together of the various threads out of which history is woven – threads which, if not seized and put into tangible shape, quickly escape altogether."

From

"Reminiscences of Old Sheffield, its streets and its people"

Edited by Robert Eadon Leader, published in 1875

Introduction to volume II

Sixty more tales of working life in and around Sheffield.

"I feel right proud about being in the book, what I like about it is – that all your life you're a number, you start work and you get a clock number, you join the Army, and you get a number, you leave school and get a National Insurance number, but now my name means something, it's like being a celebrity." Sid Morton.

"All round Broad Lane, Solly Street, Garden Street, there were little forges and cutlery works. This was in the 1950s and 60s. I couldn't imagine that one day none of them would be there." Ann Udall.

The stories in this second volume are told by all kinds of people. They include nurses, waitresses, train drivers, a drop stamper, hospital cleaners, silverware buffers, electroplaters, a sign writer, coal miners, policemen, library staff, the list goes on. Many of the stories have been written by the contributors themselves.

Making sure these memories are preserved is the reason for this book. Sheffield, has gone through an extraordinary period of change since the 1940s, from being a major world centre of cutlery and hand tool manufacture, a city where thousands of men and women, many of them highly skilled, if without paper qualifications, were employed by the steel and heavy engineering industry, to what? We're not sure yet.

As a manufacturing city, Sheffield is a particularly sharp example of the changes taking place in the British economy, and in the kinds of jobs our children will go into.

Other workplaces have also changed enormously, none more so than newspaper production, and hospitals. This book includes these stories as well.

How did we find these stories?

We asked friends, neighbours, colleagues, and relatives to write or tell us their memoirs. We advertised in libraries, doctors' surgeries, in sheltered accommodation for the elderly, at the

Sheffield Pensioners' Action Group, on Radio Sheffield, in The Sheffield Star, for people to tell us about their memories of their working lives. We also visited the Black Elders' lunch club, and the Yemeni Community Association.

Of course there are gaps. We would have liked to hear from workers at the large bakeries, the markets, from the surgical instrument industry, or from painters and decorators. So this is not a full picture, nor a carefully balanced picture, but it is a very wide picture. About half the stories are from women, which is unusual for a book about work. All kinds of people got in touch with us, and we were fascinated by their tales.

To our surprise most people had had a variety of jobs, many finishing their working lives in a job totally different from their first one. After a lot of discussion, we decided to keep each person's story all together in one place, and then fit each one into a chapter that described at least part of their working life. It has been thought provoking to read about a silverware buffer who became a silver service waitress, a waitress who went into engineering, and a train driver who later worked for the library service.

We have gathered so much material, that this is the promised volume II of a two volume book.

What people said about volume I
The wife of one of the contributors said, *"I never knew the half of what he did at work, and I never knew he felt so passionate about it."*

"You can pick something up and it doesn't enter your head how it is made."

"It is an unusual book, as it tells us about work from the workers' point of view."

In particular this volume describes the closing down, of a famous Sheffield silverware firm, of a well known precision tools firm, and of some local coal mines, from the point of view of the men and women who worked there.

"To see my father's picture actually in a book, and the lovely photo of 'D' quite overwhelms me."

"Reading the book made me cry."

"Your book is fun, and we read bits of it out to each other." A young couple.

"The Memories of Work group have produced a warm, accurate and intense account of the way we worked, which is a joy to read." Joe Ashton.

We are extremely grateful to all the contributors for sharing their memories and their reflections with us. The workplace can be a secretive place, and we tend to forget that what we take for granted as a daily routine, makes up a fascinating patchwork picture of changes at work in Sheffield in the last 60 years or so. We thank you for helping to create this record of a passing way of life.

Finally, the best words come from the narrators themselves.
"Work was a very serious business with my uncle, no skylarking, or playing the fool, too many accidents to avoid and so much to learn."

"As a newcomer I started at the bottom, literally, as I scrubbed the floors"

"My dad did not agree with all that pen pushing and wanted me to have a trade."

"From what I hear about recruitment now, none of us would have would have had a chance, you need a degree."

"In the 1960s in Sheffield there were 60,000 people who started work before 6 am."

"Another sight, which was very common in Sheffield at the time was the 'King Coal' symbol on coal lorries, all painted by hand."

"Seniority was everything at British Rail."

"This was dealt with by one man, who specialised in flicking the foreign body off the eyeball, using a sharpened matchstick."

"First thing in the morning after breakfast we had to pull all the beds onto the open air verandas."

"We had the best collection of books on steel-making in the whole of Sheffield."

"Having acquired the ability to hand draw lettering, it soon became apparent that technology was about to do away with the need for it".

"Maybe I'll settle down one day, but not yet."

"A tradition was observed every New Year's Eve. It was called 'Banging in the New Year'. On the stroke of midnight, everyone picked up something to beat, buckets, trays, tools...."

The Memories of Work Group, April 2009

Tony Allen, Ralph Basford, Irene Davy, Naomi Brent, Carl Middleton and John Nettleship

The Memories of Work Group

We started meeting in September 2005 as a WEA study group, some people joined the group later, and others dropped out. We spent until December 2007 collecting stories, and since then three of us have been arranging this material into the eighteen chapters we now have.

It has been interesting and enjoyable work. We have met all kinds of people, and learnt about all kinds of trades and professions, from waitressing to foundry work, from delivering the post to spectacle lens grinding.

We have been reminded of the optimism of the great efforts made to rebuild the city of Sheffield not only from the ravages of the war, but also from the terrible effects of the economic depression of the 1930s. Many of the stories paint a picture of a level of poverty our children will find hard to believe. But these are stories of survival and fun in spite of hardship and some very harsh working conditions.

Acknowledgements

With many, many thanks to Sheffield Occupational Health Advisory Service for their friendly support, both for their interest, and in a most practical way, by providing a meeting room, address, email, storage space and the use of a computer for three years. SOHAS have also donated money raised for them by the Workers' Beer Company to help with production costs.

We also thank David Pittaway of the WEA, who has prepared the book for printing, and has also given much appreciated advice, information, and moral support.

Sheffield City Library Service have been very welcoming, and helped us arrange meetings at Firth Park, Highfield, Jordanthorpe, Woodseats and Ecclesall Libraries, as well as including us in their 'Off the Shelf' events.

Douglas Hindmarch and his colleagues at Sheffield Local Studies Library, have been most helpful and very patient in answering all our questions.

Photos of Barrie Sheedy, Les Middleton, Christine Deakin, Opening of Greenhill Library, courtesy of Sheffield Newspapers, Ltd.

Other photos were lent to us by the contributors, or were taken by Tony Allen, John Nettleship, and Naomi Brent.

Capstan lathe operators at English Steel
Lillian Nawrocki's story is in volume I

Contents
Volume II

9

Contents

Getting to work on time
Buses, trams, and the railways

The Mill
by Sydney Morton

The rumble and rattle of a tram going down the hill,
Will surely take a young lad to the mill.
At the plate end, he stands alone, no time to chuckle,
Hot air, hot bars and a mallet, to hit a knuckle,
The conveyer starts, a 300 pounder is on its way,
Red hot as fury, you see this, you don't want to stay,
Your hands are blistered, you try to be brave,
You are captured, you feel like a slave.
Keep yourself fit, the job makes you dance,
Miss a bar, you're in trouble, you take that chance,
Lad, get used to the heat, the sweat and the smell,
At the end of the shift, you've been through hell.

In the 1960s, as Mirza Salim tells us 'In Sheffield there were 60,000 people who started work before 6 am.'

During the forties and fifties people walked or cycled to work, or went to work by bus or tram.

It was during the 70s that people started using their own car to drive themselves to work. Since then car use has grown and grown, people travel further to work, and the road network has expanded. Traffic congestion and the pollution it causes, has always been a problem in cities, and now in the twenty first century there are attempts to encourage the use again of buses, trams, and trains to get to work.

Until the deregulation of the buses in 1986, bus fares were cheap, famously so in South Yorkshire during the 70s, when Sheffield, Barnsley and Doncaster, as South Yorkshire Transport, subsidised bus fares. "Five pence to get to the city centre, two pence for the kids, and the pensioners."

On the buses

Buses and trams have to run early in the morning and late at night to get people who work on shifts around the clock to work and home again, so the drivers and conductors themselves often have to walk or drive to work.

Mirza Mohamed Salim

Proud to be a bus conductor, told us his story.

I came to England from Pakistan in 1960 when I was about eighteen, by aeroplane to London.

First I went to High Wycombe where my cousin was working. He suggested going to Middlesborough where he had a friend working as a labourer in the shipyard. I worked there for two weeks, but I didn't think it was very safe, so I went to my uncle who lived in Sparkbrook in Birmingham. I walked about six or seven miles a day looking for jobs. I walked so I wouldn't get lost. I didn't get a job, so I came to my cousin in Sheffield.

My first job was at Laycock Engineering as a hammer driver, we had to take things out of the furnace, a dangerous job again. These first jobs were my worst two jobs, because of the noise and the furnaces.

I worked there a year, then I got a job at Millspar in the machine shop, helping a machine operator. I became the first aider, with training, a badge, and the key to the ambulance room, there wasn't a nurse there. I was very young, the other workers would get metal scrap in their fingers, which would be bleeding, so they would ask me for bandages and dressings. An old bloke had a heart attack at work, I called the ambulance. After a few weeks he came back to work, and he thanked me. They liked me there.

I tried for work on the buses, but they said, "Come back when you are twenty one."

I started work at Greenland Road bus garage as a conductor. Morning shift started between 4 am and 7 am. Afternoon shifts would be from 2 pm till 11pm or midnight. There were special staff buses to take us home. If I missed the staff bus in the morning I had to walk to Greenland Road, from Tinsley where I lived. I never had any trouble, it was safe on the streets.

In Sheffield there were 60,000 people who started work before 6 am. The bus from Rotherham would have a full standing load in the mornings. The bus service between the town centre and Attercliffe, where the steel works were, ran every two to three minutes. There would be traffic jams because there were so many buses. On Saturdays it was hard to walk in town, everywhere there were human beings, walking. In snowy weather the buses, if they ran, would only run on the main roads.

Upstairs was very smoky, and I didn't smoke. In those days conductors were needed. I got my job back after I had been on a visit home to Pakistan. When I started there weren't many coloured people, then more arrived. The buses ran every day except Christmas day. I didn't mind working at Christmas, I needed the money. I worked on New Year's day. For the first few years I didn't know when Eid was. (an important Muslim festival, which changes its date slightly each year).

I lived in Attercliffe, where the houses had no baths and outside toilets. On a Saturday there would be long queues at Attercliffe Baths. I used to go after work.

I worked for about fifteen years on the buses. My favourite route was the 59 and the 22 to Holmesfield. It wasn't so busy as the 52 or the 60.

I had a full uniform, tie and a hat. I've kept my badge.

Then I worked piecework for a year at Frank Guy Lee's making drills. I moved to Samuel Peace on Upper Allen Street as a machine operator, drilling large plates of steel for big plant, where I worked for two or three years, this was my best paid job. But I went home for a holiday, and there was no job when I came back.

A friend of mine, we worked on the buses together, bought a shop and a warehouse, selling carpets on Spital Hill. Most of our customers were English. I worked there for 17 years.

My best job was on the buses, it was nice and clean, and we looked smart. It was very friendly.

A bus driver for 37 years talked to us about his working life.

Barrie Sheedy M.B.E.

Barrie Sheedy, bus driver

Born 1941, Boundary Road, Wybourn. I went to St. Oswald's School Southend Road. At the age of 15 I left school.

First job at Cockaynes as a carpet fitter

This bloke took me into a room full of women, rather frightening for a 15 year old lad. I went to open the windows, due to being very hot. Before I got to the window this woman shouted, "What you doing, leave them winders, we just had our hair dun". The room was full of material floating in the air. This made my mind up I didn't want to work indoors. Lasted two weeks.

Second job, 1956 –1969

Working for Crawfords Biscuits, depot on Canal Wharf. Then we moved from the Wharf in 1960 up to City Road, where we were taken over by McVities. Within a year we became United Biscuits Moved from City Road to Kiveton Park in 1962. Then in 1969 we got closed down. I went to Crawfords as a van-lad for £6 a week. Then at the age of 18 I became a van driver for £7.10s a week. As usual my wage was handed over to my mother and she gave me my spending money for the week.

Due to the Suez Canal Crisis, petrol was on ration, so we had to take the van on delivery as far as Buxton, come back to Bradwell, leave the van in the back yard of the Co-Op, then catch the bus back to Sheffield. This was a regular routine all due to petrol rationing.

Third job, 1969 - 2006

Worked for Sheffield Transport, then run by Sheffield Council and the chairman was Alderman Dyson.

I became a bus driver. I thought this job was a 'fill-in' whilst I got a lorry driver's job. Little did I know I would be driving buses for 37 years.

We had to go to driving school to learn how to drive buses. No matter what licence you had you still had to go to school for four weeks. Then another two weeks route-learning with a duty driver, then the final test for one day. I was driving back-loaders in 1969-71.

Ralph Basford
Lorry driver and bus driver.

Ralph, like many young men in Sheffield in the 50s and 60s had many different jobs. He could leave a job, and start a new one the next day. He finally settled down in 1975 as a bus driver, his favourite job, because of the people. This is his story.

My first job after leaving school in 1954 was at William Marsden's Meat Factory, Malin Bridge, as an apprentice butcher, although all I did was the fetching and carrying (half a pig), to keep the butchers busy. I suppose you could say I was the general dogsbody. I really enjoyed this job but the son of the owner, wouldn't tell me what my wages were going to be, so I worked a week and a week's notice. This was my first big mistake, for a 48 hour week I got £2 plus a cooked breakfast every morning – as much as I wanted, so long as nothing was wasted. If I had known what my wages were going to be, I might not have left so soon.

While here I had my first frightening experience. A young butcher about 18 years old, locked me in a cold room after we had taken some meat in on trays to be frozen for later use. If I remember right, I was in there for some twenty or thirty minutes. There was no light, no handle inside, and thick sound-proof walls so my yells were not heard. It was only when another member of staff came to get some meat that I was found. What a relief to get out! It was only my second or third day, so you can imagine how frightened I was. The premises are still there, but appear in 2007 to be a haulage yard.

My next job was at T.C. Harrison's in Boston Street. I got this job through an advertisement I had seen in the Star newspaper. Harrison's was the other side of town to where I lived. I had a bicycle so could get there O.K. Harrison's was a large Ford dealership and as an apprentice coach painter most of my work seemed to be car preparation. It was a small workshop away from the main works. There were about six other men working here.

I liked cars, but not the undersides. I was given the task of undersealing, and I was constantly covered in a thick black bostic-like substance. At this time, in the mid-fifties, the cars Ford were producing were the Consul, Zephyr and Zephyr Zodiac. All had extremely large wheel arches to allow for long travel of suspension. This meant it was difficult to reach with a paint brush.

Fitters Mate, at Langsett Lightweight Cycles. This was also on Green Lane, I got this job on my way home one day for dinner.

In 2006 the building is still there after all this time. This firm used to make one of the finest bikes. I was employed here as an assistant to a skilled fitter, making sweet wrapping machines for a company in Gainsborough, Rose Brothers. This was a job I liked, making holes in bushes for shafts to fit and putting parts in the right place, hundreds, and they all had got to work, I worked with a nice man from Newcastle, he used to work for Singer sewing machines. I would take parts to different people in the works for them to buff or paint, this gave me a chance to talk to, and watch people do other jobs.

Anyway as I have said before, I liked this job, but it wasn't to be, one day I was tapping a hole, for a name plate in a cast iron machine base, I was not having much luck. I had broken two 6 B.A. taps, and the other fitters around were having a laugh – they must have done same job and also broken taps, when the manager walked in, saw me with a smile on my face. He must have been having a bad day, he sacked me on the spot.

Machinist at N & J Wills, Albert Terrace Rd, Sheffield.

£3 and 10 shillings for 48 hrs. A sweat shop.

This firm was just down a drive way at the side of the 'Tabernacle' (now demolished) opposite the Royal Infirmary. I used to walk past or ride, anyway, one day I went in and they set me on, started the Monday. Nearly all employees were lads under 18 years old and I soon found out why. Piece work. We used to make hundreds of things on lathes and move onto a milling machine, then we would go on to a drilling machine and after a day and a half you would be moved round. There were four or five machines of the same type. All the young lads were competing against each other, if one did 200 another tries for 220. This went on every day. We had another machine which I hated, the 'fly press'. It stood on a table and it worked via a quick thread to operate a punch which cut webs out of small fork shaped metal castings. This machine had a large ball one end of an arm and handle the other end, rotation took the punch down to cut out the web. Castings used to come in half hundred weight bags, very dusty, you would tip these castings out onto the table – put the fork-end into the jig then swing the handle round towards you, take it out and throw it in a 10 gallon drum until full, and then the next drum had to be filled, hard boring work. Another thing we had to machine were the long twisted drills for shot boring down mines or pits.

I forgot to mention washing hands after work, a labourer fetched a bucket of water – most lads washed off first in the machines' coolant oil.

Dayland Garden Services, Crosspool, Sheffield.
I went to the Youth Employment this time – I never went again. The man I saw behind the desk said he would rather attend to a borstal boy than one like me, because I had had so many jobs. Anyway back to the job, landscape gardening, the firm was run from an old coach house at the back of Burntstones Hall, now demolished. This job was for me, out side, meeting people, doing something I liked, you see as a kid I had had lots of lovely times on dad's allotment up Myers Grove Lane. Dad got it long before the 1939-1945 war, and it was like having a weekend cottage.

We did garden maintenance and landscape work all over Sheffield – out to Chesterfield and east to Doncaster, gardens at big houses at Fulwood and Dore, it was great. I met and talked to the owners and families, people I had only heard about, most were well known business people, some had housekeepers and nannies. There seemed more going for them than the people I had lived amongst. Work was hard but rewarding, a job well done, and chance to see the finished garden when it had settled down. We got our 'pat on the back'. Accomplishment. I think the wage was about £5 for 45 hrs. I left when the company folded in 1957.

Samuel Osborn's Sports Ground Malin Bridge
Just before Dayland Garden services folded I was advised of their financial situation, so I got a job with Samuel Osborn's on their sports field at Malin Bridge, as an assistant groundsman at about £6.10s a week, but I would have to work over to cover games and matches, I didn't mind this as I had no ties and it gave me a chance to meet people, and I soon finished doing 80% of the work, cutting grass, rolling, marking out, about 12 acres plus. All mine, I was more or less my own boss, I put sheds up for mowers and tools, built a trailer to tow behind the mower, this proved very

useful for the groundsman who used to look after the cricket square, his pride and joy. His wife was the club stewardess and he used to help her.

My mum died while I worked there, I was about 17 and a half years old, but I was helped through the loss by the people I met whilst doing this job, they were like an extended family to me.

If I remember rightly to be a member of the sports club cost two old pence a week, we were very lucky, a big club house, tennis courts, football, cricket, netball, plus archery and motoring.

One of my jobs was to look after the boiler house, which had a Robin Hood coke burning boiler for the heating for the Sports Club. I had to sweep this place out at least twice a week. The boiler had to be stoked at least twice a day. I also used to sit down there during cold spells to get warm. I was the assistant groundsman and didn't like going into the Clubhouse with my muddy boots and wet clothes.

I bought a motor bike while here, a 250cc 'Indian Brave' nearly new, red with plenty of chrome and polished aluminium. It got me more work. Osborn's had just started a new foundry out at Halfway, Precision Castings and I got the gardening job. A very good canteen and staff.

All this came to an end when I got called up for National Service in 1959. I spent the next two years in the army, twenty one months in Germany driving 'wheeled vehicles', from trucks to personnel carriers, 'Saracens'. I soon got to like the new army mates and a different world, a trooper who didn't swear.

I was demobbed in May 1961 and because my groundsman job wasn't vacant, Samuel Osborn's set me on in the Transport Department as a lorry driver, local deliveries to other steel manufacturers and machine tools makers. This job took me into all the big steel works in and around Sheffield.

I saw all the different processes of steel making. I drove a three ton Scammel Scarab, a three wheeled tractor with semi trailer, i.e. articulated. This type of vehicle was widely used by the railways as it was very manoeuvrable. I used to take it into works that had been designed for horses and carts, not lorries.

I saw Brown Bayley's where they still used steam lorries. I used to take steel to Daniel Doncaster's where they had a giant press to forge steel that was taken there whilst still hot from our melting shop. These hot ingots were transported in large steel containers, the ingots being covered in a material called vermiculite. This insulation looked like Quaker Oats. The ingots were lifted out of this stuff and put into the furnace at Doncaster's to bring back to the right temperature. When hot enough a machine that looked like a giant lobster and must have weighed about fifteen tons, would nose up to the furnace and take out the red hot ingots, which must have weighed two tons each, and place it on the anvil of the press where it was pressed into shape instead of being hammered. It was all done by remote control so it was a lot safer.

I also drove a Standard Vanguard staff car, diesel powered, not many cars were diesel powered in the early 1960s.

I was on £10 a week for forty five hours.

I got married for the first time while at Osborn's and because my wage was not sufficient I left and went to work for a small garden firm for £11 a week. I had to get out to Bradway every morning including Saturdays. My boss had got this landscape job out at Hathersage, four of us went out there one cold morning. Having been on site for half an hour two employees went off to do their maintenance round, I was left to move a load of some eight to ten tons of rock from the road to the back of the property up steps and a steep path. When it came to about 4 pm, I mentioned to the boss that there was still a good three ton still on the road, he came to look and passed comment that he could have eaten that in the time I had taken, so I told him he could finish it for his tea. And I walked off site and went back to Osborn's and got my job back.

I have a photograph that had been taken at one of Sam Osborn's Transport Department Christmas parties, and somebody mentioned lorry drivers in neck ties. In those days at Osborn's, lorry drivers were a very important lot of men. We went around the city, and some travelled the country. We were the company's ambassadors and had to look smart. Just think of Eddie Stobbart's drivers now.

Ralph Basford, lorry driver, later bus driver

My next job after Osborn's, in 1965 was as a bus and truck brake drum reliner, for Thomas Winnard and Son, who were situated on Washford Road at Attercliffe. This was a small family run business employing about fourteen men all on piece work.

Dad put off his retirement until he was sixty eight, to show me the ropes, and we worked on machines next to each other. Dad worked at Winnard's for years and made a good living, he worked there during the Second World War doing all types of machining including gun barrels. He was a clever man he could turn his hand to anything. No qualifications or training. Just after the war he made me a scooter from wood and steel. The steel I remember he bent after getting it red hot in our fire grate. This scooter was the envy of all my school mates. And it lasted me until I was about ten when I got a bike.

Back to Winnard's, we used to reline brake drums for most haulage contractors and bus and coach operators, like Sheffield United Tours.

The lathes we worked on were old, so consequently you couldn't set the traverse control and leave the machine running but had to stand and hold the hand wheel otherwise the surface wasn't parallel.

Working with second hand cast iron wasn't easy, parts of the surface were like glass and had to be ground out with an angle grinder. I had to do as many as three cuts and broke many cutters because of the glass like areas.

There was no dust extraction for years. We only got hoists above the lathes some two years after I started work there, bracketing had been put up above machines but no-one had got round to fitting hoists, it needed someone like me to keep complaining and coming up with ideas before we got some lifting tackle fitted. I designed a hook and within days, all machines were equipped with this design. And it worked well.

I was the youngest there and continually tried to get conditions and pay rates improved, the toilet and washing facilities were dark and out of date, no hot water, the eating area was an old office in a corner of the workshop and we had a pensioner, a retired train driver, who used to come in to keep the place as clean as he could.

I started having migraine headaches while at Winnards, all I can put this down to was continual pressure, our prices for the jobs were insufficient. After nearly six years of this I arranged with the men to join a Union, we agreed a time and place and we all went to see a Mr George Caborn (father of Richard Caborn M.P.) It was agreed that we should all join. Within weeks I had another confrontation with the boss where upon he gave me the sack.

By this time I had got a wife and two small daughters, a house on mortgage and a car. Something I did notice on leaving Winnard's, my migraine ceased.

Arthur Lee's
Two men larking about one day, I tried to get out of their way, I fell onto some big coils of flat strip this winded me and I couldn't breathe for what seemed like several minutes. I couldn't finish my shift and it took me all my time to get out of my overalls and washed off. I didn't explain to the foreman what had happened

23

just that I had fallen. If I had these two men would have been sacked, I found out later I had some cracked ribs, it cost me five weeks off work and no compensation.

Later on I remember the three day week when Mr. Heath was P.M. This made a big hole in our wage packets. I think this was in 1973. I remember going to work and finding portable gas lighting in dangerous places, this was due to power cuts during the miners' strikes. One consolation of a three day week was that I saw more of my children than normal due to shift work.

One day I took a chair into work, a simple moulded plastic seat on a makeshift tubular base. It was out of my garage, and I got funny looks from the management. To me a seat, so that I could take the weight off my legs seemed like commonsense. And from then on I used it until I left in 1975.

Arthur Lee's celebrated its centenary while I was working there.

Bus Driver from 1975 to 1994

Early in 1975 I went out and got a job bus driving with South Yorkshire Transport. I had no experience and they wanted me to go conducting first, but I managed to persuade Personnel, and started on the Monday, after a week in driving school. I was out with the passengers, route training, took to it right away. In those days we still had a few back loaders, O.K. to drive but no contact with the public. And seeing I like people I didn't like these much. Got on reasonably with most conductors. I drove through areas I had never been to, and enjoyed most times.

Uniforms

In my eighteen years we had three different types and colour of uniform. The first was a very smart, navy blue serge, next we had brown trousers and dark red anoraks, and red and brown reversible body warmers. Then when we went over to be called Mainline we had grey trousers, white shirts, and individually picked top quality maroon blazers. We looked very smart. The uniform stores were at Leadmill Road. If anything got damaged it was replaced on production of the damaged item. We were issued with cleaning tokens, so no one had any excuse for looking unkempt. When I went to work on the buses every garage had a large mirror so you could check your appearance before taking the bus out of the garage. Ties were compulsory, and after several years we were given ties on elastic so we couldn't get garrotted by yobs or drunks. I am sure we gained respect because of the uniform.

Ice and hills

After a night of snow, on a bitterly cold morning I took a double deck bus on a school run, 8-12 year olds, with my conductress. I turned into a road and climbed a gradient and reaching the top of the hill, and starting to go down the other side I felt the bus start sliding, I nudged the kerb to no effect, as the road got steeper, the bus rear end slid out to the right. I was now going sideways, having some fifty plus children on board, I told my conductress to get the kids ready to leave the bus, my front doors were now over the grass verge, the kids could now get off without slipping, plus I was now between both kerbs just sliding slowly. I opened the doors and Dot managed to get all children off without any injury. Then bang, I had demolished a concrete lamp standard, still sliding I next hit a telegraph pole, which stopped me. Luckily I was only halfway down the hill. I was there for 90 odd minutes before the gritter and recovery vehicle came0. A police car came and I ushered him onto the verge or he would have slid into me. I didn't get a thank you from anyone, not even my management.

Coming down Prince of Wales Road one morning during the gritter's strike there was about four inches of snow that had been compacted. I tried to stop at a bus stop for waiting passengers and I felt the back end of my vehicle slewing round. There was nothing I could do however, the back end of the bus hit the central reservation and this stopped me going all the way round. I picked my passengers up further down the road. There's not much one can do when eight ton plus starts to slide.

Sheffield was the testing area for all new buses. Because of the hills brakes would overheat, clutches would burn out. On another occasion I lost ninety percent of my braking power whilst doing a 70/71 run down from Norfolk Park to the city. On getting near the Eastbank Road junction, with a full load of nearly eighty passengers, I could have gone through a wall and finished up twenty feet below the road. Luckily a driver doing the route in the opposite direction realised what was happening and moved to his left so that we passed each other without contact.

Leyland introduced brake retarders, it was a good idea for Sheffield's hills, apart from on ice and packed snow. When going down hills it's automatic for a driver to ease off the accelerator but in this case the pedal was also an electrical switch and the retarder responded like a brake, but the driver had got no control and it didn't take much for the back end to break away. My first experience of this was coming down the Fence Hill from Swallownest after a snowfall. When introducing new buses with modifications we could have done with ten or fifteen minutes to get the feel before they went into service but we didn't.

We got a fleet of new doubledecker Volvos, Van Hool body. They looked really great, front engined, rear wheel drive with a semi automatic gear box. These buses stood in Greenland Road garage for weeks until they had all under gone their tilt test. They were driven onto a frame, which was then tilted over until the bus being tested finally fell onto pads, and measurements would be taken. Sheffield was the testing area for all new buses. Because of the hills brakes would overheat, clutches would burn out.

Garages
The garages at Greenland Road, Herries Road and East Bank Road were all based around a similar design, all with good facilities. The site at Greenland Road is now occupied by B&Q, and Herries Road garage is now a steel warehouse. The only garage left is at Eastbank Road, which means that most buses are now parked outside overnight. The garage at Leadmill Road was old fashioned and only small, but it had an office, a medical room and our own doctor and nurse. Now only the façade remains. Queen's Road garage used to be large tram sheds and workshops. When we got rid of the trams in 1960 this workshop went over to the servicing and repair of buses. It had got every facility, engine strip down and overhaul, and other jobs like gear

boxes, back axles, brakes etc, and they could strip bus bodies down to the bare framework, do any repairs, then reassemble, and repaint

On one occasion I was called in to see Alec Lee the Chief Driving Instructor, after complaining about head-lights being fitted wrongly. Apparently I nearly caused a strike, the fitters threatened to walk out, they weren't having a bus driver tell them their job. Another time I arrived back at garage late after doing a busy duty with too little time, I complained to Mr Woodward, who said I could have more time if I took a drop in money.

Drivers' seats. I complained about these, some of the seat bases were too long in the leg so my back had no support, (these seats were probably designed for man or woman six foot six tall) on one occasion I got back to High Street and the conductor had to get help for me as I couldn't get out of my seat. And this was after only two hours behind the wheel of a nearly new bus. We had management who would buy vehicles without consulting us, the drivers.

We had a cash float of £2 when we went one man operated, losing our conductors when buses were deregulated. This was enough when fares were low, but as you can imagine when fares started to go up the change didn't last long.

Before Mrs Thatcher got into power and we had a good frequent bus service, the 52 route, which in those days carried some ten million passengers a year, had three different termini at one end. This was Handsworth, Ballifield and the most distant one, Woodhouse, while at the other side of town there was School Road and Crookes. You can imagine the fun I used to have when any of the young ladies approaching from the rear of the bus, and not looking to see the destination, would ask, "How far do you go driver?" I could come up with lots of answers, which would bring smiles to the faces of the lower deck passengers, and the odd blush from the young lady in question.

The 52 Crookes to Woodhouse via Darnall. I had almost filled the bus with passengers in the High Street one tea time, pushed for time as usual from Crookes. I picked up a few more at Waingate and the Wicker. I was driving an up to date Volvo front-engined double decker. These buses were quick, thoroughbreds.

Going from the Wicker to Norfolk Bridge, foot down, to make up for lost time. In those days Saville Street connected with Attercliffe Road on the town side of Norfolk Bridge, near Lucas Auto Electrical, making the road into a sort of chicane. I took this right, then left, at about 20/25 mph. The bus heeled over, sparks flew from the front nearside corner of the chassis when it made contact with the road. I knew I was well within the bus's safe limits, but from the lower deck a man shouted – "Who's 'e think he is – Fittipaldi?" He was, of course, talking about me.

Now if you are not into motor racing, Fittipaldi was a top driver of that time, and he was paid a lot more than me, but I had as much fun, and my conductor enjoyed it. That road is now one way, so this is no longer possible!

51 route Lodge Moor end. A smart chap carrying a brolly and briefcase, running to catch the bus, would say, "Made it", to which I would reply, "Only because I wanted your fare". This chap seemed to be late for the bus every day, and even later for work.

On a morning trip from Firth Park to the city, waiting at traffic lights, I saw smoke coming from the car in front. Thinking it might have children in it my quick reaction was, hand brake on, out of cab – heel through safety glass on extinguisher, I managed to put the fire out and sever the battery cable before the paint on bonnet had started to bubble. For this I received an award from management and a mention in the works magazine, a passenger had rung in to Greenland Garage to compliment me on my efforts.

My conductor Alan asked me if I would do an extra trip with him. I think he was in need of a bit of extra cash that week. It turned out to be beneficial for me.

We were to do the 71 Circular from Flat Street to Darnall, Manor Top, Norfolk Park and back to town. I don't normally do overtime but I said 'Yes', and I am glad I did that day, for standing waiting for my bus at Darnall was a young lady who would become the love of my life.

Rose had been doing a bit of shopping after work. She was then single and I was divorced. I had talked to her a few times over the years when she caught my bus to work or to town, but the last time I spoke to her I gathered she was engaged, and I am not one for upsetting things, so I didn't pursue her.

This was in 1983. We married in 1985 and in 2007/8 we are still married and very happy. How about that for fate? Of the thousands of young ladies I have had on my bus over nearly twenty years, I was very lucky to get Rose.

I could have had the time of my life if I had taken my commitments lightly. At 68 I can look back with a completely clear conscience. To me I didn't class bus driving as a job, although of course I needed the money. It was more like a vocation.

The Trams

The first, horse drawn trams, started running in Sheffield in 1873. After the trams were taken over by the Corporation they were electrified in 1898. There were three main depots, including the original Tinsley depot, which was extended in1899, and Shoreham Street Depot built in 1910, both became bus depots in 1960.

They were an important way of getting to work for many people, especially to all the steel works along the Don valley.

In 1951 Sheffield Transport decided to phase them out as they were causing traffic congestion.

The last tram ran on the 8th of October, 1960.

Then in 1993 the tram tracks were re-laid in Sheffield, the 'Hole in the Road' was filled in with rubble from the demolition of part of Hyde Park flats to make a central tram stop, and Supertram started to run, hopefully to help reduce traffic congestion by encouraging car users to 'leave the car at home'.

Beatie Smith *told us about working as a clippie during the war. Like many transport workers, Beatie had to walk to work, because of starting work very early or finishing very late, to fit in with shifts at the steelworks.*

I was born in 1922 in Berners Street, went to Bard Street School, left when I was nine. My Mum and Dad moved to Primrose Ave (Flower Estate), then at eleven I moved to Fitzhubert Road (Manor), then to Granville Street, and went to de la Salle Memorial School, left at the age of 14. Finished school Friday started work Monday.

First job, at **Walker & Hall,** Norfolk Street as an errand girl, then as a trainee french polisher. After working at Walker & Hall's for four years I was told I had to go to work at 'Stanley Works' Rutland Road. This was due to the war effort, making bullets and bombs. I worked there until I was 21 on 'piece- work'.

Then I moved to a factory in Soho Street off Ecclesall Road. I had to leave due to the factory being bombed.

I was given an alternative, either work on the trams or go to Skipton (Yorkshire). I still have no idea why I was asked to go to Skipton, so I decided work on the trams.

At the age of 21 I became a 'Tram Clippie', badge number 'T376'. This was 1943, a weekly wage of £3 approx. The training for this was, to be able to change points / overhead cables. One experience of emergency braking was to put the tram on an incline, I had to run down stairs, turn the brake-wheel, then put sand on the brakes, I found it very hard as I was only 5'3" and weighed seven stone.

I started work at 4.00 am and worked over eight hours a day on a regular basis. One week's holiday a year. On foggy days I had to walk at the side of the tram, then bang on the tram to tell the driver to stop at the tram-stop.

To get to work, I used to walk from City Road to Shoreham Street Depot. If I was lucky I might catch the night tram to the Depot, this would be a treat as I would be on my feet the full shift.

I remember the first day working on my own as a clippie. This was on a Sunday, from Meadowhead to Sheffield Lane Top, I felt as if I'd been thrown into it, from the start to the finish of my shift. The tram was full of children. What I didn't like on the trams, no one gave you respect for the job you were doing.

I left at the age of 24.

My father, William Briddock worked at 'Shipmans' Staniforth Road as a wire annealer. He died at the age of 51 in 1949 with a chest complaint.

And my Mum she was a loving housewife her name was Betty.

I married Norman. We had two children. Norman was a furnace-man at English Steel.

When I wanted to take the kids out at the weekend even for a walk, Norman was always working. He said he was doing it so we could have a good holiday. I wish we all had more week-ends together than the one good holiday.

Beatie Smith

"In the 1950's I started taxi-driving at the Victoria Station and Midland Station."

Ernest Squires

Ernest Squires, taxi driver

Here he tells his story.

I was born in Lancing Road, Brammall Lane district of Sheffield, in the year of 1923. Wasn't long before my family moved to Hawley Street in the Town centre. I attended the Bow Street School, back of City Hall. We moved to Leeds where I finished my schooling years.

My first job was as an apprentice engineer at Jackson's Glass Works. A friend of my father got me the apprenticeship. My wages for a week's learning was five shillings, then one shilling rise for each year after. I didn't finish my contract, as my family came back to Sheffield in 1940. My father, Ernest, became the chauffeur of Edgar Allen. My father's wages for the week - £3.

My mum, Ethel was a housewife. I remember before we moved to Leeds when we lived in Hawley Street, my mum cleaned at the Albert Hall. She would push me in the pram and I would watch the organist rehearsing. Years after, mum's done a full circle and back at the old Albert, but no pram. By the way, John Lewis's shop now stands where the music hall stood.

I got a job at Edgar Allen's as a precision grinder. We were making anti-magnetic systems which went around the war-ships and deflected the mines away from them, preventing them causing devastation. This girl called Rene caught my eye and we courted for three years, and finally married before I joined the army in 1944. I made Sergeant Squires. Came out of the forces in 1949, went back to Edgar Allen's for six months. After having a taste of the forces I realised I wasn't cut out for this any more.

Chauffeurs at Edgar Allen's

In the 1950's I started taxi-driving at the Victoria Station and Midland Station. I remember the fare was nine pence a mile and one shilling after midnight.

Once I picked up a fare in Sheffield centre, man and woman, wanted to go to Rotherham, so off we went. Got to Rotherham, then the man said he wanted to go to Thrybergh. I could overhear a conversation between them, which made me feel uncomfortable, then all of a sudden, this man grabbed me round the neck, while the woman hit me across the forehead with a joiner's mallet. The car went into a ditch, I turned round, jumped into the back and banged their heads together, knocking then out cold. Later the police told me they were wanted in London for a job.

In 1962 the manager and myself (now assistant manager for Abbey Taxis), travelled South to a place near Silverstone to buy this Mercedes Benz, which was owned by George Harrison of The Beatles – what a car! We bought it for £3,000.

When the Fiesta Club opened in the town centre I got the job of driving the Stars like Ella Fitzgerald, Satchmo, Three Degrees, and Roy Orbison. I remember having to take Mr Orbison to Newcastle on Tyne for one performance, then drive him back to Sheffield. Not a word was said during the journey.

In 1972 I managed to buy myself a Mercedes Benz car, a long base 8-seater, still taxi-driving, and a bit of security work with Parkway Markets and Midland Bank in between taxi work. Finally early in the 90's, the taxi company went bust and got sold off, and this was when I called it a day. I retired with happy memories.

My Mercedes taxi

'Kraig' *trained as an apprentice motor mechanic from 1948 to 1953. He told us his story.*

In 1932 Kraig, was born on the east side of Sheffield, the son of a poor steel worker. From an early age he was mad about motor transport especially cars. On leaving Nether Edge Grammar School with a School Certificate in July 1948, he had had enough of academic work and was determined to get a practical job despite there being very little careers advice around.

One friendly teacher offered to help and contacted Mr Frith, the area secretary of the motor industry. He was the owner of Carver Street Motor Services and proved to be very helpful. At an interview with him, it was found that the only firms with apprenticeship schemes were Sheffield Transport Department, who had no vacancies, and Leyland Motor Company in Lancashire who required a £200 bond, which of course was out of the question.

Eventually Mr Frith arranged an interview with Mr Bell, the general manager of E W Hatfield Limited of Norfolk Street Sheffield, who were main dealers for Standard Triumph and Jaguar cars. At this interview the papers were drawn up and signed for a five-year indentured apprenticeship to start in August 1948. Mr Bell stated that his firm's responsibility was to teach the art and practice of servicing, maintenance and repair of motor vehicles, whilst the apprentices' responsibility was not only to learn the trade but, also to take the necessary theoretical and practical examinations to qualify as a motor vehicle mechanic.

First year. The Head Office and showrooms of E W Hatfield were situated in Norfolk Street, opposite the Peace Gardens and the Town Hall. The Service Department was a few hundred yards away on Paternoster Row and Kraig duly arrived there on his first day to be greeted by a grunt from the Service Manager who immediately passed him on to Mr Algar who described himself as 'the clerk'.

His office was an eight by five wooden partition in the corner of the department which was about 100 ft by 80 ft and comprised of eight pits for car repairs, car hoists, machine shop and engine rebuild area and the stores department.

A wooden structure at a higher level with tables and benches was called the canteen! It had a small sink served by a gas geyser for hot water for drinks and washing for the workforce of around 20 people. All workers had to 'clock on' and 'clock off' and 15 minutes pay was deducted for being three minutes or more late.

Kraig soon realised that his eagerness to learn was tempered by the mundane tasks he was given, such as running errands for sandwiches and delivering or collecting spare parts to and from nearby firms.

The first few months were spent with Mr Algar who was a very kind and patient 'old' gentleman, wearing pinstriped suit, winged collar and a Homburg hat. He showed Kraig general office work, how to greet customers, write down their requirements, answer the telephone correctly and generally be a good receptionist.

At the end of the first week Kraig received a wage packet containing a ten shilling note (50 p today) plus a few 'coppers'! He had also enrolled on a City and Guilds motor mechanics course for three nights per week at the local technical college.

After a month he was given a white boiler suit like the other mechanics wore, but the manager insisted he stay with Mr Algar.

Towards the end of his first year, after a lot of pleading he was allowed to go into the engine bay and was shown by Roland the engine mechanic, how to clean the outside of an engine before stripping it down, logging all the parts and carefully cleaning them in a paraffin tank with a foot operated pressure pump using hands and rags to get into the awkward corners, after which Swarfega cream was used to try to remove the ingrained oil and dirt from his hands.

This work was always punctuated by doing whatever errands were required. There was a general air in the department that if too much technical information was given to someone, then their own jobs could be at risk because from time to time during the five years, some mechanics were 'laid off' when there was insufficient work around. Slowly he gained the confidence of Roland who showed him how to fit new parts and reassemble the engine, including the occasional rebore and scraping and fitting the bearings.

Second Year. This work continued into the second year together with the errands but by now, two school leavers (not apprentices) had been taken on.

At this point the service manager gave away his tools to the new lads and told Kraig to buy his own which he gradually did. By now Kraig had been given one day per week off work for the next three years to attend a technical college for Mechanical Engineering as well as continuing the three nights per week for City and Guilds. After another month or two, he was allowed to assist mechanics who were doing various repair jobs on cars such as steering systems, decarbonising engines, greasing nipples, and changing engine, gearbox and rear axle oils. Renewing the braking systems included the hazardous blowing by mouth of brake shoe assemblies to remove asbestos dust to eliminate contact with oily rag or hands.

This assistance was at first mainly confined to cleaning parts or holding something whilst the mechanic did the work, but slowly as experience and trust grew, more important tasks were given. This was very dependent on the mechanic concerned and since there was no pattern to work coming in, Kraig was allotted, by the foreman, to whichever mechanic requested some assistance, the consequence being that there was no logical pattern of training but more variety, which created in him a strong desire to learn from the good and bad situations.

When he became 17 years of age, Kraig naturally enquired about learning to drive, but was told by the manager in an aggressive tone that **he** would decide when the time was right and not for several months.

Third year. The foreman, George, was a fair person and when work conditions allowed would allocate certain jobs to Kraig which he would personally supervise, and he was a good, thorough and patient tutor but he was very busy and responsible for all work quality.

On one occasion he instructed Kraig to overhaul the brakes on a Standard 10 car from start to finish, with defined stages made for him to check progress. After certain approved stages and waiting a very long time for the busy foreman to come and check again, another mechanic wandered past and suggested carrying on with the job. When the foreman finally came he tore a strip off Kraig for disobeying his instructions even though no harm had been done. It was pointed out, that whilst Kraig was taking longer than other mechanics to carry out work, his longer time was accepted due to his much lower rate of pay.

Whilst nominal times were allocated for many jobs, due to difficulty of obtaining spares many make-do-and-mend repairs had to be made to keep vehicles on the road so scheduled times could not always be adhered to. During this year, Kraig would, at lunchtimes, practice moving the decrepit ex-army works van around in the yard without permission and was occasionally seen by the manager who ignored it until he decided the time had come for Kraig to be taught to drive by the works van driver.

Meanwhile Kraig continued to be given more and more responsibility for repairing brakes, steering, tracking, engines, gearboxes, springs and rear axles with only occasional supervision. The year ended with Kraig passing the City and Guilds examination and continuing with the Mechanical Engineering one day per week course.

Fourth year. Having now obtained his driving licence, Kraig was expected to carry out driving duties such as ferrying cars around to Head Office, the Paint Workshop, and to customers' homes, as well as collecting spares from Coventry - especially as he was paid less than the other drivers! He was now experienced enough to carry out most work unsupervised and was thoroughly enjoying the complex fault finding and overhauling of the various components to strict tolerances.

In the middle of this year Kraig was put into the Stores Department for a few months to help sort out the stock and the stocktaking, which he found to be very boring work even though the Stores Manager promised him good prospects if he would work there permanently.

Fifth year. As his experience increased, Kraig started road-testing vehicles and since Mr Algar had by now retired, he was often called upon as receptionist / tester, including fault finding and helping to arrange the work schedules. These duties were rotated with one or two mechanics returning from their National Service and in between he carried on with unsupervised work.

Around this time the service manager told Kraig to get smartened up and report to Mr Ernest Hatfield, the Managing Director at the Head Office. Mr Ernest put him in the passenger seat of his new 3.4 Jaguar MkV11 and drove to a firm of solicitors on Queen Street. Kraig was given strict instructions that if the parking time was going to be exceeded he was to drive the car back to Head Office. In the event Mr Ernest returned in time and thanked him for waiting.

Kraig was asked some time later to go on a course at Jaguar Works in Coventry to learn more about the technical complexities of Jaguar cars, which he was thrilled to do. One of these complexities was also a hazard since it involved "sniffing" exhaust gases whilst adjusting the twin carburettors, as Gas Analysing instruments had yet to be developed.

Having obtained the 0NC in Mechanical Engineering, he also attended a short course at Sheffield Technical College on welding and lathe work, which he completed before his apprenticeship ended. With a good reference from Mr Bell he went to do his National Service in the Royal Air Force in August 1953.

Kraig never returned to the motor trade but that's another story.

Due to the increased mechanical reliability of cars today, mechanics are less in demand but technicians using computers to analyse the car's electronic components are in greater demand.

The Railways

Sheffield used to have two main railway stations, Sheffield Midland Station, built between 1870 and 1905, which is still in use, and Victoria Station on the Wicker viaduct, which was opened for trans Pennine trains in1851 and finally closed in 1970. Electrification of the Manchester – Sheffield line was planned in the 30s, but was not completed until 1954.The railways were nationalized in January 1948, and at that time were the main freight carriers. All locomotives were steam engines in the 40s, and were slowly replaced by diesel engines (DMUs) during the 60s. The last regular service steam train ran in 1968. Bill Quinn, in his poem, remembers , "I hear a ghostly whistle far away in the night".

Leslie Middleton, *railway man drove steam trains until 1965, and on electrified lines until he retired.*

Les Middleton at the controls

I was born in the year of 1929 and attended Pye Bank School. My school years were interrupted by the war. We finished up going to different people's houses to be taught by our teachers. They said it was safer than all the children in one building.

I remember as a kid this railway tunnel called 'the Fiery Jack', being used as an air raid shelter. The name came from the tunnel being so low, with the sparks and smoke bouncing off the roof. All the families in the neighbourhood used this so-called indestructible shelter.

My father was the checking clerk at the Fiery Jack Tunnel. He had a cabin at the L.N.E.R. (London and North East Railway) end of the tunnel, which finished at the L.M.S. (London, Midland and Scottish) end of the line. At Bridgehouses my dad had his cabin at the Champs Hill. This is the local name for the bottom of Brunswick Road. I remember when my dad was on night turn he would take me with him to work, where I would stay, and sleep for the night in his cabin until morning. Then home with my dad after his shift was done. The reason for me going with my dad was if there were an air raid, mum would only have to look after my sister and herself.

My first job was at Greaves Cabinet and Cutlery Case Makers on Sydney Street, but with the war on we were making ammo boxes and gun cases. I realised there was no future in the job, so I left.

Then my dad got me a job on the railways at the Sheffield Victoria Station, as a messenger lad in the District Goods Managers' office, until I was 16. Then I got a transfer to the 'Loco' Depot in Darnall. I started as a cleaner in 1945. The job was to clean the exterior of the railway engines. We used inspection chambers to clean the underside of the engines. Then I became a Passed Cleaner, which meant I was a spare Fireman. In 1948 I did my National Service (two years of conscription), and when I returned to the railways I was promoted to Passed Fireman, which allowed me to drive the engine.

I had to work up through the Links. These were gradings, which were usually made up of 12 or 6 turns (shifts). You started at the bottom in the shed link. The next turn of duty was the wet pit link. That was hard work, throwing the fires out and cleaning the ash pans, and the smoke box doors. You wore clogs because to do your job properly you would walk on the hot cokes which had been thrown from the engines. Then came the Pilot Link, working on engines specially made for the Goods Yards. These were called 'saddle tank engines' due to having water tanks on either side of the engine.

The spare link meant you never knew which of the turns (shifts) you'd be working until the weekend before. On top of that, you could be called in to start two hours before, and also stay two hours after your turn, just in case someone was sick and couldn't make it to work or was on holiday. The missus wasn't too happy. She didn't know when I was starting or finishing.

There was the Slow Passenger Link, then the Fast Passenger Train Link and the Local Trip Link, which travelled to the seaside. Last of all was the Old Man's Link. You passed out as a spare driver and became a full driver as the senior drivers retired.

Darnall Depot, which was steam trains, closed in 1965 and I transferred to Rotherwood onto the electric lines. The Rotherwood Depot closed in 1980 and I went to Tinsley Depot where I retired in 1991.

The weekly pay when I started on the railways was
Messenger lad - 19 shillings and 11 pence
Cleaner - £2
Passed Fireman - £3.10 shillings
Driver - £4.10 shillings

As a driver if you didn't pass your indoor sight test you were sent to Peterborough to see if you could see the colour of the signal at a distance of 1,000 yards, and you'd be paid £12 for this.

The story of making tea in the mashing can – put a used match-stick in the mash can with the lid off. This stops the smoke going in the mashing can. When the train had stopped you'd put your mashing can filled with water on the shovel, put the shovel in the fire box until the water boiled and sweeten your tea with condensed milk. Another is boiling eggs – wrap the egg in the sweat rag and put it in the steam pipes. This method also worked on potatoes and onions – what a taste!

Holidays on starting were one week in the early 1950's, then two weeks, and in the 1970's it was four weeks. We also had six Bank Holidays a year. In the 1960's we had to work Christmas Day and Boxing Day and take a day off later when they could spare you. In the 1940's and 1950's if you were on the early turn before 6 am you would get a caller-up tapping on the bedroom window until you answered the caller.

Many thanks to my work colleague and good friend Norman Rooker for reminding me of what a time we had.

British Rail Workshop, Doncaster

Roy Barker *wrote this in 1993 and sent it to us. The workshops are still in Doncaster, they were privatised at the same time as the rest of British Rail, though they kept many of their dedicated workers, "serious minded men", as Roy describes them. Roy mentions asbestos, though he doesn't tell us that many of these workers have died over the last twenty years from asbestos related cancers.*

Coaches and power units standing in line waiting to be renovated as new, each one numbered as if named, the number describes the use each vehicle has, and registers its history. Serious minded men, with years of experience in their trades, probe and peer, inspecting every part of the vehicles, listing faults, wear and general condition.

All this information is written and entered on numerous forms, to enable an estimate of cost for repair, these forms also act as instructions for the tasks to be completed. In the interest of safety, rules and laws to be conformed to, cover every aspect of the vehicle.

The activity of the workshop starts with the cleaning of the vehicles. Dirt, oil - grease, inches thick in some areas, is removed with high-pressure hand held steam and water jets. Furniture is removed for renovation, paintwork is cleaned.

A control room monitors all activities bringing order and cohesion to the workshop. They are aided in this by a gang of workers who shunt, traverse and lift vehicles into positions where different types of work are carried out. These operations are done with great care, considering safety at all times. Renovated and new parts are placed close to the vehicles being repaired, this allows the repair gangs to concentrate on their work efficiently.

The workshop employing hundreds of personnel creates a need for services such as canteens, first aid facilities, nurses and a doctor. Safety advice and protective measures are advertised in the workshop to combat accidents to the people who are at risk in such a heavy industry.

Accidents can cause long delays to the work in progress. Blue asbestos, a deadly material if inhaled, being so small, it can enter the most minute parts of the lungs with devastating effects. Unlike accidents such as cuts etc the effects are not immediate, years after contact with asbestos dust the damage appears...

Where asbestos is known about, or found, a high priority is taken to remove it or seal it safely, this work hopefully creates a safer environment.

Safety at work is encouraged, led by a committee drawn from many parts of the workforce.

Committees are at hand to advise, judge and command all through the works structure.

A system of seniority is used in giving promotion to specified jobs, being seen as the fairest way to fill vacancies.

All the efforts of management are geared to producing a workforce that can handle any production problems turning out a high quality product, with public safety in mind.

The tradesmen and women involved are trained in many skills (coach - builders, blacksmiths, fitters and electricians) each following their own type of skills.

Other trades, coach painters, trimmers, and too many to list are employed. Unskilled workers are just as important.

The vehicles are carefully reassembled and after again being subjected to strict testing, paintwork gleaming, are ready to be given back into service at various locations. Whilst in service any faults arising are entered into a logbook, which can be studied on the vehicles' next return to the workshop.

To be employed as a cog in this large machine could be a daunting, boring and tiring experience, except for the comradeship and friends who never lose their sense of humour and are always ready to give help and advice to resolve life's problems...No matter how long it takes!

Bill Quinn *started on the railways straight from school. He remembers 'dieselisation' and then in 1988, 'privatisation', freight trains and high speed trains. And after 'retirement' he went on to enjoy working as a caretaker for the libraries. We include one of the poems he has written about his first trip on the main line.*

"There's no doubt, steam was hard work and if, during the changeover period, when steam and diesels were running together, and you signed in, looked at the roster and saw you were down for diesel, your heart leapt."

I was born in 1942, and lived in Thurnscoe. At the age of 15, in 1957, I left school. Finished school Friday, started work Monday. There were only three types of jobs for lads in our area at that time, the pits, the steel industry or the railways. I didn't want to go down the pit, and I'd always liked trains, being a keen train-spotter as a kid, so railways it was. I began at the British Rail Mexborough Loco Depot, and cycled there every day from home.

I began as an engine cleaner for under £4 a week, and gradually worked up through the grades, my goal being to become a driver. The process took years, and some men began and ended as firemen, because really you were waiting to step into dead men's shoes. Next I became a passed cleaner, which meant that you could undertake fireman's duties if required, providing you passed a small exam. It took 20-22 years to get through the grades and become an engine driver, and in some crews the driver and fireman were the same age.

I worked as a fireman on the steam trains, but not a driver. By the time I became a driver we were using diesels. Which did I like best, steam or diesel? It may be nostalgia, but I'd say that I preferred steam to both diesels and electrics. There was more companionship among the steam-men, which disappeared over the years. You relied on the other men more, for instance, when you came off duty, you had to leave your engine in fit condition for the next crew, bunker full of coal, tank full of water and the engine clean. Each shed had it's own locos allocated to that depot, so you knew them. With diesel, you just parked them, locked them up and that was it.

Driving was a high status job, and the drivers were always known by their full Christian names e.g. John William Brown would be called John William.

Shifts

At 18 you could do nights, for which you got 30 shillings per week extra pay. Normal shifts lasted 12-14 hours a day, sometimes as long as 16 hours.

The average speed of a steam-driven freight train was about 15mph, so for instance, driving from Frodingham to Scunthorpe could take 14-16 hours. You then had a 12 hour rest period before you began another shift, so you might come off duty at 10 pm and start again at 10 am.

This system meant that you sometimes ended up at night far from your home base, and some Depots had dormitories where you could sleep, but a lot of drivers preferred to make their own lodging arrangements, and booked to stay at a B&B run by a well-known landlady. Being in 'the lodging link' was only for the most senior drivers, who got lodging and food allowances, and were well-paid. These drivers were 'top of the range' , seniority was everything at British Rail. By the time I had progressed through the ranks, the lodging link had been abolished, due to diesels and a different rostering system.

Accidents

Luckily I never was involved in any of these. The most I experienced were runaway trains, and they were not really runaways, they were just overloaded for the gradient they had to attempt. This happened to me a few times, both as a fireman and a driver, but there were no tragic consequences.

The characters

One thing I really enjoyed was the diverse characters I worked with. One man, a shed labourer called George, ran a Polo Club (i.e. the mints, not the game). To be a member you had to buy him a packet of Polos every week and whenever you came on duty he'd give you a mint. Then there was a little chap called George Henry Dukes. There was a minimum height requirement for BR and he was only small, so I wondered how he got there. Rumour had it that he belonged to a well-off Mexborough family who had pulled strings. The thing about him was, that he was so dapper. He'd come to work in white shirt, highly polished shoes and immaculate overalls, and he'd look exactly the same when he came off duty, whereas the rest of us would be covered in coal dust and grease.

Most chaps had a nickname, for instance, a man called White would be Chalky. It was a hobby of mine to try to figure out how they got the more unusual ones. One driver was called Mud-eye, and he is reckoned to have got that name because, unlike most drivers, he would do any route in the country without the usual 'Road Learning' (when you went out with another driver who knew the route). Instead, he'd rely on his fireman to put him right about signals, saying – "I've just got a bit of dirt in my eye". What he was looking for was confirmation from his fireman that the correct signal on a gantry had been cleared for his train to proceed. Some signal gantries had many different signals at junctions, involving different routes, but rather than admit he was unsure of the route, he would pretend he had something in his eye, just to get his fireman (who probably did know the route), to confirm that the correct signal had been cleared for his train to proceed.

Then there was a fire-dropper called Arthur Tingle. His job was to clean out the clinker when the locos came into the depot. He was called Flipper and Flopper, because he never swore or blasphemed. Instead, if he was really angry, he'd say – "Ah, they are real flippers, I'd flipping-well flop 'em".

I even wrote a few poems about these names and characters, and I still laugh to myself now when I remember them.

Dieselisation. There's no doubt, steam was hard work and if, during the changeover period, when steam and diesels were running together, and you signed in, looked at the roster and saw you were down for diesel, your heart leapt.

Speed increased, with the introduction of HST's (High Speed Trains) and modern diesel engines, which had more braking power. It was a bit different from pottering along in a freight train at 15-20 mph.

Privatisation. This brought the biggest change of all and had the biggest impact on our jobs and lives. It took place about 1988. With British Rail, the men in all departments interacted with each other, so that you knew drivers from all over the country. Now, men who had worked together all their lives were split up between the different companies.

I would say this was a change for the worse. British Rail may have had a poor reputation in some respects, but it was far more efficient than the private system. I believe that all major industries should be in government hands and not owned by private people. Today's rail system is far, far worse even than before nationalisation, when it was privately owned.

For one thing, BR had a timetable change twice-yearly, in winter and summer, but the difference would only be that a train was about two minutes earlier or later. People knew exactly when the trains ran, because they were always the same, and the printed timetable could be consulted with ease.

Then again, you almost never heard of a train being cancelled with BR. I worked in five different depots, and went into management with BR in 1976-8, as a train crew co-ordinator. This job entailed doing the rosters for two depots, Doncaster and Leeds. It was a horrendous task, with 160 men to allocate their duties. Each week the roster for the succeeding week had to be ready by Friday morning, but then someone would ring in sick, and you'd it all to do again. The biggest crime was to cancel a passenger train. Heads rolled if this happened, but I can never recall once cancelling a passenger train. They may have been late, due to unforeseen circumstances, but they were never cancelled. Now, when you go to a station, you hear of cancellations all the time over the Public Address System.

As regards track work, under BR, one group of men, under a ganger, were responsible for a particular length of track, which they knew well and kept repaired. Now that has changed.

When privatisation occurred the freight section was split away, and I went with GNER (Great north Eastern Railway) on the Doncaster intercity route. As soon as GNER took over, they wanted to make cuts in staffing, which involved the biggest financial outlay. They decided to close the Doncaster Depot and transfer to Leeds. I didn't want to travel to Leeds, so I took early retirement – 'the golden handshake'. That was in 1998.

I was glad to go, because the work changed so much from what it used to be. They were on to you all the time. Staff were always trembling in their shoes, unsure whether they would have a job the next day. The atmosphere became terrible.

After 'retirement'

When you've been used to working all your life from the age of 15, (and I'd done 12-14 hour shifts most of the time), you can't just do nothing. First of all I bought a derelict bungalow at Wath and it took me about two years to do it up. But after that, well, you can only do so much gardening, fishing and shooting. When every day is a Sunday the time takes some filling-in.

In the year 2000 I saw an advert in the local paper for a caretaker at Wath Library, and got the job. I think one thing that drew my attention to the job was that it involved maintenance of a coal-fired boiler. I knew a bit about boilers from my steam train days and so it appealed to me. The hours were 17 and a half per week, but there was also overtime, in fact, I ended up looking after nine library buildings in the Borough, putting up shelves, replacing light bulbs and other odd jobs.

The difference was, that I didn't class it as work (not hard work), compared with what I was used to. It was a doddle – I thought it were lovely. You were not under pressure like the last years on the railways. It was more relaxed. In addition to that, I worked as caretaker at Rawmarsh Old People's Centre for ten hours a week, and I also ended up delivering prescriptions for the local chemist. I saw a notice there – 'Prescription delivery driver wanted', and spoke to one of the assistants, but did not go for it at first. A few weeks later when I went in, the same lady was there and she approached me and asked if I was still interested in the job. It only entailed one hour per day, so I thought – 'I can do that after the library job'.

I was 65 in 2007, so I was starting to think about retiring, and a lucky win on the lottery made my mind up for me. I finished at the library but kept on the Rawmarsh job, which I intend to give up in March 2008. Then I hope to have more leisure, more holidays and to spend more time with my wife.

I really enjoyed my time with the railways, though it was hard work, but in the last few years there was so much insecurity. One man was doing four men's jobs and people didn't know what the next day held for them. It made them get nasty and fly off the handle at the least thing, so the atmosphere became unpleasant. I was glad to go.

My First Main Line Trip
Bill Quinn

A few years ago when I was a lad
I used to think a train driver's job wouldn't be bad
I used to think school was a waste of time
I'd much rather watch the trains on the old H and B Line

What I wanted to do I didn't really know
So I thought on the railway that's where I'll go

I'd made my mind up so that was that
And I'd always fancied one of those shiny caps
I thought if I joined, I'd get one
I didn't really know
So I signed on as a cleaner at the old Mexborough Loco

I awoke next morning before the lark
It felt rather strange walking the streets in the dark
I signed on at the loco at six o'clock
And the size of the engines overawed me somewhat

I was met by a chap I later knew as Old Bob
He showed me around and told me my job
We went up to the ash pits, the old coal stage as well
And we talked with two chaps known as Sunny and Nigel

I remember Sunny he was just a small chap
When filling the coal tubs he had always got a bad back
They only filled the tubs when they could not use the big crane
He was sunny by nature and Sunny by name

There weren't half some characters at the old Mexborough shed
One called Big John and old Tugboat Ted
George Henry Muxworthy now there's a name
We'll never see the likes of those chaps again
I remember one day after finishing my snap

51

Getting to work on time

I'd gone to clean an engine when the foreman shouted me back
He said, "Tha's first up today lad or so it would seem"
At last it looked like I'd realise my dream

I ran round to the office
As quick as a flash
Not forgetting my can and some tea to mash
When I got there I knew my goal was in sight
When they mated me up with old driver Bill Wright

A nice old chap was old driver Bill Wright
And I knew he'd give me a hand if things got a bit tight
I slacked down the footplate till it was spick and span
·   And wired us out for Wath Frodingham

We left Wath with our train after quite some time
And just jogged along nicely down the mainline
My first mainline trip I meant to show my worth
When we dropped down behind six in the goods at Stainforth

Bill put out his food on the tender back
And I said "I think it's time that we had our snap"
Well I'd already had mine about ten hours ago
And we were a long way from Frodinghambut I didn't know

When we left Stainforth we went at quite a good lick
It was better than berthing on the old Top Pitt
When we hit Guness Bank I set to with a will
But we only got to the top by the skills of old Bill

When I got home the hours I'd worked were sixteen
I was tired but happy, I'd realised my dream
As we pass the old loco today with our modern machine
I often remember the old days of steam
I hear a ghostly whistle far away in the night
And I remember my first trip with old driver Bill Wright

Working with Metal

"Muck, noise and all!"

"Conditions were bad, but the atmosphere and the workmates were lovely."

The cutlery, silverware, hand tool and engineering trades, the lighter trades, or metal working trades have employed large numbers of men and women in Sheffield for many generations.

Back in the seventeenth century, three out of five men in Sheffield worked in the cutlery industry, and most of the knives used in England were made in Sheffield.

In 1940 there were still 200 cutlery firms in Sheffield, the same number as there had been in 1840. By 1957, out of 700 UK cutlery firms, 650 were working in Sheffield.

In 1946, 10,000 men and women were employed in the cutlery industry. By 1992 this number had fallen to 2,888.

Silversmith's tools

In 1945 Viner's, the largest cutlery firm at the time, employed 1,250 workers. This fell to 800 in 1965. They closed in 1975.

And yet some of the 'little mesters', still continue. In this chapter Stuart Mitchell, Terry Rogers, and Trevor Slngsby, all tell their stories, as do the cutlery and engineering workers who worked for some famous Sheffield firms.

There are as many different reasons for people taking up these occupations as there are people involved. Very often, a school leaver would enter a trade simply because older members of the family were already a part of it, some would spend a lifetime in their chosen line whilst others would be quickly disillusioned and look for a change.

Shortly after the Second World War, many school leavers started work at the age of fourteen or fifteen and jobs were plentiful. The jobs varied tremendously from unskilled or semi skilled to highly skilled and there were many different ways of learning a trade. It would be rare for any two people to have identical experiences, everyone has a unique tale to tell.

"My dad believed quality was everything". *Staying with a family firm can be a very happy way of earning a living. One man who started off in his dad's workshop was*

Stuart Mitchell, knife-maker.

I was born 1970. Before leaving school at the age of 15, I would go down to my dad's shop at weekends and during school holidays, helping out and also learning the trade. After leaving school I went to work full time in my dad's shop in Portland Works off Brammall Lane. We would work Monday to Friday and also Saturday and Sunday if the demand was there.

My dad believed 'quality was everything', we'd try to better our craft when ever possible. I did realise at an early age that to call myself a knife-maker or a cutler I needed to learn all aspects of this trade. At this time of my career, 'the beginning', my dad is showing me how to make table, kitchen and hunting knives. After three years in the business, I'm 18 and still learning.

After work, my dad and me liked our fishing and did a bit of shooting game. We restored two wooden boats plus a worn out land-rover which was in a bit of a state.

I think I was the only 'Little Mester' apprentice in Sheffield. Coming on for 19 years of age I found that there was a demand for Sheffield cutlery. Big changes have happened over the years, the trade has diminished greatly not only here but in the U.S.A. Now it's left to the dedicated craftsmen, who are few and far between, to carry on.

As I look round at our Brightside and Tinsley deserts of land which were teeming with steel shops, it can be very depressing. When you enter the public houses in these areas there's photos and memorabilia on the walls showing what the steel shops used to be like.

May I talk about my mum's (Mum Pat) great grandmother, born in 1881. At the age of 12, she started work as a buffer girl for Mappin & Webb. She brought up three daughters on the State Pension, plus two and sixpence (12p), due to great grandad being killed in World War 1. Later she joined G. Bisby & Sons, Portobello Street, again as a buffer, and carried on working there until she passed away in 1953.

My mum's grandmother was born in 1900. Also worked as a buffer for Mappin & Webb. After World War 2, she was still buffing spoons, forks, parachute buckles, all on piece work i.e. 10 pence a gross for teaspoons, 15 pence a gross for dessert spoons, 18 pence per gross for table spoons and the same for parachute buckles. There was a lot of resentment towards the working rules of the day. Anyone late for work, no matter how valid the reason, was docked a full month's bonus money.

My grandmother was born in 1922. She was called Mary. She joined the cutlery trade as a buffer girl with George Bisby & Co, then Mappin & Webb. Grandmother remembered walking to work at dawn after the Germans had bombed Sheffield the night before, having to pass the sights of burning buildings and corpses in the streets. Those were dark days for the people of Sheffield.

My grandfather, Lawrence 'Lol' Mitchell, worked as a collier for 15 years, and left at the age of thirty, to rent a yard in Trafalgar Street in the town centre. The yard became a working yard for scrap collection, then later, for a haulage business, then Stuart (Snr, Dad) decided to open a cutlery shop in the yard. Lol was a bit of a lad and dabbled in antiques, rags and money lending, He was diagnosed with cancer in 1970 and had to finish work, doctors told him he had six months to live at the most. Lol passed away in 2000!

A memory from Stuart's (Jnr) sister Mandy. As a 12 year old girl, she had to go and fetch her grandpa's tea, so off she went with money and a note given to her by her grandma. She went to the butchers, next to the Co-Op at the bottom of Moor. After buying my grandpa's scampi (only the best!) she decided to go in the Co-Op, and whilst in there, went to the toilet. On the way home she realised that she'd left her grandpa's scampi in the toilet. She ran back and looked in the toilet but couldn't see it, so she looked in the litter bin and there it was. She took it back in the old newspaper and nobody knew any different.

Mum met Dad, Stuart, in his early days, making kitchen knives and palette knives for Walton & Orwin. Mum and Dad started their own business by renting the fourth floor in a Sheffield run-down cutlery shop. The rent was £5 and the only tools they had were a drill, a circular saw, pinning-on bench and a belt-driven glazer. Dad paid mum two pounds ten shillings a week. They did a lot of out-work like butchers' knives and trade knives. Many cutlery firms brought work for them to finish, Wolstenholm's, Joseph Elliott, Taylor Eye-witness, Latham & Owen and John Nowill.

In 1961 Mum and Dad married. On that Monday Mum and Dad were back at the shop working, their honeymoon lasted a day. From 1962 to 1970 mum managed to have five children working up to the last minute because dad couldn't pay someone else to do her job.

Around 1968 Dad and Mum decided to go into hunting knives, making and marketing with their very own name. This was a very

Stuart Mitchell, knife maker

nervous time for both of them, but with hard work it started paying off. One of Dad's first customers was F.W. Parkes of London.

In 1975 they moved to Samuel Peace, Stag Works, on John Street, much larger premises, installing specialised machinery, which was purchased from Wolstenholm's when they closed down in 1971. They were doing well until George Ibbotson went bankrupt. My dad was making quality knives and swords for Ibbotson's on a regular basis.

Dad tells this story of his early days of making swords. With no transportation of his own, one day he set off with two swords wrapped up on his shoulder, walking three miles to the customers' office. These were still the days of "liver and draw", meaning deliver the goods then draw the cash.

The inspector of the firm noticed a minute mark on the blades. Dad had no option but to trudge back to his shop. When you have a family depending on your wages you have to be a little tongue in cheek.

At the age of 25 I took over my mum and dad's business and after ten years running the shop, I am happy and successful, and long may it stay that way.

May I dedicate this last paragraph to my mum and dad? My dad passed away in 1995 and in 1996 my mum. All the work that's been created by mum, dad and myself is stamped with the trade mark "Pat Mitchell Sheffield England" (Pat – my mum).

Eric Finbow *worked in a variety of situations, some of which were typical of the small workshops tucked away in the back streets of Sheffield. He gives us a few insights into some antiquated practices which survived well after the Second World War. In his own words, he tells us,*

"I was born 27 April, 1943. My first exposure to the world of work began at the age of 14 in the 50s. There was a workshop located close to my home at Owlerton, that refurbished bottle crates for the old Sheffield brewery of Duncan Gillmore. The owner of this firm asked if I would help him load and offload his van on a daily basis.

The Duncan Gillmore bottling plant was located under the arches near the canal wharf where the Hilton Hotel now stands. It was a very dark gloomy place and very noisy. However, the most surprising thing was the two large barrels of beer that stood side by side, one in use by means of a spigot, while the other was settling (before the days of carbonated beer). One pint glass was provided, and this was washed out with beer, and all visitors, including myself, seemed to avail themselves of the facility, yet I don't recall seeing anyone the worse for drink. These people were working with machinery, so much for 'health and safety'!

At the age of fifteen, I left school and got employment as an apprentice toolmaker for a subsidiary of Mappin and Webb. The toolroom had two shapers, a centre lathe, a universal miller, and a wet grinding wheel. The only modern piece of equipment was a surface grinder, which was motorised. All the other equipment was driven from an elevated lineshaft.

The centre lathe in the toolroom was very old, the slides were worn, and it was located very near to a wall. Behind the wall, but only three feet away, was a large drop stamp. Each time the tup hit the bed, the resulting shock wave would cause the cutting tool to dig into the work. When the finishing traversing cut was made, one had to go round and ask the stamp operator to stop work – not a popular move as they were on piecework rates. Working conditions like this and the lack of investment in modern machinery, have led to the decline of engineering and the loss of trade and jobs.

As previously mentioned, all the machines were driven from an elevated lineshaft. A number of different speeds were available by means of a stepped pulley. The usual method of changing speeds was to use a hammer shaft to force the belt off the machine pulley onto a lower step, this left the belt still moving but with no tension. Then, the belt had to be flicked to get it to climb up a step on the line shaft pulley to restore the tension. The flicking action was again done with the hammer shaft. This was a dangerous operation, the correct way should have been to stop the line shaft and then use a ladder to reach the top pulley. Moving stationary belts was much safer but this method was not used because it would hold up production for the whole toolroom.

The buffer was at the gritty end of the cutlery trade. Some people would find the job unbearable, whilst for others it became a way of life and was something to be proud of. **Gladys Macioce** *was born in Hoyle Street in 1913. She started work in 1927 and worked till she was eighty.*

Gladys Macioce, buffer girl

I was one of five sisters. I started work at the age of 14 at the silverware firm of Atkin Brothers, Matilda Street and worked there until I was 67 years old. Even after I married I still worked. Times were hard then. I started out as an errand girl, and later became a buffer girl, working 8 am to 6 pm. My first wage was three shillings per week. The Little Mester (my boss), told me to keep sixpence for myself and not to give it to my mum - it was to be my pocket money.

The firm was a big one, with lots of small shops inside, each one with it's own Little Mester. The firm did fancy-work, making the spoons, forks etc with different patterns. Some of the names of the patterns were King's, Shell, Beaded and Old English. They also made silver jugs.

My dinner would be a sandwich wrapped in newspaper and I would eat it while the machine, a slow-puller, was going. On special days we got an hour off for dinner and went out to (what is now called) the Peace Gardens or down the Moor to do some shopping.

We'd come out with our faces as black as lead from the buffing. Our wedding rings had to be covered up to prevent them from being caught in the wheels.

Occasionally there were accidents with spindles. My sister-in-law caught her finger in the spindle and had to be taken to hospital and have stitches put in, but she was back at work the next day. You were paid by results, you couldn't afford to be idle.

They were happy times. We were never miserable. They were nice friendly girls who would help anyone. I enjoyed it.

There are still people around who have stayed with the same trade for a whole working lifetime, not necessarily with the same employer. It may be that takeovers have played a part in their destiny, but in some cases, a desire to go independent has also shaped their path through life. An interesting example of this is the story told by,

Terry Rogers, hollow-ware buffer

I started work at **Walker and Hall** in 1949 when I was aged fifteen, having already tried the steel works which I didn't like.

My mother and Aunt Mabel both worked at Viner's as buffers, Aunt Mabel as a 'grease dollier' and an 'insider'.

The firm wanted me to start as one of twelve apprentice silver smiths or a silver spinner, but I decided I wanted to work as a buffer, and I was put to a chap called Harold Spencer, and worked there for twelve years, till I went into the army. The spoon and fork buffers were all women with a reputation for 'initiations'.

Terry Rogers, buffer

There was an old lady there, Mrs Murrill, aged ninety two, who wore long skirts. She worked as she felt like it. That firm really looked after its people. One day she said "I'll show thee summat", and she buffed a fork, fanning out the pumice with her hand. That fork had not a mark on it. I could never grain a fork like that, not even now.

At that time in Sheffield 20,000 men would go fishing every Sunday, travelling either by train or "Andrews" coaches. Us lads used to sit on the fishing baskets in the middle of the bus. Our boss could get a tankful of petrol for a coach as the firm did 'war work'. At this time there was still rationing after the war. At the farm where we went fishing we would get eggs and chickens to bring back. One Christmas we went fishing, with 81 orders for joints of pork, but when we got to the farm, "the butcher's got flu", so when we drove back to Sheffield we had three big pigs, unbutchered, on the back seat of the coach, praying we wouldn't be stopped by the police for carrying black market meat. We arrived back at the works at 9.30 on a Sunday night, so first we had to knock Bert up to let us in, and we carried those pigs up three flights of stone steps, across a landing, up a ramp, up some wooden stairs, over a bridge across Cadman Lane, past the hammer shop and the lasses workshop, past the finishing shop, and up some more wooden stairs to our showers, where we changed from our clean to our mucky clothes. Well, I were as strong as a glass of water then, but I carried half a pig all that way. Next day Harold said go and ask the lads to sharpen the leather knives, and ask the joiner to lend us some saws. Go down to the warehouse and ask Beattie for some tissue paper, which one of the girls ironed for us, for all the stuff we've brought back. It took us till 6.30 that evening, but we cut the 81 joints ordered, even if they weren't right.

I worked for Harold, he was not the foreman but he was called a leader. His father had died when he was 17, so he had to earn a living. He was a buffer and finisher, and he was good at everything, his work, tennis, cricket. He was the life and soul of the shop. He'd bring me his son's clothes and he'd often pay for my dinner, I paid 10 pence, and the men paid one shilling and sixpence. We didn't change our clothes at dinnertime, so ten of us buffers had a table all to ourselves, in the canteen.

One morning he said, "We're going out this afternoon." We often went to football and cricket at Brammall Lane on an afternoon. "Where?" "Never mind, make sure you come in something clean." In those days the Moor was a bombsite, Harold took me up some wooden steps, and there was a chap sitting crosslegged on a table, a tailor. "We've come for a suit apiece, make him one for £20, I want one for up to £30." So he had a tweed suit. I was only seventeen at the time, but I still wore that suit when I came out of the Army.

Piecework

At Walker and Hall silversmiths would get work out of the "trap", (the warehouse, where work would be passed over the counter). Let's say teapots, they'd take them out in twenties. At the end of the week, if the last twenty weren't done they'd take a "draw" (a wage when work wasn't completed). At the end of the month every bit of that work had got to be completed. We all had our own mark on the work. One chap was invariably the slowest in the shop, and he would hold other work up. Once it was getting to 2 pm on Friday and he needed help doing his last two teapots. They had to be in the trap by 4.30 pm. Harold, always the peacemaker asked me to help rough them, he got those pots in with five minutes to spare.

There would be agreed prices with, say, a group of silversmiths, or a group of buffers. There was a general price throughout town. We were earning good money doing piecework, women buffing and finishing spoons and forks often earned more than the management. But there was no money if you were off sick. You could decide what work you did, but not always, the firm might want to fulfil an order.

I was paid datal as an apprentice, £2 and ten shillings a week for the first six months, then £3 a week till I was 23 years old, when I went onto piecework. Harold told me that when I first started there was a heated discussion in the shop, five men had recently come back from the war, they had just got married, and got little families, and they didn't want me in the shop as I was paid datal.

At first we never clocked in, then in the 1950's it was brought in. Our shop thought it was barmy. We got sixpence an hour to be on the clock, but some workers would still be on their way home at 3 o'clock.

Mappin and Webb

After 12 years at Walker and Hall, things started to change. In late 1958 a new managing director took charge, he brought with him a first class designer. He went on to design half a dozen articles to run alongside the traditional pieces we had done for years.

We used to make silver services for all the shipping lines and the big hotels like the Savoy. It took about a year for work to fall off. One morning all the work we had was worth three and sixpence. Harold had already called at Viner's to see if they could take on 12 buffers if we were out of work. They said they'd gladly take us, so we told the departmental manager we would go to Viner's if things didn't improve.

He informed the managing director who then told us Walker and Hall would be merging with Mappin and Webb to form a new company called British Silverware Ltd.

When we got to Mappin's we were working in a 'state of the art' shop, but there were too many of us, twenty one. We worked together for twelve months. I worked two days a week for Lewis Rose, as we were on short time. Harry stayed at Mappin and Webb for a year till work dried up. He thought, "you work for a firm".

Eventually Harry and I rented an empty shop in Leah's yard for 15 shillings, I got a motor from Lewis Rose, the electrician rigged up the electrics. I worked as a buffer for two days a week on Ernest Lacey's work. He had a shop up Garden Street in Stevenson's Yard, making spoons and forks for Russell Bradley's. In no time at all we were earning good money.

The customers would bring work in big baskets. I always used to keep back one piece until I was paid. I'd work till 8 or 9 at night, Saturdays, Sundays. This trade is "feast or famine". We'd work flat out up to Christmas, and then be scratching around until the new tax year.

At Leah's yard there was a spoon and fork buffer called Edith, who didn't pay rent, but would clean the toilets and sweep the yard. I had got some cutlery, the full range, dozens of this, dozens of that, which I passed to Edith. It was all done by the following Thursday, with the prices all written down, on strips of brown paper, six spoons at eleven pence ha'penny and so on, with the total price of £5/11/9. The customer come in with £100, "How much for the cutlery?" so I says "£18", "she knows how to charge" "tha's got it cheap, anywhere else would have charged £40." Edith got her £18.

I was working at Cooper Bros on Saturday mornings, and I had an offer to go there, so I went on spec and stayed 25 years. Mr Whitely, the managing director, was a smashing man. But the same thing happened as at the other firms, and I came out on me own for 20 years. I worked in a shop at Camelot for 12 years, and now I'm renting a shop elsewhere, working for myself. I've got a talent for silver work, so I've carried on. I've always said, "These hands are mine".

Another man who has stayed with the same trade for most of his working life, initially as an employee then later going self employed is **Trevor Slingsby – pewter metal smith.** *He experienced the companionship, which develops whilst working in a large company, both in and out of working hours, he also knows how it feels to go it alone and be independent. He tells us*

I was born in 1941 at the Jessop's Hospital. Mum and dad, Laura and Walter, lived in Dorset Street. I attended Springfield School from five to 15 years of age.

At Viner's

I was two weeks short of my 15th birthday when I applied for my first job at Viner's Cutlery Company, which was successful, so the manager told me to come back in two weeks to start a six year apprenticeship. This was in 1956.

Whilst at Viner's I met my future wife Pauline, she was working in the offices, then in 1963 we got married, and in 1966 Pauline left Viner's to have our one and only daughter, Carol Jane. I didn't think the managers were very good at their jobs, due to some of the questions which they asked. If they had worked on the shop floor like their staff the questions would not have been asked.

Working conditions were very good, we didn't work bank holidays. Viner's looked after their staff.

Promotion at Viners? None of the shop floor staff seemed to want it. We seemed to go and work for someone else or work for ourselves.

Working for Viner's was smashing at Christmas. Their dinner-dance was special, I remember this Christmas they decided to hold it at the Azena Ballroom, Gleadless Townend. One of the managers volunteered to go and book at the Azena, this manager is now on the Board of Sheffield Wednesday Football Club. We didn't have transport, so someone shouted "Trevor take him on the back of your motor bike", and so I did. He wished he'd walked.

At dinner time all who could kick a ball went for a game of football, before we had to clock out, so round the corner on to the spare land. All weathers, rain, sleet, snow, we weren't bothered. This day playing 15 a side, Tommy gets injured a couple of minutes before the finish of the dinner break, so we told Tommy we'll leave you at the bottom of the steps and when the foreman finds you just say you've fallen down the steps and hurt your leg.

We all clocked in and carried on with our jobs. After a bit the foreman came round asking for Tommy. "Don't know" was the reply. Finally he found Tommy. The foreman said "What on earth are you doing down there?" Tommy's reply "Fallen and hurt my leg". The foreman came back with "You haven't clocked-in for starters and you're covered in mud".

He warned all the so-called United and Wednesday players that he was going to ban these matches. Every week he threatened, but never followed it up. Tommy was taken to hospital and treated for a broken leg. He kept his job.

Going back to the Christmas dance, all the lads on the shop floor noticed that this manager had been for a haircut. One of the lads mentioned this to him. The reply from the manager was 'You should go and get your hair cut for the dance'. So we did, all twelve of us, didn't clock out, just went to the barbers on West Street. All went to the same barbers, waited for each other, then walked back to Viner's, straight on to the carpet in the boss's office. He made his mark, "You don't go for your haircut in my time". Cheeky me replied, "It grows in your time sir". As soon as I opened my mouth I thought of what will happen when I go home and tell mum I've been sacked. The red-faced boss made the remark "It doesn't all grow in my time", then a voice from the back of the room said "We haven't had it all cut off sir". We didn't hear any more, but we didn't do it again.

My time at Viner's was enjoyable, they gave me a trade to get me through life, the trade was only learnt from work-mates, not from management, as they were not trained on the shop-floor, hands-on method.

Working for myself

I left in 1968 after 12 years, I was 27 years of age and decided to go it alone and work for myself with a mate called Bob. I rented a shop on Hill Street off Brammall Lane. We did very well, then I moved to Denby Street on my own and Bob left, this was in 1980, the premises was a top floor occupancy. This was cheaper, and less chance of being burgled. All my machinery was bought second-hand from companies going bust or someone getting a better model and wanting to sell the out of date machine.

Working on my own was very demanding, supply and demand. Each day I had a full book. I knew I was good at my job, and all in Sheffield who dealt in pewter sent blanks to me to finish, just imagine, I have to pick up 50 blanks weighing 15 kgs. At one time I would pick up four sets of 50 blanks equal to 60 kgs at one go, walk up to the top floor without putting down the weight. To make my day a financial gain I would have to carry a thousand blanks, that is 300 kgs each morning, then carry on making the pewter blanks into beautiful pewter mugs.

You may ask why I didn't start a young lad as an apprentice. This is the reason, I had no spare time and I didn't have spare pewter for the lad to train on. I only dealt in blanks, which means that if a company sends me 100 blanks I can't ask a trainee to get a blank and have a go, then he makes a mistake, I can't send 99 pewter mugs and put a sorry-note saying "My apprentice has made a mistake, is it alright?" I would lose my contract and the word would get round.

If I got big orders to complete, lads in the trade would come round to the shop after they had finished work to help me out for a couple of hours.

In time, with all the lifting and carrying each morning, the job took its toll and I had a heart attack whilst at work, which I recovered from and was advised to sell the business, which I did. That was in 1997. At present I'm doing a less demanding job.

Cutlery manufacture also needs support from other ancillary trades, one of which is cabinet case making. **Iris Guest** *tells us about this,*

I was born at Crookes in 1937, and left school in 1952 at 15 to start work with the firm of Charles Kirby & Sons on Arundel Street. The job was to make linings for canteens of cutlery - this was known as Cabinet Case Lining. The canteens might be a 24-set size, or large ones with drawers, and the linings were of felt, a serge material or velvet, with satin cushions. Most of the staff were married women, and at 15 you were the 'run-around girl'. Your job was to run errands, e.g. to and from the polisher with cases to be finished off, and of course, tea-making.

When I first walked in I thought - "I don't know if I want to do this", but the women were nice and I soon got used to it. I was quite gullible then, but my brother had warned me about the practical jokes often played on starters, such as telling me to 'go for a long stand', so I never got caught out. There was no bullying - it was a friendly atmosphere, with all age groups, men and women working together. My first wage was 40 shillings and sixpence a week (just over £2), and I was paid on a daily rate, unlike the married women who were on piece-work. The piecework ladies wrote everything down in a book and they could reckon up their wages fast.

The older workers, e.g. the French polishers, passed on their tips to the young ones.

The women worked in a big room with a coal fire at each end. Part of my job was to clear the grates and light the fires every morning. The coal had to be brought up from the cellar, and carried up three flights of stairs. We'd have two buckets of coal each and they were pretty heavy, and what's more, there were rats in the cellar. We sang as we walked down, hoping to frighten them away, but if we saw one we shrieked. The job I disliked most was on Fridays, when we had to donkey-stone the hearths. I wouldn't want my daughter to be doing what I did, but in those days I just accepted it.

Another awful job for the young ones was cleaning out the glue pots. Each woman had a pot of glue with which to stick the linings to the cases. The glue came in blocks and had to be fetched up from the cellar. It was melted in a pot which was put inside a container of water over a gas ring, and you had to keep checking the water level in your pot, and top it up if it had evaporated. The glue did not smell very good either, but you got used to it.

There was also a strong smell of French polish in the polishers' shop, and the men and women who worked there wore masks. The fitters made the wooden cases and so there was a saw mill – there was always a lot of dust flying around in there. At the end of a working day there would be perhaps 9 -12 inches of bits on the floor, from the edge trimmings etc. These had to be swept up, bagged and put into bins in the cellar.

There was no canteen, but there was an oven at the side of the fires. Each woman brought in her own food and the runabout girls heated it up or cooked it on one of the gas rings for them. My mother used to make me a little meat & potato pie the night before, which I would share with another girl I was friendly with. We took it in turns to bring a pie to share. There was a shop on Charles Street which sold plate dinners, and we would collect them four at a time. We also brought our own mugs or cups for the tea. The upstairs ladies had to be seen to as well.

Eventually, I got on the bench and a new girl took over the run-around jobs. An older lady was in charge of the bench, and she taught me the trade, which was to make the fittings for the inside of the cutlery cases. There was a rack into which the cutlery fitted, and you used a special knife to line the racks and trim off the edges. The lining material, which might be velvet, serge or felt, had to be pressed down onto the base of the case with a wooden spatula, and then the sides went in. The satin for the cushion had to be pleated and it was very important not to get glue on the lining material.

You could decide which bits of the job to do first – part of the work was done standing and part sitting, so there was variety.

There was a manager, a lovely old man called Mr Hogg, and you went to him to get your work, but under him was a young man in his twenties who was rather arrogant. There was one kind of case that everyone hated working on. They were called in the trade, 'Doodlebugs'. They were plain 6 or 12 knife and fork sets with a pleated cushion on the lid, and were not particularly hard work, but very boring, and the married women hated them.

One day when I went to ask for work, the older man was off sick and the young one gave me doodlebugs, not just once, but over and over again for a whole month. It seemed as if he'd got his knife into me. I stuck it and stuck it, but eventually I told the older lady in charge and she said – "See Mr Hogg", who was back at work once more. She told me that Mr. Hogg thought I was a good worker.

The next time I went for work, again the younger man gave me doodlebugs, so I went to the office and burst into tears. Kind Mr Hogg, who was small, bald and be-spectacled, asked - "What's the matter"- and told me to sit down. I told him - "Every time I ask for work he gives me doodlebugs, and I can't take it any more". Mr Hogg asked me - "What would you really like to do? He asked me if I would like to do a big cabinet with drawers (known as a four by four)"? I said – "I can't do that", but he said – "Yes, you can". I walked back carrying it, and I thought all my Christmases had come at once. It was an honour to be given this job. These special cabinets were never given to the piece-rate workers because they would rush the job. The lining was a special black velvet, with a pink satin cushion. It took me two and a half weeks to complete the work.

Soon after that, Mr. Hogg was off sick again, and once again I got nothing but doodlebugs, and that was the reason I left. I wasn't sleeping at nights and my mum said – "Get another job". Later I found out that the young man left six months after I did.

In those days, you could leave a job one day and get another one the next. I went to Pickering's off The Moor, making linings for cardboard boxes. The boxes were stamped out and you worked on a conveyer belt, gluing them together and covering them with fancy paper.

My third job was at The Wireless & Telephone Company on Lydgate Lane at Crookes. About half the people in Crookes worked there, and the other half worked at a laundry, also on Lydgate Lane. This was the late 1950's and early 1960's. About two hundred girls and married women worked there. I had gone for an interview at the laundry, but when I saw the big ironing boards and presses, I refused to take the job, and so instead went to Wireless. It was possible to pick and choose jobs just like that. My sister had worked at Wireless before me, also my sister-in-law and cousin, so I had a good idea of what the work would be like.

The firm made components for televisions, radios and telephones. If you worked on a winder machine it coiled wires and you soldered them together with a soldering iron. Later I got a better job in the stores there, dishing out work. We worked to targets here, so our wages fluctuated from week to week, and if you were over the target you got a bonus.

My fourth job was at Shearstone, Peters & Dunn, making components for hearing aids, and soldering transistor boards. I was married in 1962, and for a short time after my son was born I worked from home, eventually going back full-time. Whilst I had children, I needed work that fitted around them, and so I worked at the University catering for the students. This meant I had the same holidays as the children.

When the University opened the Law Centre at Crookesmoor Road, I worked in the little café there. At first there were two of us, but eventually we had six staff and I ended as Supervisor. I left there when my husband and I bought a shop on Northfield Road. It was a gift shop, but eventually there were about five gift shops on Crookes, so we gave it up. That was in 1982, and that part of Crookes never seemed to pick up afterwards.

There are many firms in Sheffield who have over the years, established relationships with overseas communities. These connections have grown naturally through word of mouth. We have a story from,

Taher Ali, drop stamper for forty years

I was born in a village outside Aden, and grew up looking after sheep.

When I was about 18 years old my uncle sent for me to work with him at a firebrick factory at Stocksbridge. I came by ship from Aden to France, then by train and the ferry to Dover, and then straight to Sheffield.

I worked with my uncle for about a year, but the money was not enough, so I got a job at a rolling mill for four months.

Then I went to T G Lilleyman, first on a machine, after that on a drop stamp. It was a very heavy job, there was a lot of noise, but it was better money. I worked there for forty years. We were making scissors and knives. We worked morning and afternoon shifts, a few nights if something happened, for eight or 12 hours.

I had plenty of friends at work, I learned English from work, sometimes I went to school on Saturdays and Sundays, after work there was no time.

In 1960 the firm helped me bring my brother to Sheffield, the gaffer liked me because I was a good worker. I visited Yemen every two to three years. I would go and come back after two to three months, and I would get my job back. My wife and little daughter came to Sheffield twenty two years ago. My sons are in America now.

Working with metal

I liked the job, but it was heavy, and hot from the furnaces. I had one accident, as I struck the hammer the die came out and injured my foot. I did get compensation.

I finished after forty years when I got redundancy in 1999.

The term 'cutlery trade' is a blanket phrase, which covers a wide variety of specialised skills. Many finished artefacts will have come into being only by having passed through many hands, each adding their own particular stage along the way. In turn, these specialists often rely on services from outside the trade. One man who eventually worked in cutlery production, but who started out at a 'Little Mester's' making saw fittings is **Carl Middleton.** *He writes about his uncle's workshop,*

CROSSCUT SAW, FOR TREE FELLING Etc.

Drawings

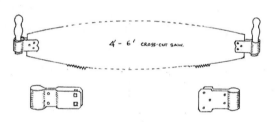

4' - 6' cross-cut saw.

PITSAW TILLER AND BOX.
FOR SAWING TREE TRUNKS OR LOGS
INTO PLANKS BY HAND.

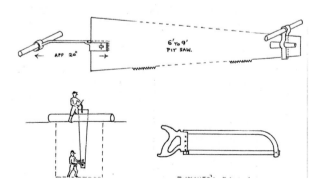

6' to 9'
PIT SAW.

APP 20°

"E.C. Gibson, 23 Court, 137, Scotland St, Sheffield 3. (established app. 1890 to 1922). On his death, business owned by Mrs E.C. Gibson, (ref. Kelly's Directory 1929) & worked by sons. All work & business transferred (probably 1930?) to son, E.C. Gibson, (saw fittings specialist) Jericho Works, Jericho St., Sheffield 3".

Sawpit

This family business was one of the very many "Little Mesters" workshops. The most employed were four workers, and my uncle and aunt (the owners). We were well known and much respected in the trade.

I joined my uncle, E.C. Gibson as an apprentice in 1937. I worked happily with him, learning a very skilled specialist trade. To shorten the six years it took to learn hand welding on an anvil, I was sent to Sheffield University, Dept. of Applied Science, to learn oxy-acetylene welding, and to study metallurgy. This allowed more time to be spent on toolmaking, for my uncle was continually modernising.

As the war progressed, (I had been in the Air Training Corps since its formation) I decided to join the Royal Air Force, in 1942. On interview, it was decided I would be trained as a flight mechanic (engines). De-mobilised, I returned to work in January 1947, and was introduced to the "Interrupted Apprenticeship Scheme", organised and subsidised by the Government.

I called in to see my uncle regarding starting work again. For four years I had worked with him as his apprentice, then four and a half years in the Forces.

MINISTRY OF LABOUR AND NATIONAL SERVICE

Apprenticeships interrupted by War Service

District Man Power Board,

To *Mr. C. Middleton.*

OAKHOLME HOUSE,

OAKHOLME ROAD,

SHEFFIELD.

16 JAN 1947 (Date)

Dear Sir(s),

Acceptance of Application under Scheme No. /

I am to refer to the application made by you and your ~~apprentice~~ employer under the above scheme and to inform you that its formal acceptance by the Ministry is contained in the enclosed form I.A.S.4/4A/~~4W~~. The form sets out the period of renewed apprenticeship to be served, the period for which the Wages Allowance will be payable and the Ministry's undertaking to pay the amount of Wages Allowance provided both parties comply with the terms of the Scheme and the Agreement entered into under it.

The form should be retained for future reference

If you wish to make any comment in regard to the particular scheme under which the application has been accepted or on other matters arising from the form, the Department will be obliged if you will communicate with them at once. The Identification No. given in the form should be quoted.

~~A copy of form I.A.S. 11(T)/11(P)/11W is also enclosed; it should be used when the first claim for the payment of the Wages Allowance is submitted.~~

Yours faithfully,

F. Bean

FOR DISTRICT MAN POWER BOARD

I.A.S.14.

G175269(A33s) M20682/3684 10/46 40M W&S 703

I had brought with me from the R.A.F. information about the 'Interrupted Apprenticeship Scheme', whereby employers would be subsidised by the Government for accepting an apprentice who was now entitled to full pay as an adult, but was not yet fully qualified.

My uncle's reply was, "Go and visit the Amalgamated Engineering Union, find out what the present full pay is, and join." This I did. The wage then was £5 or £5/5s per week, which he agreed to pay. Then he said - "there'll be no holidays with pay – this business cannot afford such luxuries". I agreed to this condition.

All went well and the months passed by. At the end of December, he told me we had had a 'good year' and I was given a share of the profits, as an incentive bonus. We had 'good years' (and bonus) until my uncle's death, when I took over the management for my Aunt, and different conditions.

I never did get 'holidays with pay', but received a better reward.

I have learned just recently that it was not until 1997 that 'holidays with pay' became law.

Working and business progressed well until the sudden death of my uncle in 1952. I continued to manage the business and work with my aunt until 1956, but we did not see "eye to eye". We had to separate, and sadly that was the end of E.C. Gibson, Saw Fittings Specialist. Following orders would without doubt go to our competitors, my uncle's cousins, who also worked in the same trade.

To describe the trade. We made any item that was used in the saw trade, and supplied to most of the saw manufacturers of Sheffield, and there were many. The bulk of our work was in the making of crosscut socket tangs, of different styles. About 15 to 20 gross per week. Next was pitsaw tillers and boxes, approximately 12 dozen per week, buckles and tillers, and finally butcher's and kitchen bows, again, many designs.

The work involved tool making to manufacture components, which were then assembled and welded. Equipment required for these processes were, two Pattinsons Power Presses, one six inch lathe, one power saw, one shaping machine, two pillar drilling machines, and two grinding machines. All these were driven by a 10 hp electric motor, through twin driving shafts, pulleys and belts. There was a blacksmith's hearth, with all hand tools, bellows/fan and two anvils.

Whilst at school I had worked Saturday mornings, and the odd hour or so after school. I was well aware it would be a manual occupation and somewhat "dirty". Some aspects I definitely did not like, one being, on a Saturday morning, delivering some of the goods made. There were two barrows, each held fifteen gross of socket tangs, or one gross of tillers and boxes, a very large load for a small lad of 13/14 yrs. Fortunately the deliveries were downhill or flat. Considering some of the journeys were to Attercliffe, (about three miles) it was a long haul. When orders could be arranged and large enough, a carter, Mr Gregg, was employed. He and his lorry cost 8/6 per hour. We also used the barrows to collect gas cokes from Neepsend, for use in the blacksmith's forge.

Work was a very serious business with my uncle, no skylarking, or playing the fool, too many accidents to avoid and so much to learn. He was a kind and generous person with an infinite amount of patience. He taught me so many things (as well as the trade).

Before I joined the R.A.F. there was no such thing as a tea-break. We worked 48 hours per week and enjoyed one week's holiday, which was Sheffield's Holiday Week. I began work for 8/6 per week (to take home to Mother) and my uncle gave me 6p per week for myself. An annual pay rise brought me to about 17/6 per week when I enlisted.

When Carl eventually left the firm of E. C. Gibson, he moved on until he eventually became linked more directly to the cutlery industry and is able to describe some of the processes involved. Although he had not 'come up through' the trade, Carl had sufficient skills and experience to adapt. He goes on to write,

I do not consider myself to be a cutler, but I did spend ten years in a very well established cutlery business. These are a few of my memories of that period. The years were 1956 to 1966.

It was a small establishment of around twenty four to thirty workers. Spoons and forks were made and finished from Staybrite Steel. Matching knives were also made, but part of this work was done by outworkers, since different plant and skills were required.

The processes began in the 'Press Shop' where sheets were cut, then formed by 'Sheffield Type' power presses and cross rolled with two huge cross rolling machines. In between rolling stages, the blanks had to be annealed, in the furnace, then 'pickled' in acid to remove scale, before a second rolling and prongs were then cut out on the presses. The next stage was the 'stamp' department where the shanks and bowls were formed, as were the prongs and shapes of the forks.

Now that the shaping was finished, all blanks were sent to the 'Polishing Shop'. First all edges had to be ground and glazed, including between fork prongs. The next stage was buffing, followed by polishing. When the polishing was completed all items were passed on to the 'Warehouse Department'. Here each spoon and fork was examined, wiped and polished with yellow dusters to remove any polishing compound, then finally wrapped in acid-free tissue paper.

Though this is a brief account of the processes, every item had gone through at least a dozen stages before being sent for finishing and polishing.

Three patterns only were made and only 'Firth Staybrite' steel was used. The finished goods were boxed, or set into very smart cutlery canteens with attractive linings. These were then sent to large suppliers, to be sent on to retailers. We depended on contracts from City Councils and Universities, also large Sheffield cutlers and silversmiths. These were household names.

The workers by and large were a friendly crowd, all knowing their own particular job, or jobs. To work in cutlery one could expect noise, dirt and conditions that left a lot to be desired. Conditions like these in many industries were common at that time. There was no issue of protective clothing or overalls, but all the workers did wear their 'own supplied' overalls, and had to arrange their own cleaning. The only protective items I recall were rubber gauntlet gloves for use when handling the acids used for 'pickling'.

Work began at 8 am though this was variable for the polishing ladies. Some started as late as 10.30 after seeing children were catered for. All had to 'clock in', and were paid by the hour, except the polishers. They were paid 'piecework', but still clocked in for office use. Someone, on arrival, would light the three gas heated boilers for tea making and washing. All were allowed to make a drink as and when they wanted (supplying their own materials). This practice was not supervised and never abused. Lunch break was more organised in as much as all machinery was switched off for one hour (then one could talk normally – peace and quiet). There was no canteen, just a small room to eat sandwiches containing two tables and four benches to sit upon. Most workers sat where they worked (on boxes usually), rather than use this facility. Another break was usual in the afternoon. Workers started to 'clock off' from 4 pm in the polishing shop. Machinists and warehouse staff worked until 5 pm.

Work in the machine shop was noisy though not particularly dirty – we just had to talk loudly. The only heating was free-standing coke stoves (not a very efficient system). In summer there were plenty of windows to open, and in the polishing department there was also a huge amount of air movement, it became quite cold, to say the least.

The annealing furnace was outdoors. No great hardship, taking only a short time to load it with blanks. These were stacked in rows in heavy metal trays, holding about three gross, and three trays filled the furnace. A pyrometer and timer situated indoors controlled the process. Cooling took place on the yard floor.

Although I stated that workers in general were a friendly lot, complaints were numerous, but very little was done about them, and they were sort of accepted as part of daily routine. One section would complain about the workmanship of another section causing them more work. Polishers would complain that inspection in the warehouse was too critical, and were sending too many units back for correction. Since these had been accounted for as piecework, returns had to be corrected without further payment. This you can imagine did not go down too well!

It is difficult to believe now, looking back, that there was no single person in charge. A woman in the warehouse (senior in work years) saw to the general routine. In the production department there were four males and each knew what had to be done. Machine tools to be set up, rolling machines to be adjusted for each batch. The one job not shared was 'stamping', which was done by one man and took up most of his time.

Through all this the two bosses (and owners) used to wander through the different sections, talking, listening and informing. They would speak of progress, the need to hasten, and offer occasionally a 'pat on the back'. There would be mention of particularly large contracts received, thereby assuring staff of security of employment. To the workers they were 'the boss', but not held in awe at all and each could speak to them 'on a level'. All workers were addressed by their Christian names and, one could say, it was a very good working arrangement that worked well.

The entire works closed for the two weeks paid holiday. The time was standard 'Sheffield Holiday Weeks', since most workers' partners would have that same period. Further holidays were allowed, on occasion, to be taken unpaid, but the practice was not encouraged.

Eventually, from there, I accepted an appointment in the Health service, as an engineer. It was then I began to look back. The difference in lifestyle! Since leaving school I had been happy on the 'shop floor', not knowing anything different. Now it was 'collar and tie and best suit'. Coffee at 10 a.m., lovely dining room, table cloths, three course, subsidised meal. Sickness (conditions applied) paid for, and four weeks holiday each year. What a difference! Why had I waited so long?

Having said that, I must say I had enjoyed my previous working life, and can look back with mostly happy memories – 'Muck, noise and all!'

Electro platers work in silver and gold for the silverware and cutlery industry, in chrome or nickel for scissors and surgical instruments, and nuts and bolts, and all kinds of engineering work.

"My job title was a wirer-upper, a preparation for electro-plating."

My name is **Mary Judge**. I was born in 1944 in Lybster, Scotland, then moved to Horsham, and in 1955 I moved to Sheffield in the district of Stradbrooke. I attended All Saints School, then Brook School and left school at 15. I went to live on Fitzhubert Road, Manor.

My first job was at Norfolk Market Hall, Haymarket (now Wilkinsons), working for Hansons Café. Then we moved to Castle Market. We changed the name of the café to Roof Top Café, due to it being situated on the Gallery. For my 5 and a half day week I got £3/0/9d. Board money (holiday money), was £4/10s. You got dinners free. My uniform was a green and white gingham smock with a white apron and white cap with green ribbon.

I left after 18 months, I enjoyed working there but I fancied a change. I went to a cutlery firm called Slack & Barlow, off Matilda Street. I got £4/15s as a warehouse packer. When I was working at the Roof Top Café my wage packet was in a dark brown sealed envelope, no way of seeing what you had inside till you ripped it open, but at Slack & Barlow wage packets had a window – much easier. My hours were Monday and Friday 8 a.m. to 4 p.m., Tuesday and Thursday 8 a.m. to 5 p.m., Wednesday 8 a.m. to 5.45 p.m. and Saturday 8 a.m. to noon. Bank holidays off, and annual holiday. After 9 months I moved into the kitchen working with my good friend Barbara, fetching sandwiches and doing teas. Friday was fish and chips day, with a lovely mug of tea and of course, bread and mushy peas. I left after four years due to Slack & Barlow going through hard times.

At the age of 21 I moved to Hartshead Plating Company. After six months we moved to Darnall off Greenland Road. My job title was a Wirer-Upper, a preparation for electro-plating. I had 3 smocks a week, what a mucky job! My wage for my 5 and a half day week was £25. All the girls looked forward to payday (Friday). It was our night out up Town. We'd put 5 shillings each in the kitty, and meet up in Fitzalan Square, then it was Marples, Blue Bell (Cavells), Red Lion, Holly Street and finish back at the Black Swan. Don't forget we were all back at work in the morning. We took our lives in our hands to run and catch the last bus out of Pond Street.

After clocking-in on the Saturday morning, feeling like you haven't slept due to the bed spinning, then to wind wire onto springs in sacks for deliveries on Monday.

In 1969 I went to work at Woolworths, Haymarket, as a stock-room girl. We had three stockrooms at Woolworths, basement, 3rd floor and 4th floor. Not a trusting company – they made sure that your uniform pockets were sewn up to stop pilfering. By the age of 29 I got married, stayed at Woolies until I was 30.

Westall Richardson was my next adventure. Their place was on Allen Street. I was put in this room, they called it the C.I.D. – Cleansing Inspection Department. I had to be trained for the job. We had a 'late bonus'. If I were on time all week I got an extra £2 a week on top of my £35 a week. By the way, I left this job at 35 years of age.

Michael was the bloke I married when I was 29. He'd worked at Firth Browns from leaving school, and this is where my next job took me, as a canteen cleaner. Not much excitement. I lasted until 1980 and in 1981 I started work as a cleaner at the West Bar Police Station. I had to retire in 1998 through ill -health.

"The silver plating which we did for James Dixon's and Viner's had to be top quality."

Ann Udall, *worked with her sister, and also Joe Fagan (as in the pub name), and next to Horace Deakin's tool shop, tells us,*

My first job at 15, was at a printer's in Neepsend Lane, working on an offset litho machine printing labels. There was a bookbinder's upstairs. The place was really old, there was even an Aga. My father thought I had a job for life, so he was angry when I left.

For the next eight or nine years (I kept leaving and then going back) I worked for The Export Box Company, part of Walter & Dobson. It was on Broad Lane, next to what is now called Fagan's Pub, it was called The Barrel at that time. Joe Fagan worked at the Export Box Co. in the 50's and 60's. Later the firm moved to Wellington Street at the back of Debenham's. We made flock lined boxes for the cutlery trades.

I got two pounds, two shillings and nine pence a week when I started.

Thirty or forty people worked there, on four landings. There were four tortoise stoves, which would burn coke and cardboard. I got two shillings and sixpence extra a week to come in early at 7.30 am to light them. In the same yard there was a joiners shop, and they would exchange wood for coke. This yard was also shared by Horace Deakin's tool shop, a little sweet shop, and a house with a family living in it. There were four toilets in the yard, which we all shared. It's all been demolished now. I worked in a cellar. It was freezing. We also stitched boxes for steel files with metal staples.

I knew Horace Deakin really well. He had always worked in the shop for Mr Turner and he inherited it from him when he died. The shop never altered at all, it had all kinds of tools. I remember my first husband's brother who was an apprentice at Norton's Glass, being sent to fetch a special tool. He had to say he was Sam Low's grandson and Horace would find him the right tool.

Twice a week I worked as the van girl. We delivered to Sheffield Steel Products at Sheffield Road, Rotherham, to Avon Tools at Maltby, Firth Brown's and Shaw's the magnet makers, which was in a little terrace house in Monmouth Street, still with a coal fire. Ralston's the file makers were also in a terrace house on Rockingham Street. Sometimes we would walk round with the boxes. It was like a day out!

Horace Deakin in his shop

We worked in what was little more than a tumble down shack, but it was lovely. We ate our dinner where we sat for work, one girl would fetch the sandwiches. We used to have a 'chip lady', whose daughter worked there. She used to take orders on Thursday, and her mother would walk all the way from the 'chippy' on Duke Street on Fridays with our fish and chips. We had a manageress who looked after us. She were lovely. On Tuesdays she would write a list of orders for us for the butcher, and the meat would be delivered to work on Friday. We did the same with fish. If we didn't have enough money, we paid the following week.

When the gaffer went out it was playtime. Fred who worked on the guillotine once cut up Mary's steak into neat little cubes, and once he cut up one of the men's ties.

Everybody was equal, we're less on a level now. It really annoys me when people say, "I'm only working class."

On one occasion, there was no coke because the boss hadn't paid the bill, and it was freezing. I went to the boss and said, "Mr

Gordon, we're going home, we can't work like this." I was about 16 years old. We thought, "He can't sack us, there's no one else to do the work". I walked out, but I thought I'd best go and tell me mam who was working as a cleaner at Robert Brothers on the Moor. Oh! me mother were fiery. She marched in to Mr Gordon, "How can you let these women work like this, and you sitting with this fire in your office?" I felt terrible, I was trying to drag her away. I did get my wages, but then I didn't dare go back to work. One other girl walked out with me.

I then worked at the snuff mill on Sharrow Vale Road, the Top Mill, for a year. As a job it was a good place to work but I didn't seem to fit in, they were all posh for want of a better word, they all came from that side of town and I was an outsider. One day I went to the pub to fetch some crisps and bumped into Mr Gordon, and he asked me how I was. He said, "The door is always open", so I went back to the Export Box Co.

When I got married I didn't work again until 1977, when I went to work for Townroe Electroplaters. My mother and my sister Margaret already worked there. I stayed full time till 1991.

For the first few years a lot of the work was silver plating cutlery, and we also used to do gold plating. We did some really beautiful work.

We used to silver plate nuts for power stations. This was 'top secret work'. Only the thread on the inside had to be plated, so we would plate them all over at first, then the silver had to be stripped from the outside. We would put rubber bungs, (bought from Preston's Chemists in West Street), in the nuts. They were then dropped into a wire basket and lowered into 'Mettex', an acid stripper. We then washed them in water, shook them over a waste bin, and tipped them out onto a table. We picked them up with eyebrow tweezers. We didn't wear gloves, but we wore goggles and a brown rubber apron, pinned with two nappy pins. Once at a meal, the managing director saw that my fingers were brown, and asked why. I said it was the Mettex that caused it. He said, "That's got to change", and soon, we got some bright yellow gloves.

The silver plating which we did for James Dixon's and Viner's (cutlery) had to be top quality. We used to plate their King's pattern knives, forks, and spoons. I hated King's pattern, I still do to this day. When cutlery came in from Viner's, it was in tins, which would be weighed when they arrived. When we plated parts for Rolls Royce jet engines, they would send someone to check how the work was done. He'd be wearing white gloves to pick up work. I remember a woman called Dot who did nickel plating for aeroplanes. She always used to worry. She'd say "There's not enough plating on these". Once, there was a plane crash and she was awake all night worrying about whether it was her fault. I used to laugh at her 'til I did the job, then I understood.

The firm used to scrimp and save. The foreman would say there were no more gloves, even when there were stacks of them in the toilet. Water was never running as it should, nor were the fans on enough, unless the Factory Inspector was coming.

Working with chrome could cause ulcers in your nose. There were a couple of young girls who were sisters, and my niece and her husband, all who had trouble with their noses. An old man, long retired, had lost the septum in his nose, and could play tunes through it. I've still got a sore in my nose, and I've got asthma now. My daughter-in-law worked in the offices and she got a sore in her nose.

Dermatitis was rife. We also did cadmium plating, and we were told "It's not as dangerous as you think", but we were not allowed to eat where we worked. A new extension was built for the chrome and cadmium plating.

We never had a break. We could just get a drink when we wanted, and we'd have to go out of the shop during our half hour dinner break. Later, there was a 'canteen' in a buffing room with a sink. We used to put our fish and chips on the hot water pipes to keep warm.

I play hell about people not wanting a job, but whilst ever there were places like that, it was proof to me that people do want to work for a living. It was hell on earth. The noise was awful.

Sometimes we couldn't breathe, sometimes we couldn't see. I hate anything that isn't right and I'm glad it's closed now. In this day and age people won't work like that, and I'm glad they don't. That kind of work proved that people would work for a pittance. But I'm sad that such a lot has been lost.

What did I like most about working? It had to be the people, definitely.

Ann's sister **Margaret Williamson** *also worked at Townroes Platers. She worked on the silver side, for seventeen years.*

" We worked with some lovely items. We used to do some beautiful cream jugs, they would be gold plated, and also fruit spoons, with fruit shapes pressed into the bowl, which would be gilded in the bottom of the bowl."

But before that, she worked with Ann at the Export Box Co. She also worked as a buffer on a wheel at Viner's for four or five months. "I walked out, I couldn't stand it, though my mother was a buffer for many years."

Margaret says,

My first job was at Homerick's on Petre Street making scissors. I worked in the warehouse for about two years. We weren't allowed to talk whilst working, and we had to ask permission to go to the toilet. After leaving, I worked at Easterbrook Allcards for about three years making dies. A lot of my uncles worked there. It wasn't strict like Homerick's. I worked first on a lathe and then as a miller. It was all piecework, so it wasn't bad money.

Then I worked at Pickerings making cardboard boxes for a short time, before going to work with my sister Ann at the Export Box Co. I had to wait for four weeks before starting as there was an agreement that there must be at least four weeks between firms. This was a common situation designed to stop different companies from poaching each other's workforce. It also deterred fickleness amongst workers.

Then I went to work at Townroes on Rockingham Street as a wirer for silver plating. The reject cutlery was thrown away in the scrap bins, it seemed such a waste, and the price now is unbelievable. I remember Bill, the gilder, he was brilliant. I've still got a silver bangle, which I was bought as a present in Spain 30 years ago. Bill plated it for me and the gilding he did is still beautiful, it hasn't shifted.

When the bars of gold were delivered, all the doors would be closed, and a woman would weigh it all in 'pennyweights'. She would put a ticket on, written in pennyweights. We called it 'Jacks little hoard'. On one occasion, some aluminium was stolen and the police were called in, but gold was never stolen.

We had a degreaser, a massive tank with a kind of fog coming out. You couldn't breath near it. It was filled with 'trike' (trichloroethylene). It was horrible job, I hated it. There was a notice, which said, "Must not be used in an enclosed space". We used to put all the workpieces in it in baskets after they had been buffed. They took the tank out about a year after I left.

I was a terrible timekeeper, always in trouble. If you were on the Late List for three weeks running, that was it, you were automatically sacked. Even when there were the power cuts, and we had to go on afternoons, 2 pm 'til 10 pm, I would still be late.

I left in 1981 to get married and moved to Retford where I worked as a childminder for about 13 years. I still see the little lad I had from 18 months old, he's 21 now. My favourite job of all was at Export Box Co. We had to work wearing our coats, hats and scarves, but it was fun. It was like home from home. Conditions were bad, but the atmosphere and the workmates were lovely".

*Over a long working life we may see many changes.
Geographical changes, for example, property which has long
since been demolished and streets which have now been built
over or changed beyond recognition. Or the disappearance of
products which are no longer in demand, due to changes in
lifestyle. A reminder of these comes from,*

Mr Wetherill, Tin plate worker

I left school at Easter 1941 and started work age 14 years on
Sycamore Street. This street no longer exists but the bottom end
was Pond Street and it led up to the present Lyceum Theatre.
Below is a photograph of the workshop of L.H. Smith Tin Smiths.

**Workshops
on Sycamore
Street**

The workforce was, Mr Smith the boss, who did the office work at the end of the shop, my father, a tin smith, a time-served apprentice and two elderly women solderers. There was no machinery that worked with electricity, the ladies had a gas ring to do their work.

My first job was to make draw plates, they were used to make the fire burn quicker after lighting on the old Yorkshire ranges. Some who would not, or could not afford a draw plate would use a sheet of newspaper to cover the aperture of the Yorkshire range, but if left unattended it would be ignited and sucked up the flue and if they had not had the chimney sweep for a long time it would set the soot in the chimney on fire and would require a visit from the fire brigade.

To make a draw plate involved taking a large sheet of metal to the guillotine and cutting it into pieces 18 inches wide x 24 inches long, then to the rollers to put a slight bend on each long side. Over to the bending machine with pre-cut strips of mild steel to make the hooks that hooked onto the fire bars, and while at the machine would make the handles from galvanised steel rivet both to the plate for a finished draw plate.

I would make a gross and as there was little room to store them I would deliver them a dozen at a time on a sack barrow. Our biggest buyer was on Exchange Street, and Machin's on Porter Street at the back of the Moor. This street has also gone. I used to pass the tobacconists Jackson's, on Norfolk Street and Tyler's in the Haymarket and if there was long queues it meant there had been a delivery of cigarettes, so I would tell the three male smokers and go back to stand in the queue. As you were rationed to one packet of twenty, I joined the queue again for the second and third packet.

Across the road from our workshop was the blacksmith's, shoeing the shire horses of the Sheffield breweries. We only got 30 minutes for dinner but I managed to spend some of it watching them. My father made friends with one of the two blacksmiths and he would bag up some hoof shavings to bring home to supplement the coal ration. They burnt alright but didn't smell very nice.

To conclude, father and son didn't work out, so I left to follow in my grandfather's occupation as a building worker and stayed in it for the rest of my working life.

A working life in the heavier end of engineering.

Syd Morton, The spring maker, and other stories

First job, shoe repairing.

Having just left school in 1954 without much education, only the three 'R's, and spotting a job in the Star, made me decide to go for it the following morning. On a day in June I caught the tram, which dropped me off opposite Coombs Shoe Repair shop on Attercliffe Road, a few yards before Attercliffe Baths.

I got the job and the very next day started work. I had a white apron and eagerness to go for an impressive start. £2.50 was my wage, £2 for my Mum and 50 pence for me. I had to pay for my tram fare out of the 50p. At 15 years old you did not need much money. Working up from me was Brian, then Dan who finished the shoes off, then John the under-manager and the boss - two good men to work with.

Dan who was eighteen tried to pick on me, but he found out he was batting on a sticky wicket. We finished up fighting, because he wanted me to get a sub (money), off the manager so he could buy some cigs. When I told him where to get off (in Manor Estate style), that's when he tried to hit me. I ducked and then hit him.

Upstairs two men repaired all the shoes, boots and ladies shoes. I remember the first time I was sent up to ask another man called John about a pair of shoes. They were having a laugh on me, for this man was deaf and dumb, and Colin, the other man, was a midget. He was having a laugh when I tried to get John's attention. (This is all true, believe me).

The manager took a liking to me for I was good at playing dominoes, and the other two were not.

A year later, at 16 years of age, my brother got me a job at the Hallamshire Rolling Mill - £11 to £12 per week and how that changed me. There were cigs, drinks, girls - which I am not saying much about, and not to forget the City Hall shuffle. Turning up at the mill was a costly mistake.

I was to work on a 12 inch mill, and at only 5 foot 1 inch tall, weighing in at 7 stone 10 pounds, that was a madness I will never forget. Standing on a long metal table of 40 feet and a rolled, red hot bar comes onto it. You use the biggest wooden mallet I have ever seen. When there is a knuckle (a kink), in the bar and I had to hit it quite a few times to straighten it. This was my first introduction to real sweat which absolutely poured out of my skin. I survived the first week, and over the weekend I could have cried till Monday morning. With the uniform of a pair of wooden clogs, and a sweat towel, I was ready to face the future in steel. With hands sore and blistered you carried on in pain. Someone advises to urinate on your hands and rub it in to harden them off.

The only consolation to all this was that their canteen did a great breakfast. I don't know when the mill shut down, because I left and joined the Army at seventeen and a half.

Fairground Work – The Boxing Booth

Apart from working in the Mill at sixteen, I also worked in the weekend at the Sheffield Show at the Farm grounds, bottom end of Granville Road. My father, Frank Morton, drove a van delivering ice cream for a Mr Addsetts of the Manor Top, who had a marquee at the show with tables and chairs, selling strawberries and ice cream. I myself walked round with a tray of goodies – crisps or lollipops, which I enjoyed until about 2 pm, when I was conned into a fight.

My namesake mate, Syd, arranged a boxing match in the fairground boxing booth, between me and him. I took time off selling, and I still don't know why I was doing this mad thing. I knew he was a much better fighter than me, never the less we stood on the front platform in front of their pugilistic boxers – ugly as sin – I just wished someone had taken a photo.

I was told if we made a good fight of it we would receive £2 each, and the referee spoke to the crowd who were gathering –

"Here we have two local lads who are going to give a good show, so roll up and see the fight".

Little did I know my mate planned for some of his family to be there. He told me to keep my arms on my chest and he would hit me on them, but as the bell went, he walked in with his arm by his side, so I punched him in his face. Then that was a case for him to chase me around the ring, like back-peddling. He won on points.

We got our £2 and the crowd got a laugh at my expense. That's when my flipping shorts fell to my feet and I stood naked. When you have on boxing gloves, the size of your head, it's hard to pull up your shorts – the Ref obliged.

Hadfields steelworks

Three years in the army, with only two nights left. Friday came and I was on my way home. With no trade or skills to my name, the world was my oyster. I started – it would be – at the bottom. Twenty and a half years old and single, I applied for a job at Hadfields steelworks, Vulcan Road. In its place now stands Meadowhall shopping centre.

For my first job I was in their yard learning to shunt, that is with a pole with a hook. You had to connect railway carriages when they were stood. Hooking a three link heavy chain was as hard as it comes. Before the week was out I was told to go and see a film – great, a sit down. The film was of slinging ingots from and to a planning machine. The overhead crane moved at my command. The two shifts were of days and nights, alternate 12 hour shifts. The week's pay (net) was £13. I was surprised to find that after that hour watching a film, I was a skilled slinger, sorry, semi-skilled.

The 1960s to my mind, was a revolution as far as employment was concerned. You could walk into any firm and most likely get a job without much fuss. Now you need higher education to work on unskilled or semi-skilled jobs. I was never asked about my education, only previous jobs.

From Hadfield's I moved to Edgar Allen's, only about 250 yards away on Shepcote Lane, which I think is still there. Stand at a steel-top table with a hammer in my right hand and a square metal plate in front of me. I had to knock it flat. Where it wobbled you had to hit it here, and then you hit it there – I was hopeless. At least it was a day shift job, only less money.

Promoted to furnaceman in the second week. It was hot and hard and fast. You pulled a red hot plate out with a long pair of tongs, and passed them to an operator who was a press tool man. He set the machine up for whatever dimensions were required. After a month this man left, and I was asked if I could do his job. This was my first experience as a press tool operator, which put me in for future jobs.

Some time later (1961), I applied for a job as a bread salesman with Fletchers Bread Company on Claywheels Lane, Hillsborough – it was my misfortune to be employed as a driver-salesman. After one weeks' training I was ready, willing and able. The following Monday morning I was clocking in at 5.30 am. Breakfast was on call in the canteen.

I had to wait two hours for my van to be loaded. Being the last did not really bother me that much. Then a bombshell was placed in my custody – a van boy. He told me he knew exactly what I needed, so we checked out the contents onto the three-ton van, and according to the boy it was all right.

Now I was ready for my big day. The shops I was to deliver to were in small towns such as Thurnscoe and Wath upon Dearne. The balance between pay (£14 gross), and the job, seemed fair, or so I thought until I arrived back at the depot. The remaining food was taken off the van and checked in, and the food put on one side for the next day. It would be put back on my van to be sold on Tuesday. The paper records were sent to the office,

The allowance for waste food was £1.50 per day, and as each day went by, I cut my order down, as anything else unsold was taken off my wages. My net wage that first time was £5.60. Stoppages for waste food was about the same. To top it all, the van boy had eaten most of the custards. This was my shortest term of employment – three weeks. Never again!

Working for Tempered Springs was a highlight in my life, first as a production worker on alternate days and nights. Shifts of twelve hours were on piecework or bonus. Sometimes ten shillings basic with bonus, or on a good week, £1 per hour, that could work out at £60 to £70 gross.

**Syd Morton
spring maker**

I was there when the paint plant caught fire, causing loss of production for over a week. We did have floods when the River Don burst its banks. The shot blaster pit would fill with water and it could not be pumped out until the river level dropped back low enough.

My first twelve months were on the production line covering many different operations in turn, some very painful. Sometimes, fingers became very swollen from holding springs on a grinding wheel which was situated between two shot blasting machines. Feeding springs into the shot blaster, whist being pelted with shot could make you shout and curse and sometimes lose your temper. Time could be lost waiting for a fitter to put some putty over holes worn through the guards.

On to the dreaded 'scrag' machine, you were lucky to escape having your fingers crushed. The scrag compressed the springs three times, testing their resilience, and was a machine feared by the best.

I think the best part of a working life, is the characters you come across in different situations. Some sad moments like the manager with only one arm, Mr Macintosh, who at the weekends went flying a glider, and sadly he was killed.

Or like the Hungarian who brought his dog to work, tied it to the back of the furnace – hot dog you might say! Like the man who took the money from the men to pay their Union dues, but kept it, then had the cheek to show off new shoes he bought with their money.

As regards progress at the Tempered Spring Company, I was promoted to Taper Forge department, then became assistant toolsetter, and eventually became Foreman.

Jonas Woodhead

While at my daughter's house I looked through a picture book of Darnall in the 1920's. One of these pictures was of a shop where Mr. Woodhead was a blacksmith. I believe this Mr. Woodhead is the same who started making springs in a barn along Club Mill Lane, Neepsend. A lot of firms were situated alongside the River Don because they pumped water from it for cooling purposes, and discharged waste water back into the river. As Jonas Woodheads grew, more people were employed. In 1970 when I joined them as a toolsetter there must have been 350 staff, with management.

The firm consisted of a Coil Spring Department and a Leaf Spring Department. There were five press machines which were used for different operations to make and assemble for a complete leaf spring.

The hardest and most fascinating machine was the main leaf operation. It was a sight to see, difficult to set up. There were only two shifts working, morning and afternoons. When orders improved they set more men on, but when they dropped they had to let them go (last in-first out). Sometimes they changed their excuse.

One year while I was doing my job the roof caught fire. They had to have a new one. I don't mean I started the fire – that was caused by something else.

To me a sad part was when I, and Jim, the supervisor, were stood together watching a man operate a cold punching machine, when the piece which was punched out shot across like a bullet, went in Jim's jaw, and knocked him out cold. I grabbed him so he would not land heavy on the ground. He survived, but a few months later he died. Afterthoughts – I was lucky - the metal piece could have hit me.

Just over 15 years I was there, then the leaf spring department was transferred to Teeside, and I was transferred into the Coil Spring Shop.

I will tell you that whichever firm you worked for, the basic pay was never any good. You had to work overtime, and a lot of the time you worked normal hours. I remember Mr Ted Heath who was in office put everybody on a 3-day working week, and at the same time his boat, 'Morning Cloud', I think, sank, so he gave himself an £80,000 pay rise and bought another boat. (swear words don't come into it!)

A day at the races seems a straightforward event – not Jonas Woodhead's day trip to Uttoxeter Jump Meeting, which featured the Midlands Grand National. I suppose it all started when I organised a syndicate. There were four men involved including yours truly, paying 50 pence each. Each Saturday one man would bet £2 on the horse or horses of his choice and the following Saturday someone else would do the same, and so on.

As we started to win, more men wanted to join, so the syndicate grew. Now each Saturday there was £8 for one man to bet with. A day at the races was mentioned, so we decided to go for it. I booked the coach, a 40-seater. The money left over went into buying 40 large pork pies for the lads to eat after the races. This would tide them over until we spent three or four hours in Nottingham for a drink.

To pick a winner is to pit your knowledge against the odds. Some you win, some you don't - it's more often you don't. Weather-wise it was a good afternoon but very soft underfoot due to heavy rain the previous night. The coach park was on grass, and to our surprise, most of the coaches had sunk into the ground. Fighting our way through a litter of losers' tickets on the ground, we then had to push the coach until it was on better ground, and those poor lads pushing fell flat into the mud.

The stories of bad luck came one after the other. Never mind, a night in Nottingham getting drunk would take their worries away, so they thought. As organiser, I insisted they had to be back on the coach at 10.30 p.m., otherwise – "We leave without you". We gave them an extra 15 minutes, then we left, leaving five behind in Nottingham.

Monday morning came and I was feeling slightly nervous of what could be in store for me, because one man caught the train, slept over his stop and finished up in Scotland (Edinburgh). Others got a taxi back, which cost them £10 each. I expected a tongue-lashing from him who finished up in Scotland, but instead he thoroughly enjoyed himself and asked – "When can we go again?" I can tell you, it was a big relief. Out of the taxi lads, two of them were my nephews, so I got a rollicking from my sister. Two months later we had a trip to Haydock Park with similar results. They were warned!

The Works Fishing Trip

While working for Jonas Woodheads Springs of Club Mill Lane, I placed my name on the list for a fishing match. A coach full of male employees will endeavour to outwit a fish or more. The one who catches the most, or gets the heaviest weight catch is the winner. I was a novice and only doing it for my two children's sake, so that when I took them to Dam Flask, I, as a bona fide angler, would know what I was doing.

A coach was booked to take us to Southery, also breakfast at the inn along the banks of the River Trent. When the coach pulled up outside our works entrance, we thought someone was playing a joke on the lads. If the police had seen that coach, the driver (an old man) would get Life in Jail. Even Wells Fargo would not have been very proud, and they used horses.

His windscreen would not stand a drop of rain, for when he turned the wipers on, they fell off. We laughed. Better still, having to go up a steep hill (East Bank Road), to pick up two of our lads, they were made to throw their tackle on to the coach while it was going. The driver said, "If I stop, we will never get going again". The steering seemed a bit faulty too, and believe me, I was surprised that we ever reached our destination.

Breakfast was laid on as usual - one sausage, one egg, one piece of bacon, one tomato, one piece of fried bread and a cup of tea. The man I presume was the landlord looked like an ex-World War 2 fighter pilot – a red face with a handlebar moustache to match. He shouted "Any more for bread?" and if someone shouted "Here", he threw the bread bun to him. A funny way to serve up bread, I thought.

The banks were pegged out from 1 to 40, I got number 6 peg. The third time I wound my line in it broke, just above the float, so I tackled again. With casting up river it came to settle down where another float was bobbing up and down. I was then accused of fishing with two lines.

I don't know who won the match – I know it wasn't me, for I had an empty net. The whistle went at 1 pm, a few drinks and a game of cards back at the pub, then a nightmare return on a coach you would not get ten bob for.

I am only 5' 2" – a sense of humour is my life, says my wife and family. I love telling jokes, but I have a serious side to myself. In this world, who does care?

The cutlery trades share many processes with the edge tool, hand tool and engineering industry, so people moved between workshops and factories making knives or accessories for musical instruments, or hand tools.

Edna Allen – Capstan lathe operator

I was born in Arbourthorne Road, Sheffield, in 1930 and attended Arbourthorne Central School. I left this school at the age of 14 on a Friday started work on the following Monday.

My first job was at Wardonia Works, Clough Road off Brammall Lane, as an assistant packer of razor blades. It was paid weekly. The management was very strict and we very rarely had a laugh with them.

Each week the staff had to take it in turns to scrub the workshop floor. We had a bucket of cold water, scrubbing brush, and worked on hands and knees, (no knee pads). When we finished scrubbing the floor we were in no fit state to go dancing. For this job you were given no extra pay. I stayed at this company for three years and it was a good grounding for working life, miserable gaffers and scrubbing floors.

I moved to Harlow's off Broomhall Street as a trainee capstan lathe operator. I enjoyed my time at Harlow's. There was a nice warm family atmosphere, totally opposite to my first job. I stayed at Harlow's for three years, but before I left, I met a bloke called Frank. We went to the pictures four times a week and dancing three times a week, but didn't bother with the pubs. Eventually we got married. After four years we had a son called Stephen. When Stephen started school I had to go back to work, so Frank's mum who was called Nora, looked after Stephen whilst I was at work. I was 28 years of age by this time.

I found a job at True-Tones on Eyre Street as a capstan lathe operator, making musical instrument accessories. All lathe work was paid on piecework and bonus. It was good socially, and True-Tones had some lovely family trips to the sea-side. We went to places like Skegness, Cleethorpes, and Mablethorpe. We always had a good time.

After four years I moved to Blenheim Works off Glossop Road, once again as a capstan lathe operator. This is where I found I had a nickname. I was 4ft 10" tall, built on the lines of Barbara Windsor, with the blond beehive hairstyle. In all the lathe shops where I've worked, no other operator has been able to work faster or earn the same money as me. That's how I finished up with the nickname of 'Flash'.

The company closed down and I had to leave. From there, I went to Pneumatic Components on Eyre Street, now demolished, once again as a capstan lathe operator. We had Christmas parties, seaside trips, coach trips to pubs around the areas of Sheffield, and I stayed with this company for 30 years.

I must have enjoyed my time at Pneumatic Components, because after retiring, I went back for part-time hours. As for gaffers, I didn't bother with management, just got on with the job. While you're talking to the gaffer you're not earning, and the first experience with the management at Wardonia Works really stuck in my mind. They were sour-faced and demanding, not my type at all.

Shirley Vallance *spent 24 years in precision tools, but her favourite job was as a waitress. She tells us how it all panned out.*

I was born in 1937 in what was then called the Sheffield Women's Hospital, later the Jessop Hospital for Women. I was the second of eight children, the eldest girl. The whole of our family, lived with my grandma on Ridgeway Road, so I was partly brought up by her.

My dad worked nights at Firth Brown's, where they could sleep on shift when they had finished their work.

At fifteen, I left school to go to a job starting on Monday as an apprentice at Stephenson Blake, the top print foundry. It was a trade I was learning. I worked on a machine that traced a letter onto a brass block, and you would then remove metal to different depths, it could take a day to make the mould for one letter.

The firm was in an old building on Upper Allen Street with lots of windy passages. Actually it was very clean. As teenagers we were well looked after, we got a three course meal in the canteen for our dinner, very cheap. I was earning two pounds, two shillings and sixpence a week, a good wage for that time.

There was a brass foundry, and other machines, which the men worked on. Then I was given a job, machining brass, I didn't know, but when I went downstairs where the men worked, they said, "You're a right one." Apparently, I was unknowingly doing a man's job for less money. That upset me and put me off. I decided to give in my notice but was offered ten shillings a week (a lot of money then) to stay. After only nine months there, I got a job at Woolworth's for Christmas, for the same money.

Then I went to work at Mellor's for three months, making fittings for windows. That job was not at all nice. They tried me on a new machine and said "Whatever you do, hold the safety guard when you put your foot on the pedal". I hadn't got the knack, and as I leaned forward, I pressed the pedal with my foot. The machine broke and it took three days to mend it. They didn't put me on it any more.

We used to make brass washers by stamping them out. It was a very painful job, the washers cut our hands.

From there, I went to Gordon Tool's. The conditions weren't good, even though we cleaned up every week on Fridays, but it was a laugh. That was in those horrible Camp Coffee days. The boss was dead against the union, and he favoured the men. At Christmas they would be given a bird, the women didn't get one.

I worked in the chrome shop, wrapping spanners with wire, on a frame ready for plating. We had some fun there, we used to sing all day, and we'd talk for hours about the pictures we'd seen, it passed the time. Sometimes we would work till 7pm.

For some extra money, after work on Mondays and Thursdays, I'd go and sell ice cream at the pictures, and I had a Saturday job in Woolworth's at Attercliffe.

I worked at Gordon Tool's till I was five and a half months pregnant. I was 20 when my first son was born.

We were living with Harold's mother at that time on the Flower Estate. When my son was four and a half I got a cleaning job at C and A's, but those old fashioned mop buckets were so heavy. My friend said, "Why don't you come back to Gordon Tool's?" The manager sent a message, "Tell Shirley, she can come and see me, or start next Monday, she can have any hours she wants." I worked there near enough full time for about two years until my second son was born, my mother in law used to take my little boy to school.

When my second son was about one year old I got a part time job at Tuckwood's, waitressing, I had gone there for a washing up job! Of all my jobs this is the one I enjoyed most, though the money wasn't very much, the tips were as much as the wages, and it was hard work. I stayed there five years, working from 5pm-8.15pm. You got to know regular people, I got satisfaction from serving good food.

Then when my younger son was seven, I worked days as a waitress at Rabone Chesterman's dining room in Ecclesall Road for the main bosses. My neighbour would come in and stay with the kids till my husband got home. But it was boring, I was on my own most of the time.

I went to Moore and Wright because I could get the same Works Weeks holidays as my husband. He worked at English Steel in the stamp shop. One day, when our Peter was eight years old he went to work with his Dad. When he got home he said to me, "Mum, I don't ever want to work in a place like that, the noise is terrible, it closes in on you." I told him he'd better get his head down at school, and get some decent marks.

I worked in the photo etching room at Moore and Wright's at Handsworth, making steel rules. It was very clean, but there were lots of chemicals, including trichloroethylene fumes when you lifted baskets of work out of the degreasing tank. In the dark room, there were photographic chemicals. They found out the dark room extraction wasn't working when I couldn't breathe in there. The worst job was acid etching at the end of the process. You would leave the work in the acid for so long, then get it out and scrub it off with trichloroethylene. My husband brought a book home, which said I shouldn't be doing this. I told the foreman, who replied, "If you report this, you won't have a job."

You had to check the steel rules with a magnifying glass, and cover over any spots with fine brushes. It would hurt our fingers holding such thin brushes so carefully. We used to keep the solvent for rinsing the brushes in old Tate & Lyle treacle tins. I remember some Japanese visitors coming round, trying to read the name on the treacle tins!

In our jobs you had to work very carefully, otherwise it wouldn't come out right. There were three wage rates for women, and the union negotiated a skilled rate for us, until at a later date they changed and we were all put on the same money.

Only the women worked hard there, the men saw to the machines, and then laid about, reading the paper...

About ten years before I finished, James Neill's bought Moore and Wright's and came up to Handsworth. They were slapdash, compared with how we were used to working. Most of the work was coming from Japan and we only put our name on it.

All in the name of progress they also converted one of our canteens where we could eat our sandwiches, or play snooker in our breaks, into offices, leaving only one canteen, which gradually deteriorated, so eventually, we had our dinner where we worked.

At the end, when they moved to Napier Street, the canteen was just one small room. When the firm moved from Handsworth, there were lots of rumours, but we only got to know when I was on holiday in the Cotswolds, someone I met there told me that Asda were negotiating for the site.

Working for Moore and Wright we all had to pay into a pension scheme, it was the best pension scheme in Sheffield. Even the women had to pay in, there was no option. At that time women weren't usually in a pension scheme. It was a better pension than my husband's, and I'm better off now, it makes the difference between managing and struggling.

I finished when I was sixty, after 24 years, because the firm was moving again. The firm is in Attercliffe now, and employs Polish agency workers, so they are earning less now than we did.

The shop steward

As she says, **"Some battles we won, and some we lost."**

A.G. *Hammer linisher*

"Prior to 1976 women's wages were always less than men's, and the Union did not do much about it."

I was born in 1936 and left school at the age of 15 in 1951. My first job was at Marks & Spencer's, but when my first marriage ended and I was left with a son to bring up, I needed a job that did not involve working all day Saturdays, which is how I got into factory work. Being a lone parent in the 1950's was hard, with no benefits as there are today. My first experience of factory work was at James Neil's, in the late 1950's – it paid better, and there was no weekend working - I never worked excessive overtime, shifts or nights. As you can imagine, it was a bit of a culture shock going from Marks & Spencer's to factory work. Later I moved to Motor Control Centre.

Meanwhile, I re-married, moved to High Green and had another son. My husband, Basil, was a miner and during the 1971 pit strike we were left with nothing (we had no savings and I was not working), and two boys to bring up.

During that pit strike, when Basil was not earning, we had £10 a week Family Allowance, to pay the £2 rent and feed the four of us. The lads had free school dinners, but at one school the miners' kids had to stand in a separate queue, with their tickets for a free meal. When the electric was off I'd cook on the open fire. My mum would come up with one and a half pounds of shin beef and I'd make it last us three days, and I always had soup on the go.

The very house we lived in was a tied house. Originally built for Thorncliffe's, a big firm which made Churchill tanks during the war, our row of terraced houses had been sold to the Coal Board. A few years later, in 1974, we were able to buy our house very cheaply, so it was paid for in five years, and meant that when the next pit strike occurred in 1984, we were in a better place financially.

After the strike I got a job cleaning at the local club. Stanley Tools were advertising for linishers (a hard job) for the twilight shift, 5-9 p.m. and in February 1973 I started working at Stanleys.

I kept a low profile for a long time, but this led to a bit of bullying. You had to stand up for yourself or go under – it was a hard life, and hard times for women, especially the piecework, with everyone scratting for two and sixpence more.

My job as a linisher, hand-finishing hammerheads, involved standing for eight hours daily at a grinding wheel. It was hard, dirty work, you breathed in the dust all day, and I reckoned that during the course of each day, I lifted three tons in weight. The movements were also very repetitive, swivelling round to take a hammerhead from the box at my side continually. This is probably what led to me having an arthritic hip.

Hand finishing hammer heads

Many people doing this kind of work ended up with tenosynovitis, or other kinds of repetitive strain injury. I wore goggles and thick gloves for protection – the wheel was revolving at 3,000 revs per minute, and had open sides. If the hammerhead was at all rough, you had to put a lot of body weight on it to get it to a smooth finish.

I went part-time until 1976, then full-time, leaving in 1996 after 23 years and 10 months, just short of the 25 years service, which would have got me a gold watch.

I will say that the women at Stanley's never took part in the kind of rough initiation games played on new apprentices. The men did sometimes take their trousers down and daub them with paint, but the women did not join in, and tended to 'mother' them a bit.

Prior to 1976 women's wages were always less than men's, and the Union did not do much about it.

There was a male-dominated attitude of "Gi' 'em five bob". Skilled men saw women as a threat, so they were always lower paid in industry. Women were their own worst enemies, as when asked to describe their job, they would minimise the skills involved. The men, asked to do the same, would make it sound more complex and skilful and get a rise. I challenged the union about this and stood for election as a shop steward.

Once equal pay came in, firms could no longer advertise for a male or female machinist so they tended to pay the lower, women's rate to everyone.

The big closures of the Thatcher era caused many redundancies and men who were out of work would take anything. Some men pooled their redundancy money and formed Co-ops. There were five or more in Sheffield, the most successful being Traffic Systems. Most national apprenticeship schemes were stopped by the government, but Stanley Tools kept them on, but with many fewer places. They would advertise for an apprentice and a skilled man, such as a toolmaker, would apply – it was heart-breaking.

Stanley Tools had four factories, each with it's own shop steward's meeting. There was also one big meeting for all four together, which I chaired - some men didn't like a woman being in charge. The first thing I noticed was that the management meetings had coffee and the shop stewards did not, so we started having coffee and biscuits and a bit of a laugh first. Prior to my arrival meetings with management had been characterised by a lot of shouting and table-thumping, but I said -"If you lose your temper, you've lost the argument" – I also didn't allow swearing.

I found I was able to argue our case with management – you use your ability for what you want to achieve. At first I had some stand-up rows with John Gilbert, their Personnel Director, but we soon came to a good understanding, and now that we are both retired, are good friends. A better understanding between them and us was reached – it was all about compromise, and negotiating for what you both want. One manager called the workers greedy, but I said - "If it weren't for us, you wouldn't have a job".

Our union was the AEU, later to become AMICUS, and I stood up at Conference and challenged them about the discrimination against women. Then I represented women for 15 years on the District Committee, and eventually, I represented the women of Sheffield, Rotherham, Doncaster, etc at the Women's Conference. Our Union brought in a policy of positive discrimination.

When I was running for the first full-time National Officers' position I travelled all over Britain – Glasgow, Dundee, down South and Lancashire. At the Aerospace Factory near Preston they were on strike for the shorter working week. I went on the picket line at 6 a.m. in the morning, in support of their claim, and also at my own factory in Ecclesfield. We were on strike for the forge men who were threatened with dismissal for working to rule.

With all this travelling I needed to learn to drive, so at 55 years old I took lessons and am proud to say I passed the test first time. I think the examiner was glad to get me out of the car due to my chatter! I lost the election for N.W.O. (National Womens' Officer) by 10,000 votes, which in context was a very good result, as nationwide I polled 56,000 votes.

Some battles we won, and some we lost. The Shop Steward Committee discovered that our Pension Scheme only covered 'widows', but not widowers, so I threatened to take the firm to an Industrial Tribunal and won. I also fought for the men on low incomes, who were stopped £3,000 because of paying the full stamp, whereas women, who could opt out of the full stamp, did not get the £3,000 stopped. I said it was unfair because the men had no choice, but were forced to pay the full stamp, but I lost that one. Nowadays women are not allowed to opt out.

I paid AVC (Added Voluntary Contributions) so that when I retired I'd get more pension, but I discovered that if I, and a man were paid the same, he'd get more money because women are deemed to live longer than men.

When I finished paid work, I wanted to give something back to the community, so I took up various kinds of voluntary work, and now I have three different roles

- On the Management Committee for Wortley Hall, the Trade Union and Labour Movement stately home.

- Two days a week at the local primary school helping young children one-to-one with their reading, so that they not only learn to read, but to comprehend what they are reading. To read without understanding is not progress.

- At the same school I am a Governor, appointed by the L.E.A. Part of my responsibilities is to be History Governor, which means I monitor the history projects of all classes. I am also on the Staffing and Finance committee, part of which includes an interviewing panel to appoint new teachers and other staff.

I guess I could have had an easier life at work if I'd 'looked the other way', but it wasn't my style, so I ended up as I'd begun, as a linisher, and retired in 1996.

Long service with one company is fast becoming a thing of the past, but there are still some people who can claim to have spent most of their working life in one job. Inevitably, they will have seen many drastic changes, and survived several takeovers, but could still be manufacturing the same basic product." I liked working for Record and stayed there for 45 years".

Great pride can be taken in producing an article, which can be labelled 'Made in Sheffield'. *This describes a man who prefers to be known here simply as* '**KB**'.

I failed the 11 plus, a big disappointment to my parents, and so went to Brook Secondary Modern School. There I began to brighten up, doing well at maths and science and extremely well at technical drawing (now called Engineering Drawing – I think). This is now done on a computer, but at that time done on a large drawing board with pencil, tee-square, compasses etc. I could complete a three hour exam in this subject in half an hour. I decided this was the job I wanted to take up – draughtsman.

At school I also did woodwork and metalwork, using tools made by the very firm I was later to work for, and I knew these were tools of the very best quality. I was offered an apprenticeship at Davy United – Darnall, but could not start until September 1959, and as I disliked school I left in March 1959. I learned that C & J Hampton (also known as Record Tools) had a vacancy for an apprentice draughtsman so I applied and got the job - to start immediately. My starting wage was £2/1/11 (£2/7/6 gross). I only intended to stay for six months till I could join Davy United, which was a much bigger firm, but I liked working for Record and stayed there for 45 years.

C & J Hampton was formed in 1898 by two Hampton brothers – Charles and Joseph, and became a public company in 1948. Management was passed down the Hampton family until the1980's when the then Chairman - Anthony Hampton (later Master Cutler) retired, and none of his six sons worked in the company. The company grew and as a result of mergers and take-overs over the next 20 years, was involved in the manufacture of a very wide range of products with many top quality brand names including Ridgeway (wood and metal cutting tools), William Marples (woodworking hand tools), Gilbow (snips), Bulldog (horticultural and contractors tools). They then started to manufacture and distribute wood and metal working machinery – Record Power and Startrite. All top quality. They also owned and ran companies overseas.

In the 60's the firm moved into the new head office and factory – Parkway Works. Some of their manufacturing processes were the best in the world. The products were not cheap – but they were, we believed, very best quality. Here I was involved in the manufacturing processes from start to finish. We were self-contained, including foundry and machine shops. I was not a bound apprentice with documents, but my apprenticeship lasted till I was 21. It involved drawing, design and manufacture.

My training involved day release and evening classes. This is how I learned engineering. At school I learned to draw, but at work I learned the complete package – how to design so the product could be manufactured. I got my ONC (Ordinary National Certificate) in Mechanical Engineering. I did rather well here and the college recommended my employers to allow me to do the HND course (Higher National Diploma) in Mechanical and Production Engineering. This was a three year full time sandwich course followed by two further years evening classes.

Record did allow me to take the course, which I really enjoyed.

At the end of this study and with a few years hands-on working experience, I was qualified as a Member of the Institution of Mechanical Engineers and Member of the Institution of Production Engineers and then Chartered Engineer. These are now postgraduate qualifications. For someone who failed his 11 plus I was quite proud of this. During this time I also taught myself the German language. This came in very useful. For the rest of my working life I regularly used this – as interpreter and regularly in communication with German speaking customers and suppliers – both in the office and in Germany.

Back at Record Tools, I worked as Production Engineer – finding better ways of manufacturing our products – mostly metal working processes. At 30, I was offered the job as Quality Manager. This was a position I held until my retirement although I did take on additional responsibilities and functions over the next 30 years. As the company grew I was responsible for the quality functions in all the companies in the UK, and some overseas.

When I took on the job I had a staff of over 30 people. When I retired I had only three. This was because the process of quality management changed very positively.

Originally quality management was mostly inspection i.e. sorting the good from the bad after manufacture. Now quality management incorporates all processes from design, through manufacture and on to customer services and even end of life disposal. With correct quality management, people are trained to do the correct job first time, and inspection is not usually necessary. I have, unfortunately, had to make people redundant and this was always very painful to me. Mostly we were able to redeploy people rather than dismiss them. I found quality management very rewarding. It concerned protecting customers from bad products and bad service management, and protecting the company from bad suppliers and bad practices in-house. Very worthwhile I believe.

One of the most amusing episodes of the period was when I went to investigate a complaint about one of our tools. The Irish really got some use out of their tools, getting ten years of work out of tools in only one year. When I eventually found the little workshop, in Dublin, the manager was so overwhelmed that I had come all that way, he assured me our tools were absolutely wonderful and it was quite an effort to get him to demonstrate the problem. However, through this visit we learned that a design change introduced many years previously was not the improvement we had believed it to be, and we immediately took corrective action.

I saw quite a few changes in ownership and management of the company. The first big change was 1981 when C & J Hampton Ltd was taken over by Bahco Tools – a top Swedish tool manufacturing company. Although we worked well with Bahco, after a few years our Managing Director persuaded them to allow him to organise a management buyout. I remember getting a phone call from our MD asking me to see him in his office on Boxing Day. I could not imagine why he would want to see me so urgently. I learned from this appointment about his proposal. He had selected his team, of which I was to be a member. There were two conditions to our offer being accepted. We were sworn to as much secrecy as was legally possible, and the matter had to be concluded in what seemed an impossibly short time.

My problem was – I didn't have the cash. The MD did a deal with one of the big national banks, who did a great job lending us the necessary funds, but they would not lend more than they knew we could repay. I had to take a second mortgage on my home as security for the loan. I remember saying to my sister, "If this fails, can I pitch my tent on your lawn?"

I was fairly reassured by the fact that our Chief Executive and Company Chairman - both successful prominent businessmen – were putting a lot more money into the company than I. If it's a good risk for them – it's a good risk for me, I thought. It was very successful – the company took off – expanded – acquired lots of other companies and became profitable and very respected. In 1987 we were a Stock Exchange listed plc.

During the next few years we had our ups and downs but always made a profit and offered shareholders a return on their investment. Despite this, our share price fluctuated and once, when very low, American Tools Companies – another top quality tool manufacturer, made a very good take over bid, which was too good to be rejected by our shareholders – and this was successful. This was felt to be good for the company and good for the shareholders. American Tool Companies were very good with us. They were rich, prestigious and helpful. We worked very well together.

After a few years American Tool Companies was itself taken over by another American company - Newell Rubbermaid, a very large, very profitable company with a wide quality product base including Pyrex tableware and Parker pens. Newell Rubbermaid quickly got involved in our company operations. They correctly pointed out to us that we needed to reduce manufacturing costs and could not survive in the modern world unless we changed our manufacturing base from the U.K. to Eastern Europe or Asia. If we didn't, then our competitors would. We knew this was true and reluctantly agreed with their proposals.

As quality boss, it fell to me to ensure that this process was successful as far as product quality was concerned. We had to find factories abroad, which could make tools to the consistent high quality of our own Sheffield made products. I visited factories in the Czech Republic, India and in China. While we still buy some items from the Czech Republic and India, we finally settled on China as the main production base. With our purchasing manager I visited many factories, checking their operations, management systems, product quality etc. It was essential that products made for us would meet our own technical specifications and high quality levels. In all cases their own specs and quality levels were lower than our own.

After two years of very hard work – on their part and on ours - they achieved the standards we required. Unfortunately, it was necessary for us to disclose our manufacturing secrets to these companies, who were previously our competitors, in order to ensure they achieved the quality levels we had developed and achieved in the UK over the last 110 years. It was a very big risk, but we had to take it and it was, I believe, successful. I was very impressed by the dedication and hard work shown by these people during a very intense learning process.

Two problems I encountered in China were language (I had to do everything through a Chinese interpreter, who did not always understand the engineering aspects nor the local Chinese dialects), and the matter of "not losing face". This meant that if I asked - "Do you understand, and can you reach the quality level we need?" they always said yes, but initially results proved otherwise.

The Chinese always showed great hospitality, and every evening we were taken out to dinner by the company's top management. They would also invite civic VIP's like the Mayor, Chief of Police, Chief Magistrate of the town. We'd be in a private dining room at a large round table with a big turntable in the centre. On this would be placed, altogether, the starters, main courses and deserts.   These meals with lots of drinks for all the necessary toasts often lasted three hours.

Although there is still some manufacturing left in the Sheffield factory, most of it is now done overseas. This is obviously sad, but by moving with the times, Record Tools has remained a profitable UK company, supplying quality products to its customers,

I have always been proud of working for Record Tools, but at the age of 60, after 45 very hard but enjoyable years, I decided to call it a day, take life easier, and I retired.

Record Tools was 100% Sheffield born and bred, and was associated with all that Sheffield is famous for.

Some people would enter a trade and believe it was the start of an occupation, which would last a lifetime. Some of them would stick at it through thick and thin, even though in some cases, they did not like what they were doing. Others would move around constantly searching for something better. The ideal is probably when a job is enjoyable to the point where it almost becomes a hobby. One man who came closest to achieving this, but only after many years, is

Kenneth Hawley Tool dealer & collector

Ken's first experience of going out to work was during the school summer holiday in 1940. Ken was a pupil at the Junior Technical School in Sheffield where a condition of admission, was that parents were required to sign an agreement whereby, the pupil would complete the three year course of study. The age at admission was 13. He spent that holiday time working in his father's factory where the main product was **wire mesh guards**

for industrial machines. This was in the early days of the Second World War and many of the work's employees had been called up for service in the forces. The loss of skilled labour plus the useful contribution from Ken in the factory, led to him being 'bought out' of school early and taking up full time employment at the age of 14.

Ken started as a 'Wire Worker'. Much time was spent as general dogsbody, but at the same time, he was expected to learn how the various products were manufactured. This was mainly through observing how other workers performed.

Most of the work consisted of bending steel rod to form a skeleton frame, tailored to shape and size for its intended purpose. The skeleton would then be covered with a wire mesh, thus forming an enclosed guard to cover moving parts of machinery.

Much of the process was carried out by hand and could lead to very sore and damaged fingers. Like many trades, when the skin was soft it was painful to hold tools or any materials, but as time went on, the hands hardened to cope with the job. Eventually, calluses would develop in the appropriate places and one could then just get on with the job without too much suffering. It paid to very quickly learn how to use tools rather than fingers for forming the wires.

Handling materials could throw up some challenges. The bulk of stock was stored on the ground floor in a space which had an unusually high ceiling. This was convenient for stacking rod and tubing, which was supplied in approximately eighteen foot lengths, against the walls. The top ends would be prevented from sliding sideways by steel rods projecting out of the walls. There was nothing to stop the material from falling away from the wall if it was not stacked correctly.

When the material was needed for production, it had to be moved up to the workshop on the first floor. This was achieved by carrying a bundle of rods out into the yard and lying it with one end against the factory wall. The far end would then be pushed up to raise the bundle into a vertical position against the wall, and one could develop the knack of utilising the springiness of the material to make the task a little easier. The next stage was to raise the bundle high enough off the ground for it to be passed into an open door in the wall at first floor level, obviously a two man operation. The man on the ground would lift the bundle as high as possible, whilst his mate leaning from the opening above, would catch hold of the top end and drag it inside.

Occasionally, a new bundle of rods would be required at short notice and it was quickest satisfied by going directly to the suppliers. Usually, a man and a boy would walk to the Rolling Mill in Blonk Street to collect the material. They would then hoist the eighteen foot length bundle onto their shoulders and carry it back to the workshop in Pond Street.

Not all material came in straight lengths, the smaller gauge wire would be in coils which usually weighed half a hundredweight. These could have been hoisted up from the yard to the workshop level by means of a block and tackle, but this would have taken time to set up. The 'real man's method' was to load a coil onto a shoulder and then run up the flight of steps to deliver it to the workshop. An occasional 'showoff' would sometimes do this with a coil on each shoulder.

The workshop was a cold place to work in winter, the only source of heat was a 'Pot Bellied Stove' in the centre of the room. Lighting it first thing in the morning could be very difficult and often filled the workshop with fumes until it eventually began to draw properly up the cast iron chimney.

The assembly of machine guards involved welding and grinding with the result that it was not unusual for a worker to get a spark burned into an eye. This was dealt with by one man, who specialised in flicking the foreign body off the eyeball, using a sharpened matchstick. He would use a live match, which he would first strike and then blow out the flame. That action would supposedly sterilise the wood, the charred end then being sharpened to a point thus forming the ideal 'instrument' to perform the operation.

In summer, the hot dry atmosphere could cause hammer shafts to dry out and shrink so that the head would work lose. This problem was overcome by soaking the hammer head in a bucket of water overnight.

After mastering the manufacturing aspect of the work, the next step was to go out to customers' premises armed with tape measure, callipers, chalk-line and sketchbook etc. The chalk-line was a particularly versatile piece of equipment taking up very little space in the pocket. It could be used for lining up related parts, for marking out areas on a wall or a floor, and with a weight tied onto one end, could be used as a plumb line.

Out on site, it was necessary to observe a machine in use to be able to design appropriate guards, and then make accurately measured sketches. All this was sometimes done in dark and dirty conditions and great care was needed to make sure the information was reliable. This would then be taken back to the factory where a custom shape could be made up. These visits were to become a very useful source of contacts later on in life.

Ken was eventually conscripted into the army towards the end of the war, but typically, his practical skills were not utilised during his period of service. He left the army after serving three years in the Pay Corps in various parts of Britain.

Returning to civilian life and with his interest in hand tools, he went to work as an assistant at Wilks Brothers, a well known ironmongery business in Norfolk Street. He was already well versed in the use of metal working tools but knew very little about woodworking. Some of his early encounters with customers proved embarrassing for him when they asked him about various specialist tools, proving that he had to be a very quick learner if he was to survive in the job.

In the years soon after the war, everything was in very short supply, and if a customer asked for an item not currently in stock, it was not uncommon to tell them there could be a twelve month delay on delivery.

Because Wilks Bros. covered such a wide range of household goods, Ken preferred to deal and specialise in tools for practical crafts. In 1948, he eventually found an attractive position advertised in a trade journal, but the job was based in Manchester. He sent off a letter of application and was able to arrange an interview for his next half day off. This involved a train journey and an interview with a sympathetic business man.

Ken obviously made a good impression at the interview and was provisionally offered the job, but was advised to talk it over carefully with his parents. He had recently been away for three years in the army, now after a short time back home, he was contemplating moving away again. How would this go down with his family? It was agreed that he would find lodgings in Manchester for five days per week and would return home at weekends.

The experience turned out to be very valuable as regards gaining knowledge of the tool trade. Ken became capable of recognising and explaining the use of a very wide range of hand and machine tools, relative to many different trades. He stayed in this position for three years, all the time gaining knowledge of the trade but growing tired of the weekend commuting.

In 1951, he heard that a similar business based in Rotherham, was looking for a shop manager. He successfully applied for the position, which he held for the next eight years.

By 1959, Ken felt confident that he would be able to run a business of his own, rather than spending the rest of his career managing for other people. The big problem was finding suitable premises, preferably in Sheffield. Many sites in the city centre were still derelict from the effects of wartime bombing raids. Some had been redeveloped with temporary buildings being erected, but the rents on these were prohibitive for a new, untested business. Eventually, Ken found a run down property in Button Lane, a back street off The Moor, now completely erased. The previous owner of the shop belonged to the Plymouth Brethren, a religious organisation who strictly observed the Sabbath as a day of rest. So strict was their beliefs, that they would not allow 'window shopping' on Sundays. As a result, Ken's window display of tools had to be covered over with sheets of brown paper every Sunday.

Ken promoted his new business by making use of his earlier contacts gained in his days of machine guard making. His rented shop was eventually made the subject of compulsory purchase when the whole area was cleared for redevelopment. By that time, able to afford better premises, Ken took over a shop in Earl Street. This was conveniently close to The Moor without having to pay the top rent and rates, which were demanded for the main shopping street. He eventually retired from this in 1989, but that was not the end of his interest in tools.

Over his working life, Ken had always made a point of looking out for and collecting, unusual tools. This interest has resulted in what is possibly the most comprehensive collection of tools in the country, and even now in retirement, Ken spends much of his time maintaining, cataloguing, and still adding to, his vast collection.

A final word from Ann Udall

"They say "History is now, isn't it?" but we were living through a period a lot of people will never know about. All round Broad Lane, Solly Street, Garden Street, there were little forges and cutlery works. This was in the 50s and 60s. I couldn't imagine that one day none of them would be there."

Cooks, waitresses and pot washers
Working in restaurants, canteens, pubs and clubs

From the 40s till the 80s the large employers provided subsidized canteens serving hot cooked meals for their employees, some of them, round the clock. At the same time most schools had their own kitchens, providing hot, cooked, healthy meals for school children.

"A pub on every corner" is how the older areas of Sheffield have been described, and the Working Men's Clubs were an important part of family life on the housing estates, organising trips to the seaside, football matches, as well as putting on entertainment. Pubs are now closing every week, and only a handful of the clubs are left. We now go out for tapas or Vietnamese noodles, and buy our booze at the supermarket.

These are the stories of the women who made sure we were well fed at school and at work, enjoyed gala meals in elegant restaurants, or a quiet drink after work.

Ada Lorriman's *favourite job was as a* **Silver Service waitress**, *after she had spent 14 years in the cutlery trade as a buffer and a dollier, trades that contributed to the manufacture of the beautiful silver plated spoons, forks, and knives, as well as the silver plated teapots, cream jugs, and salvers, "Made in Sheffield", and used for 'silver service'.*

Ada Lorriman

I was born in 1915 in Fitzwilliam Street, Sheffield. Attended Springfield School, then at the age of ten I moved to Park School, Duke Street. At the age of 14 I finished school on Friday, started work on Monday, as errand girl at J G Graves, Shoreham St, this was my first experience of the world of buffing. Within a year I had started on the wheel, and lasted for four years.

I moved to Ryall's on St Mary's Road as a 'dollier', stayed at Ryall's for ten years. I was poorly for a long time and didn't work for over six years.

My most pleasing job was at Fretwell-Downing Catering as a 'Silver Service waitress'. Two women I knew, who were already working for them, introduced me to the firm.

The staff called Mr. Downing 'father' because he looked after us so well.

Serving royalty

I must have got the knack. I started working on the top tables at the Cutlers' Hall, the City Hall, and the University.

I was at the opening of the Hyde Park Flats in 1966 by Her Majesty the Queen Mother. The dinner was held at the Hyde Park Community Centre, where I served Her Majesty.

I was at Weston Park Hospital when it was opened by Princess Anne. I was so frightened of knocking Her Highness' large green hat off!

I then travelled to Port Talbot to a special opening by the Queen, I had the greatest of pleasures to serve Her Majesty.

A couple of memorable moments

We travelled to the Fattorini family home on Ilkley Moor, for a very important dinner with important guests. One of the guests came into dinner with this backless dress. She sat down, and Hettie my friend was serving sauce. She arrived at the beautiful lady with the backless dress, and by accident spilt the sauce down her back. Poor Hettie was in tears.

We went to Brighton on the coach to a dinner. After a successful night we started to make our way home from Brighton to

Sheffield, sleeping on the coach. When the coach stopped, the driver says "the radiator is broke". The village garage was closed at this early hour of the morning, but we realised that we had milk bottles on the coach, so we went looking for puddles of water to fill the radiator. Whilst filling the bottles, someone in the village must have called the police. They came, heard the story then asked "has anyone got any chewing gum?" 'No' was the reply. The policeman made us stay until the garage opened, due to no one having chewing gum to seal the radiator.

In contrast, **Mrs Phyllis Hoole** *started work at the Sheffield Transport canteen, before joining the School Meals Service.*

"As a newcomer I started at the bottom, literally, as I scrubbed the floors"

I was born in Crookes in 1919 and went to Crookes Endowed School, leaving at the age of 14. My first job was at the Sheffield Transport Canteen, which was at Hartshead. The pay was eight shillings a week, eight hours a day spread over a seven-day period. Because the trams ran seven days a week, so did we, working shifts on a rota basis, either afternoons or mornings. Even at Christmas and Bank Holidays the trams kept running and we covered those times too, on a rota system. My stepmother took nearly all my wages. I was lucky to get a tanner (sixpence) for myself.

As a newcomer I started at the bottom, literally, as I scrubbed the floors. It was a nasty job, as the floors were filthy — I think the men spat on them. Next I graduated to washing pots, and finally to serving food at the counter.

The tram drivers and conductors brought their own tea and sugar in brew cans, which we filled. If they could not manage to get into the canteen, we had tea boys (young lads straight out of school), who took the cans from the men on the trams, brought them in for filling, and delivered them back to the men.

I worked in the canteen till I got married at 18 or 19 years of age, and had my first son. My husband was away in the army during the war. We had two sons, and once both of them were in school I started work again – you couldn't afford not to. We were living at Southey and I managed to get a job at the same primary school my lads were at, helping with the school meals. Again, it was mostly washing up and serving food and I don't remember having much trouble with the children, they behaved pretty well. This was very convenient for me, as I was at home when the boys were out of school and had the same holidays they did. I worked there until some time after they left school.

Christabel Cameron *started* **washing pots** *and pans in a hotel, and went on to work for a total of 42 years as a cook at Lodge Moor Hospital and Bent's Green School.*

I was born on Myrtle Road, Arbourthorne in the year of 1916. My father's name was John Edward. He was a joiner all his life. My mother was called Maud Mary – she was in Gentlemen's Service before marriage. I attended Lowfields School and left at the age of 14.

My first job was a pot and pan washer at the Albany Hotel, Surrey Street, above the Yorkshire Bank. The first wage of my working career was seven shillings and sixpence for six days.

In 1939-46, the war years, I was parachute packing, also working with barrage balloons.

After this I was employed at Lodge Moor Hospital, the so-called Fever Hospital. Once again, I started as pot and pan washer. I applied to go on a cook's course at Middlewood Hospital, which lasted for 12 months. Returned to the Fever Hospital as cook and stayed at Lodge Moor Hospital for 23 years.

In 1975 I went to Bents Green Special School as cook, looking after 300 pupils on a daily basis. There were 55 boarding due to illness, and the rest of the pupils went home. I spent 19 happy years at this school and in 1981 I retired.

Marian Chapman *came to Sheffield from Leeds, to get away from her violent husband.*

"I started a new life in Sheffield around 1956"

Despite her sadness at leaving her first family, she has spent much of her working life in Sheffield serving customers with food or drinks during their leisure hours.

I was born in 1925 opposite Armley Prison, Leeds. My father Clifford was a butcher at Blubber House Moor Farm and my mother Doris, was a weaver, club singer and housewife. I went to Farsley School on Weston Street, Leeds.

Before I left school my mum taught me to be a weaver. This was done at weekends. The company I was to join when it was time to leave school would pay me an allowance for my learning time. But when I did leave school World War Two had started and we weren't allowed to work for whom we wanted. I remember my first job was to get on this charabanc in Leeds with many other workers, then travel to Bradford. Sorry I can't remember the company, but my job was as a seamstress making military uniforms and raincoats, sand buckets, Bren Gun covers and worst of all, diving suits.

The smell of rubber was dreadful. You soon found out who your friends were! Even the smell of rubber on your sandwiches was enough to make you feel poorly. I worked five and a half days a week for 16 shillings. Mum had 12 shillings and me four shillings. This paid for my visits to the pictures and the dance nights. Mind you, when you had been working on the rubber, you might as well have stayed at home! After one year of travelling from Leeds to Bradford I was allowed to leave, so I started at the weaving company at Woodhouse Mill, Leeds as a weaver and in the mending department. This lasted for only twelve months.

Then I became a seamstress at the H.F. Brown Suit-makers in the district of Bramley. Paid on the Friday £2.50 for a five and a half day week. Worked on Saturdays, closed on Wednesday afternoons.

I met a Canadian serviceman in 1942 at a dance hall in Leeds. We started courting and I became pregnant. This was in 1944. The soldier promised to marry me, but he didn't keep his promise. Then in 1945, alone with a child, I met this man who later became a violent alcoholic. I had three children by him. He worked, but kept his family hungry. I had to give the children sugar with water to stave off the hunger pangs. One night he beat his eldest son for giving his younger brother a piece of bread. I was always beaten in front of the children.

Saturday night he would say - "Get your coat on, we're going to the pub". I'd reply – "What about the children?" and he'd shout – "Leave them". I'd put my thin summer coat on, this was in the middle of winter, and there I'd sit in the pub shivering and crying with worry, while he'd have his quarter and the snooker. In the pub was this man called George who I knew from school. He'd ask if I was O.K. I had a feeling he knew of the heartache I had living with a man who couldn't keep his hands to himself.

Every day was the same, struggling to feed the children, and me having to take very violent beatings from this monster of a man. I could see the concern in George's face, that if I didn't get away from this man I would be dead within weeks, so on the spur of the moment, George and myself decided to leave everything behind us, even my children. We ran to the railway station, George searched his pockets for money, then he asked – "How far will this take us?" The reply from the ticket office was "Sheffield", and that's where we finished up, in the clothes we stood up in.

I started a new life in Sheffield around 1956. No one knew where we had gone to. I know that if my husband had found out, he would have done his worst. In later years I found out he'd put the children in care. My first job in Sheffield was at Mary Gentles Chips & Fish Shop, Howard Street, and George got a job at Ward's on Woodseats Road, as a precision grinder. George and I had three lovely daughters, Lesley, Susan and Jane.

Then I worked at Nether Edge Hospital as a cleaner for four years, and then in 1966 I got the job as Club Stewardess at

Broomgrove Private Club off Ecclesall Road. At the side of the club was this lovely cottage, which was our living quarters. I remember you were not allowed out of the snooker room without your jacket on. In the evening George would work in the Nether Edge Dance Hall as bartender and at the weekends he'd help at the club with me, as cellar-man.

We married in 1973 after I found out my first husband had passed away. I spent 10 lovely years at the Broomgrove Private Club, made some very good friends and plenty of good memories. In 1976 we moved on. We went to live on the Winn Gardens Estate in a maisonette, which we bought later on. I worked at the Park Hotel off Leppings Lane as a bar-maid, then as a care assistant at Middlewood Hospital. I left at 60 and became a cook at Rosebank Nursing Home.

Whilst living at Winn Gardens, George passed away in 1994. He had worked at Ward's for 28 years and as a mark of respect, the company of Wards closed its' doors for the day for George's funeral.

On a lighter note, I used to play darts, dominoes and crib for the Beeley Wood Pub. We won trophies, that's how good we were.

Marian passed away on 2nd August 2007. Her daughter Jane, thinks that her mum was not totally happy when she came to Sheffield, due to her regret at having to leave her children back in Leeds. Jane knows, through speaking to her mum, that she would not be alive to care for the children she loved so much, if she had stayed there. By the way, her children that she left behind in Leeds attended their mum's funeral.

Coal mining, and afterwards

> THIS COLLIERY IS NOW
> MANAGED BY THE
>
> # NATIONAL
> # COAL BOARD
>
> ON BEHALF OF THE PEOPLE
> JANUARY 1ST 1947

This notice was posted at every colliery in the country on 'vesting' day. The National Coal Board took over 958 collieries, and 796,000 miners, 4% of the British work force. Mining communities throughout the country marched in their thousands behind banners and colliery bands to the local pithead. They believed there would be safer working conditions, decent wages, and long term security.

Modernisation of the industry lead to pit closures in the 60s, by 1969 there were just under half the number of miners and a third of the collieries there were in 1947.

However the 1974 'Plan for Coal' made plans for the future expansion of the coal mining industry in the face of rapid rises in the price of oil.

During the seventies every pit in South Yorkshire had the pithead steam engine replaced by electrical winding gear. One man remembered Bill the steam engine driver, who kept his machine beautifully for thirty years, weeping as it was dismantled and cut up with oxy-acetylene torches.

But in 1984 plans were revealed to close collieries on economic grounds, rather than the exhaustion of coal reserves, and to replace coal for power generation with gas and nuclear power.

The strike, which started on the 12 March1984 and lasted until March 1985, was the culmination of the longest and bitterest industrial dispute in British history. 10,000 people were arrested, and the cost of the strike to the taxpayer was £7 billion.

"Some pits never re-opened due to flooding".

The National Coal Board was replaced in 1987 by the British Coal Corporation. By 1992 there were only 53 collieries left in Britain, and in 1994 the Coal Industry Act returned the last collieries to private ownership.

Fred Haddington *writes about working at Orgreave Colliery before and after its modernisation, and about becoming an NUM Branch official.*

Fred Haddington, and colleagues.

Twenty years in the mining Industry

On the 8th October 1943 I made my debut in the world, the seventh child of a family of ten. My parents weren't too well off, they had lost nearly all their possessions in the blitz of Sheffield in December 1941. I can recall a tale my mother used to tell about returning home the next morning after the blitz to find the street completely demolished. The only thing left standing was the gable-end of their home. Hanging on the wall was the birdcage and inside was the canary singing for all it was worth. To think the Germans had blown up a gas tank and flattened a complete street and the little bird had survived. Incredible!

My parents were re-housed in the Broomhill area of Sheffield and that is where my memories began. My childhood was very full, always plenty of places to go. At three years of age I was attending Broomhill Nursery, and a few years later I moved on to Western Road Junior School. At the age of ten I was on the move again. The house where I was born and had lived all my life, was reclaimed by its previous owners, so we had to move across the city to Shirecliffe. My education continued at Shirecliffe School where I failed the Eleven-Plus examination. I was only an average scholar but I really excelled at sport. Football and cricket were my games and I represented Sheffield at both junior and senior level. Looking back, if my brains had been in my feet I would have been a professor by now.

The day most school kids look forward to finally arrived, December 1957, I was fifteen years old and leaving school. I went straight for an interview at Orgreave Colliery, I was going to be a miner.

Orgreave Colliery is the oldest in South Yorkshire and lies in the valley of the River Rother, six miles east of Sheffield and five miles south of Rotherham. The shafts were originally sunk in 1851 to the Barnsley seam at a depth of 137 yards. This was engineered by Sir Frederick Jones who was employed by the Sorby family, the owners of the colliery company. Between 1887 and 1890 the shafts were deepened and extended to work the Silkstone seam at a depth of 510 yards. Since then the Haigh

Moor, Flockton and Pargate seams have been worked at Orgreave, the latter being exhausted in 1976.

Following the formality of a medical I started work in January 1958. My first job was assisting in the pit-head baths but after completing my training I was moved to work on the screens working on the picking belt. On this job you had to sort out lumps of rock from the coal. I hated this job. It was very dusty and noisy and sometimes the lumps of rock were covered in shit and you got it all over your hands and clothes, but I managed to persevere until I was sixteen and old enough to go underground.

My first job underground was in the pit-bottom coupling empty tubs together before they were sent down the roads to the coal workings. After a few months of this I was moved further out into the workings to learn the art of chaining. Chaining was a very difficult job, not manually heavy but you had to acquire the knack of looping the chain around a wire rope while the rope was moving. The chain was coupled on to a run of six tubs of coal and if you weren't careful you could lose your fingers very easily. The old colliers used to say that a man never made a good chainer until he'd lost a couple of fingers. I never lost a finger but I did finish up with a few flattened finger ends.

After two very enjoyable years on the haulage the chance to go coal-filling arose and I grasped the opportunity with both hands. It was every pit lads dream to go filling coal on the face and the opportunity could not be missed. I was in the big money – or so I thought! At first you shared a break of coal with a collier but as time went by you finished up filling off a break of coal on your own. A break of coal was seven and a half yards long, five feet high and five feet thick. In total weight it made about twelve tons. As you can well imagine, it was bloody hard work and there weren't many fat colliers in those days.

In 1966 there was a complete change in the method of coalmining at Orgreave. It was like starting over again. In a matter of months hand-filled coalfaces were phased out and mechanised faces took over. The first mechanised face I worked on was a district named 20s. This coalface was some two-hundred yards long and the machinery consisted of a 125 horsepower Trepanner (this was the main coal-cutting machine) and around a hundred and fifty hydraulic five-leg Dobson roof supports. The Trepanner would travel down the length of the coalface, cutting coal at a thickness of two feet. When it reached the end of the face it was pulled into the stable-hole (a place at the end of the coalface which colliers had worked in front of the machine-cut face to allow the Trepanner to move forward to its next line of cut). The Trepanner had cutting elements at each end, which enabled it to cut back down the coalface without having to turn round.

This new type of mining was far in advance of anything I had ever seen before. It was a great step forward and a lot easier work, the age of the pick and shovel was on a downward spiral. As the years moved on the machinery got better and I graduated from a stable-hole man, packer, machine driver, charge-man and into a maingate ripper.

It was while I was working on the ripping lip that I had my first taste of the Union. It was just before the 1972 strike, I was charge-man on the backshift and I was working in the ripping. On our shift there was no coal turning, only maintenance and ripping duties, so we decided to ask the gaffer for 12.00 o'clock afternoon shift on a regular basis (down the pit by 12 noon and out of the pit between 7,30 and 8.00 p.m.). The manager agreed to our request without any hesitation, great!

That's what we thought until the next day. I was sat in the pit canteen having a cuppa when the union secretary came up to where I was sat. "Fred" he said, "you had no right to go and ask the Gaffer for afternoons regular, I have been and cancelled them". Well, I just saw red. The next thing I remember was the union secretary lying fist out on the canteen floor. Needless to say I came within a hairs-breath of getting the sack, and a £25 fine – we didn't get afternoons regularly after all.

Following my costly experience with the union I decided it was my time to get involved in the running of it, so in June 1973 I put up for election to the NUM Branch Committee and topped the poll. I don't know if it was beginners luck or the events of the previous year but after a very interesting year on the committee I decided to try for bigger things and stand for the position of Branch Treasurer. I didn't realise what the job entailed but I was soon to find out and it was a lot harder than I first thought. My apprenticeship was anything but easy. I was arrested on the first lobby of Grunwick (a dispute about union recognition in North London) but it didn't deter me from attending another three times. Come to think about my six years involvement in the union, it's really been the most satisfying years of my working life and who knows what the future may hold – a Branch Secretary's job maybe!

Throughout my twenty years at Orgreave Colliery I've made many friends and we have had some great laughs. Times may have been tinged with a little sadness but when you've been in the mining industry for over twenty years you learn to take the rough with the smooth. Looking back, if I had the choice of jobs to come again, a collier boy I would have to be.

Clive Hoyle *started work at Manvers Main Colliery in 1946, 12 years earlier than Fred Haddington started at Orgreave colliery, just before Nationalisation. He describes the old system, and later changes, his smallholding, how he (and his son) got through the strike, redundancy and new work.*

I was born and went to school in Wath upon Dearne, leaving school in 1946 at the age of 14. Finished school Friday and started work Monday, at Manvers Main Colliery. I worked at the pit top, a nine hour day, five days a week, seven hours on Saturday and the pay was £1.19s.6d. This was at the time the coal mines and all public utilities were being nationalised. The process in the pits started officially on 1st January 1947.

My job involved driving a loco, which was pretty good. When I reached the age for National Service I had to make a choice, either the army or underground at the Pit. I chose to go underground. You hadn't much of a say then. Bosses were bosses. There was no backchat. I was pony-driving underground. There was no machinery then, all the work was hand grafted.

When I reached the age of 18, the overman in charge of underground work asked me "How old are you, lad?" I told him - "I was 18 last week". "Right, see me on Monday and go contracting", was his reply. Contracting meant that I no longer had a set daily wage, which was the rule for under-eighteens. Now I had to earn my money. If you didn't work, you didn't get paid, and the amount of your pay depended entirely on how much work you did. I was given a kind of training at the coal -face for three weeks, then I was on my own. The target was to fill 25 tons of coal per day, and for this you earned around £2 a day.

I did that job till I was twenty, but then I said to myself – "Clive, are you going to be doing this for the rest of your life?"

There were 4,000 men at Manvers, including pit top and coking plant, and there were some men still working at the coal face at the age of 65. I didn't want that, so I went to night school (at my own expense) and got a shot-blasting Certificate. As soon as I'd qualified I found there was a vacancy for shot-firers (blasting stone and coal) and I began that at the age of 21. This meant that I'd transferred to the Management side. Due to my youth, I had to do 6 months on approval before I could join the Coal Board Superannuation Scheme. This was a good thing, as it was something for the future.

Hardly anyone my age went in for qualifications. They usually waited till they were about 30 or 32 years old. At 24 I went to college to qualify as a Deputy.

I'd work nights and go to college in the daytime. There'd be about 40 men in the class at the start of the course, and it would dwindle down to about ten.

For three years I was a Deputy. This was the kind of job you had to wait for, until someone retired or died, but at 27 I got the job.

Then a production overman until I was 45, then colliery overman until redundancy. The pit sent me to college full-time for two years on the overman course. It took me three to four weeks to get back into studying, for instance in the Maths exam you had to do 16 sums in 15 minutes, but at first I'd only do 12. The teacher said -"It's not that you can't do them, but it's so long since you studied. You've got out of the studying method. In 2-3 weeks you'll be O.K." - and he was right. It was the same with projects, after two to three weeks you got into it.

There were three Overmen, one for days 6 a.m. – 2 p.m., one for afternoons, 2 – 10 p.m. and one for nights 10p.m. – 6 a.m. I was normally on afternoons or nights, because the day Overman ran the whole pit.

Then came the time when I had a health scare. About ten years before I finished, I was doing a lot of hours at work, seven days a week, and I started with chest pains and went to see our doctor. When he told me to come back in the afternoon with my wife (because he was pressed for time), I feared the worst, and thought I must have heart trouble. Dr Foster was a good old-fashioned doctor. If you were really ill he would put you right, but if you were 'flannelling', he'd chuck you out of the surgery. We were there about an hour, and he went into every aspect of my life, work, marriage, finance etc, and his verdict was – "You are bringing your work home, and you've no hobbies. Get a hobby. Now go home and take your wife to bed". So, I started a smallholding and I was fine after that.

We kept beef cattle mostly, and Mavis (my wife), helped by feeding them when I was at work. We had a few chickens too, but they got pinched. We even got geese thinking they would scare off thieves and protect the chickens, but they too were stolen, so we stayed with the cattle.

The strike – 1984/5

This was a terribly trying time. I was in management but my son worked at the pit and was on strike, and picketing. The Underground Management were in favour of the strike, but we were still expected to go in, and were getting our wages. Every day we went in to work to register and then were sent home. It wasn't so bad on afternoons and nights, but on days you had to run the gauntlet of the police and picket lines. I used to leave the car in Wath and walk down to the pit, because these were men you'd worked with and you sympathised with them.

During the strike we never went out socialising. I thought it was not fair to go to the pub and buy a drink, knowing that the miners outside could barely afford to eat. Mrs Thatcher stopped all benefits for miners, except Child Allowance. Even ones already on Sickness Benefit were turfed off. They were hard times. After the strike dreadful stories were heard of unpaid bills for gas, electric etc, and mortgages which had been halted during the strike but were now in arrears. Men were up to their ears in debt and marriages broke up under the strain. It was very rough mentally as well as practically.

After the strike

Within six months of the strike she (Mrs Thatcher) was shutting down pits in rotation. I was offered redundancy due to long service, and only worked for six months after the strike. By then lots of men were leaving on redundancy pay or being transferred to other pits.

After 12 months Manvers closed and my son Adrian went to Frickley , but that shut after five years. Luckily I knew Tony Lawson, the manager at Silverwood Colliery, because he had been at Manvers previously. He'd worked his way up and we got on well. He was the kind of chap that if you did your job well he supported you. If not, he'd be down on you like a ton of bricks. I rang him about my son, and he said - "tell him to come on Saturday morning and see me". Adrian started at Silverwood on the Monday, but in 12 months that pit closed too.

Adrian signed on for about two weeks, got a job warehousing, but then he met a recruiting officer who asked – "Would you fancy the Police Force?" Adrian had not thought of that before but he went in for it. There was a four or five-month process to get in, with exams to take, and meanwhile he was still doing the warehouse job in Barnsley. Finally he was accepted and joined the West Riding Force, based at Castleford. He loved the job, but there was too much paperwork, so after about four years he left.

Next he got a job at St Catherine's Hospital in Doncaster, went to college for three years, and qualified as a nurse. He took to nursing like a duck to water and is now a Staff Nurse at Rotherham District General. He has got two degrees and is doing another for a doctorate, which will qualify him to teach nursing.

When I finished at the pit in 1986, I met a lady called Joyce, who said there was a job going at Wath Library, for a caretaker. During the dark nights of winter I'd kept myself busy for four months with decorating and suchlike jobs, but now I was getting bored. I went for the interview on Friday morning and at 1 p.m. Gill Gardner (the librarian), rang to offer me the job, saying – "If you want it, it's yours, and can you start on Monday morning?" I accepted, and went in on Saturday morning to find out about my duties.

Mostly these involved looking after the coal-fired boiler, and covering the building when it opened for evening classes. However, very soon the Area Librarian, Steve Carney, asked me if I would work at other libraries, particularly Maltby, doing a variety of odd jobs, and from there it snowballed. When the regular caretaker at Maltby was off sick, I covered not only Maltby Library, but the Town Hall and Social Services offices. At one time I was covering seven buildings.

I did this job for 13 years up to the age of 65, and they were very happy years. You worked in your own time – no-one was bossing you about. It changed our whole lives at home too. At the pit it was a men-only environment, with language and attitudes to match, and I tended to carry these same attitudes home with me, whereas at the library they were all women.

I began to change my manner and language and this was noticed at home. Both my wife and the children noticed the difference, and commented on it. When I was at the pit, I worked such long hours that I hardly saw my older children, and often rarely saw daylight, but with the youngest I could spend much more time. I remember when my eldest son told me he was getting married, I had no idea he'd even got a girl-friend. We have four children, two girls and two boys, but it was only the youngest lad that I was able to watch grow up.

Reflections

The fact is, that the place where you are working rubs off on you, and by working in a different atmosphere, I brought that home. From bossing men about, I found myself in a totally different and much better atmosphere. It's surprising how a different job changes your attitudes and outlook on life.

When I was at the pit I really loved the job, even though it was seven days a week, and I was disappointed when it closed, but now I don't regret the closure at all. Within two years at the library amongst the people I worked with there, I realised what was available apart from the pit. I'd only ever thought of jobs at the pit or in the steel industry, and I said to Mavis – "I wish they'd shut the pits 50 years ago". Those 13 years working at the library were gorgeous, and I was disappointed when I had to retire.

It is true that there are some men around here who have never worked again since the pits and steel works closed. A lot of men I worked with spent their days getting up late, reading the paper and watching T.V. and they are full of ailments or have even passed away. It is possible to change if you want to, either for better or for worse. Working at the library was a big change for me, but a good one, both for myself and for the family.

When the pits closed, I did a rough calculation, that 450,000 men lost their jobs in South Yorkshire, but within ten years there were that many jobs again, if not more. Lots of work came up from the South of England. Miners were used to working three shifts to cover the whole day, but in the South and Midlands most people did 8-5 jobs. Their factories only worked to one third capacity, but by moving to Yorkshire with a workforce accustomed to covering 24 hours a day, they could increase their capacity.

On my opinion South Yorkshire has changed for the better. Since the pits and steel works closed, families in general enjoy improved health, and also other improvements from looking at life from a different point of view. Once, young people were brought up to follow the same jobs as their dads and mums, but now they can go to College and learn different trades and professions, leading to improved lifestyles. The younger generation are doing things their parents never dreamed of, whereas if the pits were still open, they'd have gone into them.

Even after I retired from the library at 65, I started something new, in addition to the smallholding which I still have. I had a friend who was a qualified brickie, and about two weeks after I finished at the library, he said – "Would tha' like to do a few jobs for me?" So I started as his labourer, fetching materials for him from the suppliers, and this grew till I became handy at bricklaying, plastering etc. I built an extension to our house, and now I build extensions for my sons and daughters. You can learn something new at any age.

There is plenty of work out there if you want it and are prepared to graft. Whenever I am working on a house, all the neighbours start coming to ask if I can do jobs for them, and a fully qualified plumber, electrician or gas fitter can earn good money. In this area a bricklayer can earn £14 an hour, a joiner £16 and electricians and gas fitters £18 an hour, and they could treble that if they moved to London.

The demand is there, but often, young people don't want that kind of work. One of my sons-in-law works at the P&O warehouse, and they can't get staff, and have to employ foreign labour due to the shortage of English people wanting the jobs. My bricklayer friend tells me that Henry Boot set on about 20 school leavers each year, but in two or three months they've nearly all left.

Since the pits closed our area has been transformed. What I like is that when they shut the pits and the railways, they didn't just leave everywhere derelict. The government and the EU poured money in to regenerate the area and the pit sites have been landscaped, so we have open spaces, which can be enjoyed for free. Pollution has gone, and the environment is 200% better. For instance, years ago, you could hardly distinguish one bird from another – they were all dirty brown. Now we have abundant wildlife and the trees are green. The old railway has become a cycle track and provides pleasant walks. The Pennine Trail runs past our house and Mavis and I have an hour's walk most mornings. This is now a nice place to live, whereas before, it was rough.

Ken Frost *worked for fifteen years for the Coal Board as a fitter. Here he tells us about hard times during the strike, and then his job driving for the mobile library service, a job with a woman as a manager, and more women as colleagues.*

When I first left school I took a variety of jobs, starting in an accounts office. From this job I was made redundant at the age of 19. Next I took a stop-gap job as a driver-warehouseman, then a milk round, taxi-driver and a pop round. Then I got married and felt the need of some serious money, so went into engineering. I stayed there for two years, but didn't really enjoy it, so in 1979 I went to work for the Coal Board, where I stayed until I was made redundant in 1993.

My work was not underground. I was a fitter's mate in the Coal Preparation Plant, in charge of servicing and maintenance of conveyer belts and gear boxes and other fitting jobs.

The strike

This lasted for 52 weeks and was a very hard time. My wife was seriously ill, so could not work to supplement our income, and we had two young children. We got a bit of help from both our families but the bills mounted up. Our mortgage was frozen and we had just £29 a week to live on. We lived in a big old semi-detached house, and while I was on strike we all lived in one room, because we couldn't afford to heat it properly. We got one bag of coal a week because one of our children was under five years old, and that was it.

After the strike

Some pits never re-opened due to flooding. Basic maintenance was carried on during the strike, but if there was major problem with rock-falls or flooding, nothing could be done.

Six months afterwards my pit (Brookhouse at Beighton), closed down, and I transferred to Fence Workshops repairing electric cables, but in 1988 that also closed. I felt a false sense of security at Fence because there was plenty of work, but it was actually work that had piled up during the strike. Then pits began to close down, one by one.

I moved to Shafton, between Barnsley and Pontefract doing the same job. It was quite a long journey (one hour), as opposed to five minutes to Fence, but we got subsidised transport. We were given the chance to move house, but we'd only just moved house as it was, my wife was ill, and what's more, I could see that pits were closing all over the place, so there seemed little point in moving.

As soon as McGregor was put in charge of the mines, it was pretty obvious he would do to us what he'd done to the steel industry. First of all the Shafton job was OK, but then the Yorkshire Coalfield began slimming down. You didn't need to be a brain surgeon to work out that the job was coming to an end. In 1993 the light went out at the end of the tunnel. The Coal Board were quite good, and several options were open to me. I had the choice of moving to Derby or Middlesborough, but I decided against it.

I felt particularly sorry for the older men, in their 50's, because it would be hard for them to get a new job and start all over again, but I was in my 40's.

The thing that did make me feel rather bitter was the way my employment at Shafton ended. The union had been negotiating to get us the best deal, and they tried to keep us in touch with developments, but from the moment we decided we were going, it was one hour to leaving for good. We were called into the office, asked to sign a piece of paper, and asked to leave the premises within the hour. I felt like a condemned man. I had worked 14-15 years for this firm, and at the end they got rid of us so unfeelingly.

When I think of all we suffered in the strike, I'd like to think that we achieved something, but I'm afraid we did not, because eight years later our industry was more or less over. I gradually lost touch with most of the men I'd worked with. Fence had been very localised, though some men had been brought in from the Elsecar and Birdwell Workshops, but we lost track of each other after we split up. I know that one man never worked again, because he was very ill, but the fact is that you moved on and lost touch.

I finished in June 1993 and the redundancy money helped at first, but when you are in your early forties you can't live on that forever and a day. It was a strange feeling.

Rotherham Library Bookability driver

There was no immediate pressure to get another job. I was waiting for something to take my fancy, and joined a Job Club, applying for several jobs, none of which I obtained. Then I saw an advert for a Relief Driver for the Rotherham Library's Bookability vehicle, and I got the job. I knew nothing about books or libraries, but I could drive, and I was later told that that's how I got the job. The vehicle was a mobile library with a special wheelchair lift, and was designed to travel around all the Care Homes, Nursing Homes and Sheltered Accommodation Units for the elderly.

Because of my ignorance about books, it was like being back in the accounts office in my teenage years, but it's the kind of work you pick up as you go along. Fourteen years later I can easily recall the titles of popular books and their authors, the kind of things we are often asked for. Mills & Boon romances are as popular as ever, albeit in a Large Print format. Luckily my past experience on the milk and pop rounds had enabled me to pick up the knack of chatting to customers, and this is really important with the old people. You might be the only person they see that week and you've got to listen and try to empathise, and show sympathy. It's not just a library service, more of a Social Service.

We always try to encourage people to come on the bus and choose their own books if at all possible, but some are not confident about using the lift, and others really cannot move from their homes, so we select books in advance for them and deliver them in person. I've met some real interesting characters, such as the woman who was a trapeze artist in a circus, a lady whose husband was Ringmaster at Billy Smart's circus and a qualified draughtsman who had taken up painting and produced some marvellous paintings and pencil sketches.

The work has changed a little over the years, because at first all of the library assistants could drive the bus, in addition to the full-time driver, but they don't have to do that now. I obtained the post of full-time driver when the previous driver retired, and we have relief drivers who cover all the mobile libraries and the delivery van. We have about 80 stops on our round, and no waiting list, although it takes some effort to fit in new stops.

What were the differences between this job and what I did previously? Well, for one, it meant working in a much cleaner environment. Another strange thing for me was that all my previous jobs were male-orientated, but now there was a lady in charge, and most of my colleagues were women. That wasn't a problem to me, but it was something I had not experienced before.

Not many people have the luxury of job satisfaction, but I really do enjoy this work. I'm out in the fresh air driving around, seeing some nice countryside (if it's fine), and meeting different people every day, not to mention the characters! I think I acclimatised well, and I'm pleased to be part of a service that is so well-received.

When Ken finished at British Coal he says, **"The day I finished work we went on holiday, but it was odd to think – 'I've no job to go back to".**

An old fashioned Bobby

'A policeman's lot is not a happy one' – so goes the well-known Gilbert & Sullivan song, but the two men whose stories are recorded here give the lie to that. Amazingly, their careers in the Sheffield Police span the years 1928 –1994. Both men began 'on the beat'. Charles Haddon, who joined the force in 1928, retired as an Inspector in 1958, whilst Barry Sorsby began his working career as a 'Beat Bobby' in 1962 and retired as a Sergeant in 1994.

These two men's careers covered many of the major events of local life – the Blitz, the visits of royalty and other VIP's, the pit strikes and the Hillsborough disaster.

"It was a sad business. I've often thought about those young miners and wondered how they managed to support their families and pay mortgages when the pits closed."

Barry says that when he joined the Force, the job was, in essentials, much the same as when Charles joined all those years before, but since the 1960's, the pace of change accelerated to an amazing degree.

Did you ever long to know what was inside those mysterious police boxes? (Apologies to Dr Who, but it was not a spaceship)

How did they check whether someone was over the drink-driving limit before breathalysers?

Read on....

Charles – Police Force, 1928-1958

I was born on the 19th of May 1906 in Walkley. My parents were Charles and Josephine Harrod, and I had one sister called Alice. At the age of 14 I left school and began work as a clerk in a solicitors' office near the Cutlers Hall. However, my dad did not approve of 'all that pen-pushing' and wanted me to have a trade.

My uncle was a woodworker, so I left the office and became a carpenter, which lasted for seven years. It was quite a change going from working in a nice navy suit to overalls, and from a 9 - 5 working day to an 8 am start.

The first job in the morning was to get the old gas engine going to drive the circular saw! During the first two years I was unhappy, but gradually grew to like it. I couldn't leave because I was bound for seven years. This training has stood me in good stead as I have made many items of furniture for our home. I was not sure that the boss would want to keep me on when the apprenticeship ended, but he asked me - "Are you happy?"

I said - "Yes"

Then - "Do you want to stay, because I am happy with you"

I accepted, and did I skip home that night!!!

In 1927 a chance remark changed the course of my life. One summer morning, a little chap called Chris, a plumber, passed me on the road. We knew each other through working on various jobs together, and he said – "I wish I were as tall as you"

"Why?" I said.

"You don't think I'd be here if I were, I'd be in the Police Force".

"Well," I said, "The boss has kept me on, the sun is shining, why should I join the police?"

His reply was, that it would be O.K. while my boss had work, but if there were a slump in trade, I'd be out of a job.

One hour later I walked up the steps of the central police station at Castle Green in my old work overalls and said - "I'd like to join the police". I was told to go up some stairs and knock at a door. I entered a room full of smart looking men who looked at me as if I was something the cat brought in.

In reply to a sharp –"Yes?" from one of the men, I said –"I'd like to join the police force". I was asked where I lived, and when I said "Walkley", he turned me down at once, with the words "You can't be a good policeman and have friends". I was too local, and he suggested I apply to the Force in another town. I didn't want to leave home, so I thought – 'well at least I've tried' - thanked them very much and left.

One month later I received a letter inviting me to come for an examination, and later, on finding that I did not have flat feet, I was in. Just a chance encounter and a few words. I retired 31 years later as an Inspector. I thank God every night for little Chris!

When I started my career, the Chief Constable was a wonderful man called Captain P. J. Sillitoe (known to us all as 'P.J.'), who broke the Sheffield gangs.

These were the Mooney Gang and the Garvins. Before he came to Sheffield the previous Chief Constable had formed the Flying Squad with just four men. 'P.J.' got all the magistrates together and told them – "You do your job and we'll do ours". By the time I joined the force the two Fowler brothers had been hung and it was nearly all over. Three years after 'P.J.' left I saw him in the street, saluted and said "Good morning sir". He said straight away, "I know you". I am the last one left who worked under this great man, who was later knighted and became head of MI5.

I began my police career at Attercliffe Station as a beat Bobby, with a weekly wage of £3.10s plus a rent allowance of four or five shillings. I lived at Walkley so had to take two trams to get there. Of course we worked shifts, including nights, and the worst was when you finished at 6 a.m. and then had to be back by 2 p.m. to change over to the afternoon shift. I remember standing in a passage at the end of Cricket Inn Road on a rainy night, soaking wet, and thinking 'I'm not sticking this', and I had to be back at work with a dry uniform by 2 p.m. We also worked Sundays, Bank Holidays and Christmas, always immaculately turned out in uniform. No matter how hot the weather, you dare not undo even the top button of your uniform.

I always remember my first time on traffic duty. It was at the bottom of Staniforth Road. You put your hand up and all the traffic stops – that's power!! But then you think - 'What do I do next?'

I was in the Force when the Box System was introduced, i.e. Police Boxes (as in Dr Who). They were great! Before that when we did our rounds, we'd leave our food and drink with the nightwatchmen at the little steelworks, and they would have it all heated up by the time we came back. They were only too glad to have us call in.

Inside the boxes was a stove where we could leave our mug and by the time we returned there would be a nice hot drink ready. The boxes also had a telephone, with a button which you pressed when you reported in. If no button was pressed, the operator knew that a member of the public was using the phone, and assistance would be sent

I was once involved in a battle royal with a man on Leopold Street and a woman who saw it ran to the police box and used the phone to get help for me. I got a broken nose out of that encounter. My other injury, a broken leg, was also got when I was on duty. The Box System involved the policeman ringing in at a certain time every hour. It meant you could choose one of about six routes around your 'patch', instead of going the same way each time, so long as you rang in at the expected time.

One miserable night I was followed all round my Section by a big dog, so when I called in at the Box on Manor Lane, I tried to get rid of it, by letting another policeman who called in go out first. I waited quite a while, but when I emerged, the wretched creature was still there. It followed me down to the Market Place where I called in at another box. Suddenly I heard the screech of brakes – the dog had run under a bus.

Before joining the police my favourite pastime on Sunday mornings, was hiking in Derbyshire, and it was on one of these occasions that I met my future wife. It was pouring with rain and I had walked round Kinder Scout and landed in Castleton for refreshments. There was a party of young ladies from Manchester, one of whom attracted my attention. We were married in 1932.

The thing I enjoyed most of all was when I was transferred to the Motorised Section. In the 1930's this consisted of a car for each

Division, with three drivers allocated for emergencies. Some days we just spent time polishing the cars and sweeping up the yard etc. My job was to drive another officer to incidents and help in the arrest if necessary. Our first cars were Alvis Narrowtrack models, custom-built, expensive and good, and they were wonderful to drive. We also had George Brough Motor Cycles built in Nottingham.

I moved to Hammerton Road, Hillsborough. One day I was sitting eating my packed lunch (there was no canteen then), when the Superintendent told me he'd had an urgent phone call from a lady at Fulwood and I was to take him there as fast as possible. This was an excuse to show what the Alvis could do and we shot along Fulwood Road, pulled up at a big house and rang the doorbell. A maid answered the door and showed us into a large entrance hall, where we stood for some time. A lady came out of one door, walked past us without a glance, and went in to another room, into which we were eventually shown.

She sat there like Queen Victoria, flanked on each side by her two daughters. "My daughters and I are going to be away on a cruise for six months. I want you to look after this house". My Superior said - "Madam, I understood this was urgent. There are policemen passing your house four times a day who could deal with this, and you have called out a Superintendant".

"I don't deal with junior ranks" was her reply. "Madam, I am in charge of this whole area, and you have called me out to something a constable could do quite adequately". Once again – "I only deal with senior people. We shall have to pay off the servants when we go away and you never know where they have come from. They might have been born in a slum". My boss stood up and said, " Madam, on Sunday morning you will go to Ranmoor Church and kneel down and worship a man who was only born in a stable. Good day", and we left.

Another time it was just gone 10 pm when the Super came through to announce "An accident on Manchester Road". It was a milkman who'd just fetched milk from a farm on Carsick Hill Road. It was 1930, just after the First Road Traffic Act came in. A Rolls

Royce had hit the milk cart and quite a few swear words came from the driver of the Rolls. The Super said to me "Harrod, can you smell anything?" "Yes sir, he's had too much to drink. Shall we take him in?" We did, (there were no breathalysers then), and the language that 'gentleman' used was beyond belief. When we got to the station he rang a top lawyer and top optician (before breathalysers, we laid a straight line of coins on the floor and they had to walk along them. If they 'wobbled', we knew they'd had too much to drink). They bailed him out, but he was convicted for 'drunk driving'. Next was to go back and see about his car. When we got there my boss asked me -"Have you ever driven a Rolls Royce? No? Then now's your chance." We parked it in the man's drive, as we thought, but three quarters of an hour later the Super said "Harrod, where have we left that car?" It seems it was not his address at all, so back we went and I drove the Rolls for the second time. What a wonderful experience.

During the Sheffield Blitz I was based at West Bar, and recall standing in the doorway there that night – but not for long! About 4 - 5 weeks later on a Sunday morning, the Chief Inspector came down, which was very unusual. I thought - 'Something's happening here'. Then the Assistant Chief Constable came, dressed in plain clothes, and I thought - "Crikey, what have I done?"

He said "Harrod, come here, close that door. You are to get the car and go to the Town Hall. You will find a gentleman on the corner. Bring him here. Don't say a word to anyone, just do as you are told". I did this, and when they had all got in the car they told me to take them to the City Hall, and they began looking at the bomb damage. I realised from the conversation that in four days' time the King and Queen were coming to see the damage and try to encourage people. When we reached the City Hall, the Assistant Chief Constable sat beside me and spoke as if I would be present when they came. I said - "I won't be there", but he replied - "Yes you will", and there I was, escorting the King and Queen around Sheffield!

At the end of that year I was made a Sergeant. In 1950 I became an Inspector and moved to Hammerton Road Station. One day I went out on a call. I didn't have to go, I could have sent someone else, but it was a nasty job. A young man had committed suicide. He was a public schoolboy with a lovely home and was apprenticed to a solicitor. His mother was a widow and had gone shopping, as it was Saturday afternoon. His brother was out playing sports. He had cut his wrists, then put his head in the gas oven, where we found blood, and finally gone up to his room and drunk photographic fluid, which killed him. Suicides were always very sad.

In July 1958 I retired from the police, and I took on a totally different job. I went to Winter Street Hospital as a clerk. This was completely new ground for me. It was a difficult time at the hospital as staff never stayed long. I ended up being promoted to the job of Secretary (nowadays called Administrator), running the whole Hospital. The matron was very strict indeed, but fair. However, when a new matron came, we did not agree, and I resigned and retired for the second and final time in 1966.

In some ways I think more of my time at the hospital than in the police, because I had no knowledge of hospital work at all. I was an utterly raw recruit, but I ended up as Secretary. Altogether, I can say that I have met some wonderful people and have many wonderful memories of my working life. Indeed, the above is a very small collection of episodes. There are many, many more which could be recounted.

Barry Sorsby – Policeman

I was born in 1939. We lived at Norfolk Park and I attended Arbourthorne North Secondary Modern School. Our teachers were mostly ex-military men and very tough. My first job was at Edgar Allen's Sales Department from 1954 to 1960, and whilst there I was sent on an Outward Bound Course at Aberdovey – that were brilliant and was the start of a change in me.

Next came National Service from 1960 -1962. I was in the Army Pay Corps, but spent most of my two years playing sport. This, along with the Outward Bound experience, was a really formative experience, and when I left the army I only stayed in my old job at Edgar Allens for one month. Partly it was for better money, and to enable me to get a mortgage for a house, and partly because I'd changed. You are never the same when you've been in the military.

Entering the police force was easy then, you just took an exam. At that time the police were recruiting lots of ex-miners, ex-steelworkers and ex-military. From what I hear about recruitment now, none of us would have a chance – you need a degree.

I started at Attercliffe Police Station, which covered a huge area, including Darnall, Tinsley, Firth Park and the Manor, which was then quite a respectable area. We lived on Hurlfield Avenue. You worked a beat on foot or on push-bike – I had a bike. The Division possessed one car and two motor cycles. I was on the motor bikes for about two years, and because you were mobile you got all the accidents, sudden deaths and suicides.

The sort of stuff we were dealing with was mainly break-ins and fights. There were a lot of fights in Attercliffe in those days, but no knives or guns. I only made one arrest where the man was thought to have a gun, but he did not use it and we never found it. There were very few murders then. If there was a murder it was so unusual, everyone in Sheffield was talking about it.

When you joined the police you did two weeks together on nights, but the changeover to afternoons was hardest, because you went off night duty at 7 am and the same day went on in the afternoon. They were very strict about time-keeping. If you were one minute late the sergeant would report you. When personal radios came in they gave you more freedom, you could just disappear, but before that, you had to be somewhere every 20 minutes or else!

The beat system worked like this. Every man had a Beat Book with the beat numbers in, for instance, C Division was numbered 1-24. I-6 was Firth Park, 7-14 Attercliffe, and 15-24 Manor, Woodhouse and Handsworth. This would show the starting point each day from Monday through to Sunday and everyone started at the same place so the Sergeant could locate you if need be. It showed the B Points you had to go to, and your third one had to be at a phone kiosk or police box. You would do two hours, and every third point, i.e. every 20 minutes, you stopped to phone. After two hours you went back to the station, spent 10 or 15 minutes writing a report, then out again for another two hours. Then it would be meal-time. The Police Boxes had, in addition to a phone (which the public could access in emergency), a table and chair for writing up notes, and a small stove on which you could heat up food and drinks. One chap left something on the stove too long at a box in the city centre, and it burnt down.

Without fail, you checked every property on your beat, by shaking the door handles, and going round the back of shops (a bit dodgy after dark) and if you didn't, and there was a break-in, you'd be in trouble. This is no longer the practice. My first turn on nights on the Manor was in January or February 1963, one of the worst winters for years, and there was deep snow. I found that Manor Social Centre off Prince of Wales Road had been broken into. I called out the report that the safe had been stolen. It hadn't snowed all night, but there was fresh snow on the floor. I could see they had taken the safe away on a sledge, so followed the tracks to a house where subsequently an arrest took place. The CID pinched that job off me though I'd done all the spade-work, and my sergeant said – "You'll learn as you go on"

I did the beat for five years, then two years on motor cycles, and then one year in plain clothes, in the Crime Intelligence Department, which I found extremely boring. I got caught in a car in the wrong Division, and though I thought I'd dodged the Chief Superintendent, he'd seen me, and when I got back to Attercliffe Station there was a reception committee awaiting me, and I was back on the beat. I liked it much better, I liked being outdoors, and not cooped up in an office.

I was a great practical joker. Once at Attercliffe Station, we found an old tin of black paint, and painted the seats of the two toilets, but told no-one. The first chap to sit on the loo was an Inspector, a really nice bloke. I think he twigged it were me - I usually got the blame for practical jokes. They sent me off to the Manor for a month, as far away from the station as possible, so I couldn't cause any more trouble.

The Mounted Police

In 1970 the best thing happened to me - I met some pals at the Bakewell Show who were in the mounted police and I managed to get into that department. I'd had some experience of horses as a pal had a farm where he broke in thoroughbreds from Ireland, and my daughter was learning to ride. They were amazing creatures. They put me on one once and it ran away with me, but that didn't put me off, it made me keener to ride.

Barry Sorsby on Glayva

154

The mounted police was a whole lifestyle. Your horse was your responsibility. You groomed it, mucked it out, cleaned the kit etc. I had some wonderful horses. The one I rode from 1977 to 1993 was called Glayva. He was 17.2 hands, an Irish draught cross-thoroughbred. I won loads of dressage and jumping competitions with him, but it was the horse who won, not me. He had throat cancer, and went out to grass until it was necessary to have him put to sleep.

About 1992 or 3 we had a lovely horse called Sandhurst, which became very lethargic and wouldn't work, so the Chief Inspector, who was going on holiday, gave orders for him to be humanely killed. After the C.I. had gone on holiday, I changed the report to say that he was all right to be put out to grass, and he lived happily at our house for the next four or five years. It didn't do me much good with the Inspector.

We were on patrol every day in problem areas such as Broomhall when the new students came up. They were always getting mugged, so we'd step up the patrols there. We also did a lot of schools work – the kids loved stroking the horses. In 1979 they sent me on an advanced riding course at the Met (London) where a horse rolled over me, but I was O.K., and in 1981 I was promoted to Sergeant.

Of course, the main work of mounted police is crowd control, at football matches, royal visits, and other occasions when large crowds gather. We would lead off the students Rag Day Procession, the Lord Mayor's Parade and the Star Walk

When the Queen and the Duke of Edinburgh opened the new police H.Q. at Snig Hill I was on duty, on a big grey horse called Baron, and was one of the protection squad when Princess Anne came to Lord Scarborough's place. When Mrs Thatcher came to the Cutler's Hall, we were kept standing too long, and one horse got fidgety, spun round, reared up and put it's feet through the back window of the police car that followed Mrs Thatcher, right outside the Cutlers Hall.

Football matches were, of course one of our main duties, as we covered not only the two Sheffield grounds, but also Rotherham,

Barnsley, Doncaster, Chesterfield, Scunthorpe, Derby City and Leicester, none of which had their own horses. That kept us pretty busy. I did every semi-final since 1970 on horseback, and before that, on foot.

The pit strikes

These were hard work. We'd go to work at 2 am, and the horses were saddled and in the boxes by 3 am so we could be at the first pit by 4 am when the protesters came. This was usually Silverwood. We'd have a fight there and move on to Kiveton Park by 5.30 am - another fight, then Brookhouse, near Treeton and finally Yorkshire Main at Doncaster. We'd have had four good scraps by 9.30 am. Sometimes we went to Nottingham pits, but usually it was these local ones.

A lot of the protesters were not miners, they were 'professional activists' from all over the place, and local lads who just fancied throwing bricks at the police. One horse called Argyle, lost an eye at Stainforth Pit because of the bricks, but he was not put down. Instead he went to Edinburgh where he was ridden by vets in training.

We had a lot of trouble at Kiveton Park, where crowds of lads (most of whom were not miners) took the opportunity of chucking bricks at us. They would then run away into a nearby housing estate where we couldn't catch them and they would pull up drain covers to try to cripple the horses. We decided to sort them out, so one day we blocked off all their usual escape routes so that the only place they could run was a field in which we had them trapped. So there we were at 6.30 am chasing these brick-throwing lads around a field, in the middle of which was a copper from Thames Valley driving around in a 'Pig'(a transit van with reinforced floor), with the 'Ride of the Valkyries' music blaring out from the stereo.

I was at the battle of Orgreave. I was a sergeant then, on a big grey horse, and I was a marked man. I never got knocked off, but one bloke did, because they put trip wires down. One of my pals, a really nice chap on a horse called Dragoon, was set up by a photo which looked as if he was hitting a woman with a stick, when in fact she was some distance away.

The big day was the 18th of June, and the police were using their last resources. They bussed in coppers from all over the country. Units from Thames Valley and even as far away as Plymouth came up the M1 in convoys. Our tactics were, that when they began throwing bricks and shoving, the Superintendent told them to stop or he'd send the horses in. When they did not stop, we were sent in at a fast canter, almost a gallop, head-on. We had once tried the sideways 'football shove', but it didn't work in this situation. It looked just like a medieval battlefield, with the front line of police making a shield wall, the opposition charging at them, and us, the cavalry, charging through from the back.

It was a sad business. I've often thought about those young miners and wondered how they managed to support their families and pay mortgages when the pits closed.

The Hillsborough football ground disaster, 15 April 1989

First you need to understand where and how supporters were located. The Penistone Road (Kop) and South Stand were where supporters from teams coming up from the South were located, whilst supporters coming from the North or West, e.g. Manchester or Llverpool filled the stands opposite the Kop and Leppings Lane. The problem on this day was that the stands allocated to Liverpool supporters i.e. Leppings Lane, held 5,000 less people than the Penistone Road ones, but there were far more Liverpool supporters than those from Nottingham Forest.

I'd done every semi-final from 1970 on horseback and we never had any trouble at these matches. This seemed like a normal semi-final. I was a sergeant and had twelve men on horseback at the Penistone Road side, and everything went like clockwork. This was usually the hardest side to police because whereas Leppings Lane was closed to traffic, Penistone Road was not, so you had buses and other vehicles to deal with along with the crowds on foot.

By 2.50 pm there were no supporters left on Penistone Road, they had all gone inside in an orderly manner, but I was puzzled because from 2.15 pm onwards, Leppings Lane kept asking for more horses. By 2.45 - 3.00 pm there were only two of us left to work my side. I went round to Leppings Lane at 3 pm and I couldn't believe what I saw. It was as if two games were taking place on the same day, and the place smelt like a brewery. It was that side that people got crushed when non-ticket holders got in. I couldn't comment on the rights and wrong of it, enough to say that something went very wrong.

I was not involved within the ground, although I remained on duty outside the gymnasium and saw all the bodies brought in.

My view is that police shouldn't buckle under the strain of sights like these because that's the job. I'm not into this counselling at all. Once I went to an accident at Shire Green, when a bread van ran out of control and crashed into a little car containing a man and his small daughter. The child was killed, and I carried her into a nearby house. When the ambulance arrived they said she was dead, and I had to go and tell her mother. What that woman suffered – that's stress. Later, when I was doing charity work in a Rumanian orphanage, children were dying all around us as we worked, and two of my lads cracked up.

Charity work.

The police do a tremendous amount of work raising money for charities, and if you have a horse, that's a real crowd-puller. In 1990 when the communist regime in Rumania was overturned, my wife and I saw on T.V. the terrible plight of the children in orphanages. With publicity from the local Press, we gathered a team from British Telecom and South Yorkshire Police, and got started. Over the years we took several teams to the orphanages, and also helped the Rumanian police to bring their Force into line with modern European methods of policing.

At the same time we were raising money for charities here in England, and though I retired from the police in 1994, my links with Rumania continue to this day, along with much other charity work.

In 1994 when I was 55 years old, I applied for an extension of service, which was refused. The reason given was that 'riding horses is a young man's game'. Six months later I climbed 3 mountains (Snowden, Scafell and Ben Nevis in 22 hours), just to prove how fit I was.

Safety pins and paper clips
Hospital and Care Work

"First thing in the morning after breakfast we had to pull all the beds onto the open air verandas."

When Clement Attlee's post-war Labour government launched the Welfare State, of which the National Health Service was the lynchpin, it changed forever the way in which 'care' in its' widest sense, was delivered in the U.K.

Some of these memories cover the time before that great change, but most relate to the developments which have taken place over the last 50 or 60 years.

One change locally has been the gradual closing down of a proliferation of smaller hospitals in favour of a few large ones, including the building of the entirely new Royal Hallamshire Hospital, the expansion of the Northern General site, and the removal of the Jessop Hospital for Women to a new unit on the Royal Hallamshire site.

The caring role of doctors and nurses in our hospitals can only be effective if backed up by countless others. Here we see the contributions made by cleaners, laundry workers and secretaries. In the still wider context we see the work of the National Blood Donor Service, Social Workers and Care Workers.

Whatever problems the Welfare State may have, few of us would want to go back to those 'good old', bad old days before it existed.

Eleanor Hickinson began her nurse training in Northern Ireland in 1940, in the days before penicillin, when Sister's word was law. Marriage brought her to Sheffield, when she moved into the field of mental health nursing, at the vast Middlewood Hospital complex (since closed down). Eleanor tells of her early struggle to understand the Sheffield dialect – and an acute shortage of cash!

Eleanor Hickinson - nurse

I was born in 1924 in County Leitrim, Ireland. My working life began before ever I left school as we had a farm. Ours was a ten-cow farm (the size of Irish farms was measured in the number of cattle, not acres), and I had to see to the cows before I went to school, where I'd arrive smelling of cows.

I left school in the spring of 1940, after being off sick with diphtheria (it was a serious outbreak and some children died). I had no desire to work on a farm, so went to Northern Ireland to train as a nurse, and this was where I met my future husband who was stationed there with the RAF. He came from Hathersage.

He was moved to England so I went there too, to nurse at Botleys Park Hospital in Surrey.

Nursing

The Sister-Tutors were old devils, very strict on punctuality and manners. Once I asked Sister for something, saying, "Can I have?" and was immediately corrected - "May I please have?" The sisters and matrons were perfectly immaculate in their dress and very particular - I always thought no wonder they never married, no man could live with them. If you were two minutes late for lectures there would be trouble. There was more respect in those days, and less money.

Our training was very much on etiquette and procedures, such as 'don't run', the making of invalid food and old-fashioned remedies. Penicillin was not heard of in those later war years, and people stayed in hospital longer. It was a good rest for them. Learning to take temperatures showed up my poor eyesight and the need for glasses, as I couldn't see the thermometer properly. Hygiene and cleanliness were very important.

Middlewood Hospital

When my future husband went back up North I came to Sheffield and got a job at the big mental hospital at Middlewood. This was a world of it's own, like a small self-contained town, with laundry, workshops, social centre and church. At first I had trouble understanding the local dialect. One day I was sitting by the fire in the Nurses Home when a porter came in and asked me

"Dust need some coil?" "Pardon", I said. He repeated this and I said I didn't understand and he swore at me. I don't know just when the penny dropped and I realised he was saying, "Do you need some coal?"

We lived in the Nurses Home receiving free board and lodging and our uniforms, but we had to buy our own shoes, stockings, underwear, and toilet articles. There was no wage, we received an allowance, and it was not much, perhaps about £3 a month at most. My sister in Ireland used to write asking for money and I tried to send her £1 now and again. Sometimes I had to go out without any knickers on, because I couldn't afford to buy them. The hospital was quite remote then, with no shops near.

My ward was FLG (Female Low Grade). The women were all ages and many different kinds of mental illness from schizophrenia to dementia (it was not called that then, and Alzheimers disease was unheard of). They could be violent and would dot you one as soon as look at you, but I was never hurt and I was not afraid of them. I learned to be careful, which became a lifelong habit. Even now when I am walking along the street, I never let anyone come up behind me, but always stand aside and let them pass.

Some trusted patients were allowed in the kitchen but all the doors were kept locked and we never left knives or other potential weapons lying about. I had keys on my belt and locked and unlocked doors everywhere I went. I knew all the patients well, they were like neighbours to me. One girl was a hermaphrodite – she was related to a notorious Sheffield family. I met some beautiful people in there, particularly young girls who had been put away for having illegitimate babies. They were banished for life and became institutionalised. Once a girl had to have an operation, and it was done at Middlewood, all the equipment being brought to the designated room.

School Caretaker

I gave up working at Middlewood when I got married and went to live at Edale, and stayed at home caring for my two children. My husband was a railway signalman, working shifts so he couldn't help with the children. His pay was very poor, and my daughter used to drive tractors for local farmers to earn the money to go on school trips. There was a mortgage to pay so I got a job as caretaker at Edale School, and another job at Losehill Hall, Castleton, doing domestic work. While I was out at work an elderly neighbour would take sandwiches for my husband's lunch – she knew we were hard up.

Sadly my husband became ill with heart disease, which ran in his family, and died in 1973 in his early fifties.

Edale School was Infants and Juniors, with 30 pupils and two teachers. The children were lovely, very well-behaved and you got no 'lip' from them in the playground. They all called me Mrs Hickey and still do to this day. The job was a heavy one, involving making, and stoking up coal fires and shovelling coal into the big boiler. I did it for 21 years.

Mrs C. came to Sheffield from Jamaica and spent 28 happy years working at Middlewood Hospital. Like Eleanor Hickinson, she experienced the shock of discovering perfectly normal women who had spent their whole lives in this hospital, for no better reason than that they had given birth to illegitimate babies.

Mrs C. - mental hospital nurse

In 1956 I came to work in London from Jamaica, I was 34 years old. My brother was working in Sheffield, so I came to help with his little girl, and started working at Middlewood Hospital in 1956, looking after mentally ill patients. I finished working there in 1984 when I was sixty. If I had been in good health I would not have retired.

I got my State Enrolled Nurse (SEN) qualification through my long experience.

In those days staff were more disciplined, not like now. We all got on very well. We had five or six changes of uniform, it was blue, with aprons and caps, all washed in the hospital laundry. Some of the patients worked in the laundry.

I enjoyed my work, I used to look after the patients, bathe them, dress them, and sometimes take charge of them for the day. Some of them were cheeky and would call you names, but you can't take any notice. Some people you feel sorry for. There were some women patients who had been there all their lives. It seems they got pregnant and nobody wanted to be bothered with them, so they were sent to Middlewood Hospital. I remember one old lady who kept telling us she was fed up and wanted to do away with herself, and eventually she did commit suicide. Very sad.

At the finish I did two years of working night shifts. Before that I worked from six in the morning till two pm, and from two pm till ten at night.

After I retired I went home for eighteen years, but I didn't have any close relations there, and my children sent for me to come back to Sheffield. One of my daughters is now working as a staff nurse in Nottingham.

Middlewood Hospital has been knocked down now, and they have built houses on the site.

Esmee Heywood was another of the many people who came here from Jamaica in the 1950's and 60's, and made such a tremendous contribution to our city's life.

With her hard-working, no-nonsense approach, she plunged into working life in Sheffield and made a go of it, first at Franklins, and then as a nurse.

She highlights the changes seen by so many in the NHS, starting in the era of strict discipline and high standards of cleanliness, and ending with computers and vast quantities of paper work.

Esmee Heywood - nurse

I came from Jamaica in April 1962. My boyfriend sent my air ticket and warm clothes for me to wear when I got to England.

Getting my first job

There was a lady who rented properties to West Indians. She used to tell me to come to her house in Ellesmere Road just to talk. Her friend said I should get a job at Batchelor's Peas, so she took me up to the office. That was a joke, I'm sitting waiting when I saw a great crowd of people working, the noise, the behaviour! I thought – 'no way is this for me'- so I walked off without waiting any longer.

There were a load of families in the house where we were living, and when I told them I don't want this, they all said - "Who does she think she is?"

But the landlady says, "Look in the newspaper". There was a job at Franklin's on Ecclesall Road. So I say to my friend, "I think I'll apply."

Back came the reply - "You're mad, they don't employ black people."

So I applied and I got a letter back to go for interview. I went to the interview.

Now listen carefully. I was green, I had just arrived and I didn't know about Social Security. I thought it was what we at home called handouts to paupers.

As I went into the interview, I was asked - " Where do you come from?" "Jamaica."

"Why did you apply for this job?"- it was Mr Alfred Franklin.

Well, the man didn't stand a chance, I said - "I don't want any pauper money, I want to work."

"How long have you been here?"

"Only two weeks."

"We have never employed any of your people before, I'll have to talk to my brother William."

Anyway I left. Coming home I stopped in the market for a chicken. I got off the bus at Burngreave Road, and as I was walking up the road a Franklin's van drove by, stopped and asked, "Do you know where number 23, Burngreave Road is? Anyone there called Anderson?"

"Yes, me."

"Letter for you" - Start Monday morning.

I stayed there for two years and I got on smashing. I earned three shillings an hour, which was good money then. Loads of people worked there. I would check in loose covers and curtains, to go to the dry cleaners. When they came back we would iron them. Then the van drivers would deliver them to the customers.

I applied for nursing. I needed two references, so I gave one from Franklin's and one from my neighbour. I kept asking my neighbour if she had heard. For weeks I had to wait. Then I got a letter from matron to go for an interview, and she told me I hadn't needed the second reference, the one from Franklin's was sufficient.

In 1964 I started my training at the City General and Firvale Hospital (now the Northern General Hospital).

I stayed there till 2000 - 36 years! I enjoyed my job.

The wards were big, long, Victorian wards, with 30 or more beds. Those wards were clean! We would start by carbolizing beds on Monday morning. The cleaners were there at all times, when you needed them, but we were short staffed all the time. Right up to me retiring after 36 years we were short staffed. I can remember feeding six patients all at the same time. We managed by the good nature of the nurses.

At the beginning patients didn't get out of bed. Most patients had pneumonia, bronchitis, senile dementia. Those old doctors used to understand old folk.

There was no union, Matron was everything. She could sack you on the spot.

After finishing my training I wanted to work in Geriatrics. I remember one man telling a nurse he used to be paid sixpence to kill black people, but I didn't take any notice, that's not what you are there for.

At the same time I've always done agency work in the London hospitals. They are different. I wouldn't put them anywhere near as clean as Sheffield hospitals.

Nurses are hard working. They've got a lot to put up with - the doctors to put up with, the relatives to put with - and now all the changes ever since the 1980's. Too much time on the computer, too much paper work.

Sheila Gilbert's early desire to be a children's nurse was thwarted at first, but wartime work in a nursery led on to nurse training, thus enabling her to experience at first hand the change of attitude brought about by the introduction of the NHS.

After her marriage and a spell as a Home Help, she once again gravitated to working with children, first as a school dinner lady and then as a Child Care Assistant.

Sheila Gilbert – child care

Just before we left school at 14, we were asked what we wanted to do. I desperately wanted to be a children's nurse, but I would have been the only girl in the class to say that, so I said the same as all the other girls, shop work, which is what I did.

So my first job was as a butcher's girl at the bottom of Rawmarsh Hill. I used to walk to work, and stayed about a year. I was paid ten shillings a week, and gave my wages to my mother who gave me half a crown for myself. I had a bicycle with a big basket, and delivered weekly orders of meat to customers. The load was heavy, but I was pretty strong. One of the worst jobs was slicing up the beast liver on a frosty morning with the door open. We used to boil the cotton muslin that wrapped the lamb, to give to regular customers, ideal for cleaning windows.

My next job was in a shoe shop in Rotherham, which I remember as a dark shop, and as it was war time we drank cocoa made with water at our break times.

Then I went to a grocer's, the Home and Colonial, as a cashier taking money, which had to be exactly right at the end of the day, and as general dogsbody. This was the only job I have ever left without giving notice. The under manager made my life a misery, and being young (15) I walked out. I went to my aunt, as I daren't go home and tell them. I've always regretted I didn't stand my ground, and work my notice. My mother said I must always have another job to go to, but "you can change your job as often as you like".

War time nursery

So then I got the job I always wanted, I went to work in a war-time nursery, in Denby Street, Rotherham. The nursery was open twenty four hours. Some of the children were brought in by their mothers (who worked in munitions), on a Monday morning and they stayed till Friday night. I remember bathing some of the children on Mondays.

Then, when I was 16, my family had to move to Chesterfield because of my father's job on the railway, and I had to leave the nursery. I was so disgusted I went to work at Woolworth's.

Hospital nurse

I applied to work at Jessop Hospital in Sheffield. I was a pale child, so Matron sent me up to the annexe at Norton Hall, where there was a special ward for patients with infections. We were allowed to talk to the patients and treated them well. Some women who came in had had back street abortions, I remember one woman was there for months and months, sadly she died the day before she was supposed to go home. There was a relaxed atmosphere at the annexe and when it was hot the sister let us go for a walk at night in Grave's Park.

A friend and I decided to go down to Cornwall, in general nursing, so we wouldn't have to go home on our days off! We wanted a life.

I was training at Truro Hospital when the NHS was set up in 1948. Some of the patients' attitudes changed - "We're paying for this". They expected a private service. The hospital was always short staffed, one patient wanted to tip me to look after her more, but we weren't allowed tips, not even chocolates. We were overworked and underfed, and my health went down, I got bad anaemia. I came back to Sheffield, engaged to be married but not fit enough to work, and lived with my parents.

Home help

When my son was four years old, I wanted him to go to nursery, but they wouldn't take him unless I had a job, so I worked as a home help, which paid for the nursery. We started at nine, mostly cleaning, though we weren't allowed to clean windows. Of course we had to do things as people wanted them doing, one man said I had to put tea leaves on the carpets before I brushed them. We didn't use vacuum cleaners, we used brushes. You went between extremes, from beautiful homes to homes where people had nothing. You went wherever you were needed.

In about 1957 I applied for a job as caretaker for the Methodist church behind the Central Library in Surrey Street, as it had a house with it. I was glad to have a home of my own.

Child care assistant

Two years later, when my second son was a year old, we finally got a council house in Firth Park. We were told on Friday that we had to move on Monday!

My third son was born in 1960, and I didn't go back to work till he started school when he was five years old. As I wanted to work with children, the head teacher suggested I take any job with the Education Department, then I would be able to move jobs. I started as a dinner lady - it was awful. My face didn't fit. It took two years before I was accepted. In those days the tables had tablecloths and we served nicely cooked food.

I finally did get the job I wanted at Hartley Brook School as a child care assistant for ten years. It was hard for the first three months, the teachers had to get used to me and I had to get used to the teachers. I started in January 1980. It was the time of redundancies in the steel works, some men did the mother's job, while the women worked in several part time jobs. I got a lot of pleasure from helping the older children, who hadn't learnt to read yet.

That was one of the best jobs I had. I regretted leaving it when I had to give up work to look after my mother, who had Alzeimers.

Sylvia Graham was drawn to nursing as a result of childhood illness, and also a strong family tradition. In the 1950's TB was still a scourge, as was polio, which caused many deaths and left others crippled for life, before the Salk vaccine was introduced.

Sylvia Graham – nurse

Nursing was the only thing I wanted to do. My mother was a nurse, my eldest grandson is a nurse, even my great great grandmother was a nurse at Stirling Castle where she was matron at the Army Hospital. I had TB twice as a child, and was in Winter Street Hospital for three months during the war. During air raids we had to get under our beds. I think being a child in hospital may have made me want to be a nurse.

In 1950 I went straight from school at 16 into orthopaedic nursing at King Edward's Hospital. After I'd done 18 months there I was sent up to Lodge Moor Hospital during the polio epidemic. Being young we weren't allowed to nurse men at King Edward's, so it was an eye opener when we went up to Lodge Moor!

First thing in the morning after breakfast we had to pull all the beds onto the open air verandas. Some of the adult patients slept all night on the verandas. It had to be bad weather, or bed baths, to be indoors. There were specialist nurses for the iron lungs. As juniors, after pulling the beds out in the mornings, we had to clean lockers and window sills ourselves.

Some of the patients spent five to six years in hospital, so we got attached to them. A lot of patients came in with TB, and there were some with Spina Bifida. Some patients got better slowly, others were crippled more or less for life. Some of them died, mothers with young children, some patients only in their teens. One or two of the nurses caught polio.

Training lasted five years, and we lived in, two to a bedroom, in the nurses' home over the top of the hospital. We had one day off one week, and a day and a half the next week. After being away on holiday you never went back to the same room. If a nurse was taken ill you worked half the next shift to cover, but you still had to come back on duty for your next shift at the usual time. We wore blue dresses, white starched aprons, and caps. We had to have a clean apron on when matron did her rounds. If you wanted to get married, you had to ask matron's permission, and you had to leave nursing. I still have friends from my nurse training days.

I left when I was 23 to get married. I had to learn to cook when I left the nurses' home. After having my children, times had changed and I could go back part time on permanent nights, at the City General Hospital, now the Northern General Hospital. I worked for three nights a week for six years. It was hard, because as I was going out to work my husband would be coming in.

A friend of mine told me about a job at the dentist's. For the last 18 years of my working life I worked fulltime as a dental nurse. I enjoyed it - it was an extension of doing general nursing.

The best thing about nursing, it is a hands on job, and you see patients at the end going home, some of them after years, especially at King Edwards, even though a lot had callipers. There's more choice in nursing now, but hospitals are less friendly, you are a number these days, not a person.

Felicity Hampton *tells of her determined struggle to be a nurse, despite the crippling after-effects of a severe illness as a baby. Although she fulfilled this ambition, increasing disability forced her to abandon that career, though she soon found a new outlet for her talents in voluntary work. Now, nothing daunted,* *she hopes to fulfil her desire to be a 'carer' in a totally new direction.*

As a baby I was affected by encephalitis, a condition which causes pressure to develop on the brain. In my case, this led to paralysis down the left-hand side. Subsequent treatment controlled this, but I have always been subject to brief periods of loss of control in the left arm and leg, which can happen at a moments' notice.

My father, who had been a pilot in the R.A.F., left the forces in 1966 and was sponsored by the Air Force to study computers and electronics. He chose Sheffield, which had a good reputation for his chosen subjects. I still had to complete my education and had ambitions to become a nurse. My mother, who was a nurse, was convinced that my medical history would bar me from nursing and also that I would not be able to stand up to the stresses of that kind of work. She was convinced that I would be better off working as a secretary in an office environment, and as a result, managed to find me a place at King Egberts Comprehensive School, which had reputation for preparing girls for secretarial work.

On leaving school, the Youth Employment Service found me a position as office junior at The Mount, where I was used as little more than the general dogsbody. After a short while I went to work at Lodge Moor Isolation Hospital as a junior accounts clerk, but I did not find this kind of work satisfying.

Soon after starting there, a serious flu epidemic struck down most of the nursing staff and the wards were severely undermanned. Office staff, including myself, were brought in to help out on the wards. This meant that I had the opportunity to sample the kind of work which I really wanted to do. Around this time the treasurer at the hospital expressed the opinion that I was not suited to office work, but had heard good reports from nursing officers about my time on the wards.

Despite my mothers' advice, I began initial training in the United Sheffield Hospitals School of Nursing. This was the beginning of a three year S.R.N. training course which was served partly on the wards and partly in blocks of theory in lectures. Theory work was carried out in lecture theatres and the practical side of the work on the wards, was tutored by the ward sisters.

The illness which I had suffered as a baby began to assert itself in the form of attacks of paralysis down my left side, which caused me to drop things and also to lose balance. These attacks were very brief, but severe enough for me to be limited to day shifts and on wards where the physical work was lighter. The day shifts meant that there would be more staff on site in case I should get into difficulties.

At Nursing School, a tutor, without asking my consent, made an appointment for me to be examined by a doctor in the Student Health Service who knew my medical history. He referred me to a consultant neurologist in connection with the partial paralysis problem. In addition to the loss of feeling down my left hand side I also developed joint problems in my hands, knees and ankles which made it difficult for me to handle certain items, which were a necessary as part of my nursing work.

I also saw a junior doctor in the rheumatology department, but he simply told me that I should go back to work and stop worrying. However, simple tasks became more and more difficult, and eventually I was forced to give up my nursing career.

This could have meant the spending rest of my time sitting back as a disabled person. I felt that I needed some constructive purpose in life, so began to take on some voluntary work. I now spend one day per week as a volunteer teacher and assistant in school, which enables me to sit and hear the children read. I also spend one day per week helping in Saint Luke's Hospice.

I would still like to work full-time and am considering counselling as a career. My thoughts of becoming a counsellor were first directed by the experience of seeing a fellow student whose life was being made miserable because she was continually taunted about the colour of her skin. I was able to comfort her and to boost her self-confidence which in turn taught me that I might have a talent in that direction.

I feel that my experiences in the past both as a carer and as a patient give me the ability to see other people's problems from both sides of the sheet.

Mrs Jeffrey is one of a legion of unsung heroines who keep our hospitals clean, working hard like so many new immigrants at a low-paid job.

Mrs Jeffrey - hospital cleaner

I came from Jamaica in 1955. I worked at Mappin and Webb for a couple of years, grinding spoons. It was hard on those machines - pure dust. They didn't give me anything to cover my nose.

I worked at Nether Edge hospital for a long time, cleaning.

We came just after the war when Sheffield was all mashed up, all dirt and dust. We cleaned it and made it nice.

People didn't understand us and we didn't understand them. They weren't used to us, we weren't used to them. At work you get the worst work. Wages were so small, but things were not so expensive.

Sheffield is a hundred times better now than when we came here.

Ellen Davis was also a hospital cleaner, though for her, that was the last job in a long and varied working life. Recent visits to her former place of employment draw forth some interesting comments on the changes she sees.

Mrs Ellen Davis

I am now 85 years old. I was a farmer's daughter, and came from a big family. When I left school at the age of 14, I stayed at home for two years to help on the farm. I hated farm work, because even while we were young, we had to help with the hay and harvesting crops. There is nothing worse than digging up potatoes and turnips when the frost is on them.

However, my first job at age 16 was also on a farm, a large dairy farm at Rivelin owned by the Thompson family. I'd get up at 6 am to start with, and begin filling up the bottles from a churn (they had just started selling milk in bottles then). There were three of us, Mr Thompson, Fred and myself. Mine was the smallest delivery round, 20 gallons, and I delivered around Fulwood, Broomhill and Crookes. At the end of the week I'd collect the money, which in the big houses would be paid by the maid or cook. At one house on Marlborough Road, Broomhill, which belonged to Becrofts, who ran a big china store in town, they had a little Scottie dog. It would let me in, but wouldn't let me out, and I'd have to call "Would you please take your dog in?"

The winter mornings were dark and cold. When I got back to the farm I would start cleaning the churns and glass bottles, which had to go in the steriliser. At night, after the men finished milking, I would wash the milking buckets, eventually finishing work at 10 p.m. I lived in and received board and lodging so my pay was just 5 shillings a week. This was before the war.

I left there and went to a farm at Handsworth, the same job but not such hard work and the pay was seven shillings and sixpence a week. Then I went into domestic service, as a maid to a Mrs Gowers at Thornsett Road, Nether Edge. She took in lady teachers as lodgers, but when the war came the schoolchildren and teachers were evacuated. My next job was with Westbourne Prep School, which had been evacuated to Broomhead Hall, out towards Ewden Valley. The boys slept in big dormitories, and I also lived in. There was no public transport, so I cycled to and from my parents' home on days off. Eventually the school returned to Broomhill, and I got a new job, at the Blind Home at Crosspool, as a domestic assistant. I stayed there two years and enjoyed it very much.

During the war I had a complete change and went to work in a factory, C.J. Hampton's Record Tools, as a capstan lathe operator, and it was here I met my husband John, who worked for Record Tools all his life. I was 24 when I married and we went to live with my husband's mother. Our family had the great sorrow of losing my brother Joe in the war. He was with the Seaforth

Highlanders, 51st Division, fighting in North Africa. We heard that on 6th April 1943, he had been killed at a place called Safax in Tunisia. Many years later my husband and I went to see his grave, and it was a very moving experience to see all those white headstones in that far country, and so beautifully kept.

It was too long a journey to Record Tools, so I got a job at Stoker Drill on Langsett Road. It was machine work again and quite repetitive but the wages were £4 a week. We had to be careful about safety, wearing overalls and hats, but I don't recall any serious accidents, just cut fingers and burnt feet. This happened when the 'turnings' fell off the machine and dropped on our feet. There was some piece-work and some day-work.

I left there when I was expecting my son, and after he went to school I got a part-time job at the Bendix Launderette, which lasted 12 or 13 years.

My next job was that of a ward orderly in the Renal Unit at the Northern General Hospital. This involved cleaning, dusting and running errands e.g. taking blood samples to and from the labs. People there were on regular dialysis and so you built up relationships with the patients. I went to visit someone in hospital recently and I thought the ward did not look very clean, and seemed shockingly untidy. There was nothing nicer than to look down a ward and see everything looking clean and tidy. I could hardly believe my ears when I heard a nurse calling a doctor by his first name quite casually. They were stricter in those days - fancy a nurse calling a doctor by his first name! Dr Flint and Dr Moorhead wouldn't have had that!

I stayed at the Northern General 12 years, until my husband had a stroke at the age of 60. They asked me to stay on past 60, but I had to leave to look after him. This was in 1982.

Nellie Hicks *worked as the' In Service maid' in a private house until her marriage, after which she took up a back-breaking job in the laundry at the old Royal Infirmary (since closed). This job left her with health problems, which affect her to this day.*

My name is Nellie. My father's name was George and my mum Charlotte Mary. I was born in the year 1915. We lived at Hackenthorpe, which was in those days a rural village near the city of Sheffield. No public transport, you had to get the tram to Intake, then walk the rest of the way. I went to Hackenthorpe Council School until the age of 14. We were not well off – as children, my brother Jack and I had to stand at the table for meals, because we only had two chairs.

Coming up to the age of leaving school with not much prospect, my mum noticed an advertisement in The Star newspaper, so she wrote off for it. The job was 'in service' for Mr and Mrs Warriss of Grove Road, Millhouses. Mr and Mrs Warriss had a silversmith's shop on Moore Street. We thought it quite strange, that the Warris family came to our house to speak to my parents about the job. Finally I got the job, so I left school on the Friday and on the Monday I'd moved to Grove Road as the in-service maid.

I was shown where I'd be sleeping, in the attic, then my chores on a daily basis. Get up at 5 am from a very cold attic bedroom. Go down to the wash-house which was in the yard. Then at 6 am I had to make sure that the kitchen fire was lit, also the living-room fire.

Seven am was breakfast. At 14 I had to be able to cook to requirements. After breakfast, clear and wash up and re-lay the table, then my morning continued with the black-leading of the kitchen stove.

Twelve noon was dinner-time. This was always a warm dinner. Afterwards, wash up, re-lay table. In the afternoon was cleaning the silverware. At tea-time this was nearly always a cold tea. By this time I'd been up over 12 hours, with no break. After tea this was supposed to be my free time, but Mrs Warriss always found something for me to do, like sewing buttons, darning socks, patching.

I had two uniforms. In the morning it was blue with apron and white cap. In the afternoon, black, with apron and white cap. The uniforms I had to buy myself and the upkeep was my responsibility. My rest days were half a day in two weeks, and a week off in the year. My half day was always going to see mum and dad. Tram to Intake tram stop, then walk to the village. By the time I got home it was time to come back.

Before leaving the house I gave my wage, which was five shillings a week, to my mum. I got two shillings in my purse. Don't forget my two shillings was for two weeks' wages. My father and brother were miners. My father told me he got seven shillings and sixpence a week, but had to pay a filler to load his wooden barrow while he mined the coal.

I stayed in service until I was twenty-one, when I married Owen in Beighton Parish Church. Mr and Mrs Warriss gave us a canteen of cutlery as a present (my daughter now has the canteen), and Owen went off to war.

Then I started at the Royal Infirmary Hospital, Infirmary Road, Sheffield, working in the wash-house on these machines called Hydros. I got seven shillings and sixpence a week. Meal breaks were a frightening experience, with a kitchen and tables in the basement with rodents running across your feet. Even worse was the fire watch, having done your shift, then staying to do your stint, and having to sleep in the basement with rats running over you, with no lights on. I always slept near the light switch.

The job was very demanding - high-sided washing machines which spun. The blankets and sheets had to be placed in machines a certain way or they wouldn't work. The sides were nearly as tall as me, so when it came to getting the spun sheets out of the machine, I found it very difficult, even though I had a bloke working with me. Then we would pass the sheets on to the couple of girls who put them into the calendar. There were only four workers in the wash-house to keep the whole hospital clean.

By this time we were living in Crookesmoor, so I walked down to work to start at seven in the morning. On my feet all day, with the exception of half an hour's meal break. Then at five o'clock, time to walk up to Crookesmoor. Got home, had tea, and a bit of knitting and darning before bed.

Owen came home after the war and went back to be a butcher – loved his garden. My job at the hospital was taking it's toll health-wise, pulling and tugging day after day, so I left and decided to do private cleaning. Word of mouth was my recommendation. I worked in Crosspool and Millhouses - W. Gunstone's (bakers), and Isaac's the watchmakers. They were some of my clients. I charged two shillings and sixpence an hour. I was in a situation where I could take days off when I wanted. At the age of 78 I retired, with pain in my shoulder and arm from that blessed hospital job.

Carol Hill, beginning her nurse training in the 1950's, survived the rules and regulations, took part in some very modest rebellions, and even managed to get some fun out of it, despite the hard work and long hours.

No disposable syringes or disposable anythings meant that instruments had to be sterilised and re-used, but on the plus side there were no antibiotic-resistant superbugs.

So strictly was the need for hygiene drummed into her, that she decided to enforce it at home, with comical results!

Carol Hill, nurse training, 1957 onwards

I left Secondary School before Christmas 1956, celebrated my 15th birthday on 23rd December and started at the Pre-Nursing School on Clarkehouse Road in January 1957. We were given material and had to make two uniforms in the sewing class. At this stage we were called by our Christian names.

The School was much like ordinary school, teaching subjects such as English and Maths, but also Anatomy, Physiology and Biology. During our first year, in addition to our studies, we worked one day a week either in a hospital or Nurses Home (i.e. the residence where nurses lived), helping out in very basic ways such as cleaning. We did not go on the wards, but perhaps in the outpatients department, helping with very menial tasks i.e. cleaning and directing patients.

**Trainee nurses at Clarkehouse Road,
Carol Hill is in the middle row on the far right**

In the second year of training we had two days a week out of school and this time we were allowed on the wards, doing menial tasks such as cleaning, folding gauze bandages, preparing cotton wool balls and swabs for sterilising. These had to be placed in round steel drums and sent along to the sterilising department, along with instruments and syringes.

By the third year we had three days out of school working mainly on the wards doing tasks such as washing and feeding patients and making beds ('hospital corners' - which I still do – I cannot make a bed without now). At the end of our three years pre-nursing course we took our Preliminary State exam Part 1. At this stage we also decided which hospital we wanted to do our three year training at, as student nurses, before taking our finals. The choices were, The Royal Infirmary, Royal Hospital and Children's Hospital (the latter was four years training). I chose the Royal Infirmary.

In January 1960, at the age of 18, I began nursing properly, starting with a three months block in Nursing School learning how to bandage, give injections, take blood pressure and temperature, set up treatment trolleys, and to carry out various treatments. Each nurse had a book on the ward in which she wrote what procedures she had carried out, and this had to be signed by the Sister or Staff Nurse in charge. By this stage we were always called 'Nurse'.

Another new uniform came at this time, provided by the hospital and not made by us, along with a wonderful warm navy blue cape lined with blue. You needed this because at the Royal Infirmary site there were many outside wards and departments, and though there were underground passages connecting these, they were a bit scary, and we never used them at night. We were also supplied with an overcoat to wear outside the hospital over our uniforms, e.g. as we travelled to and from work. A beret had to be worn at all times with this coat. I only lived in for the first three months at Ranmoor Residence, which was compulsory.

Rules, Regulations and Routine

A strict hierarchical system was in operation. No first names were used, either to each other or the patients, and I would be addressed as Nurse Hill. Matron was a terrifying figure, who could turn up at any time without warning, to check on us. If we knew someone important was coming we made the beds, got everything perfect and told the patients, 'Don't move until Matron's been'. Most patients knew how terrified we were of Matron and did as we asked. When matron did her inspection all the wheels on the beds had to be turned inwards in the same direction, and the bed corners look identical, so that she could see the rows lined up with military precision.

At night it was the Night Sister or Night Supervisor who came. We were not allowed to eat or drink on the wards, and though at night we would sneak off to make tea, someone had to keep a lookout, for we'd get into trouble if caught. We could not leave the ward without permission. There were separate dining rooms for doctors, sisters and nurses, but at night we were allowed to use the doctors' dining room.

Clothes

Our dresses came with a laundry box containing separate white starched collars, cuffs and caps, which were flat and had to be folded into the correct shape and pinned into place. The collar was pinned at the back and also at the front with one of my dad's collar studs, and all the buttons were taken off for washing, using a hook. We tried to fold the caps to be as small and neat as possible. Aprons also had to be pinned on, i.e. the bib part, and buttoned at the back, and had to be removed, every time we left the ward, even just for a tea break. A watch with a second-hand was pinned to our shoulders, and the whole was completed with black shoes and stockings.

We tried little rebellions to make our outfits more fashionable or easier to wear, such as hitching the long skirts up round our waists, or shortening the sleeves, but it depended on the sister in charge whether we got away with this. All these clothes took ages to put on, and I would get up at 5.30 am to be ready for a 7.15 am start.

On the wards

We girls all wanted to work on Ward 6, Male Orthopaedic, which would be full of young lads from bike or sporting accidents, and there would be great rejoicing when we saw the rotas if this ward was allotted to us.

There were three shifts, morning, afternoon and night. Night shift was from 10.00 pm to 7.15 am. At 19 years of age, I was once left in charge of the brain surgery ward at night with just one Auxiliary Nurse. We'd get two nights off per week, and sometimes the rota worked out that you got four nights off together, which was wonderful.

Meals were brought in for the patients in big trolleys, and the orderlies would set out trays with knife, fork and salt and pepper pots for each patient, but sister would dole out the meals, ensuring special diets got to those who needed them, and that patients unable to feed themselves got help, often a job for pre-nursing students. Patients fit enough to be out of bed ate at a long table in the centre of the room (these were the very long 'Nightingale' wards).

Drugs were wheeled round in a big covered trolley and doled out by Sister (using a Kardex system) to the nurses to administer. In those days there were no antibiotic-resistant bugs and after the injections were given, syringes and plungers were sent to the sterilising unit for sterilising and re-use.

Giving my first injection was a terrifying experience, and I don't know who was more frightened, me or the patient, as the staff nurse told the patient it was my first time, and asked if she minded. The first attempt failed but the second was O.K. The thigh was the only place you were allowed to inject at that time. I was supervised one more time and then went it alone, and I found that my confidence and skill increased from then on. Needles were bigger in those days, and the quicker you gave the injection the less painful it was. Some people got so good that the patient didn't know the procedure had been done.

Cleanliness was drilled into you, and no corners were cut. One day I came home from the Pre-nursing Course full of zeal and boiled up all our toothbrushes, utterly destroying them, much to the annoyance of my older sister, and my mother, who had to buy us new ones. Though I only recall wearing gloves in the Operating Theatre, we never touched things with our bare hands, but picked them up with tweezers. Each ward had it's own two cleaners and an orderly, so you knew each other and worked as a team. Wet dusting and floor mopping were done daily. In the Sluice Room where the bedpans and bottles were kept, lived the steriliser, a large steel cabinet full of water in which these were boiled. We used big clippers to remove the hot items and how we did not get scalded is amazing. Nowadays they would have Health & Safety down on us like a ton of bricks. This room was hot and steamy and when we went in at night and turned the light on, all the cockroaches would scuttle away.

Christmas Day - all routine admissions were cancelled so we only needed a skeleton staff, and there were only two shifts, day and night. Each ward had a Christmas tree and was decorated. We had our Christmas dinner there, and each person received a small gift. Our gifts were useful rather than luxury items – I recall getting a hairbrush.

Punctuality - Getting to work on time was vital, and sometimes involved walking all the way from home at Meersbrook, to Infirmary Road, for instance during the bus strike and in snowy weather, then doing a long tiring shift and walking home. I remember the night of the great gale in the winter of 1962, coming home absolutely shattered and sleeping right through the noise and chaos. It was only when I set off to work next day, and found myself walking through streets of rubble, past roofless or chimney-less houses and over fallen trees that I realised something awful had happened.

The work was very hard, and during the long training years we had lectures, homework and essays to do in addition to working on the wards, but I loved it, and from the start took a great pride in being a nurse. Right from the beginning we were made to feel part of a team and when I put on my first uniform I felt wonderful. Nursing was all I ever wanted to do and it was a very proud career.

Another aspect of caring work is the vital job of Home Help or Community carer, as it is now known. Carole Jackson has tackled both, and also worked in a residential home for the elderly. She recounts some hilarious experiences with her delightful, if confused clients, and then in her 50's moves on to work with 4-11 year-olds in After-school Clubs.

Carole Jackson - carer

After travelling for 17 years as a service wife, with four children, I found myself enjoying being home in Sheffield once again, settled at last.

I decided a job caring would suit my age and temperament, so I joined the Home Help Service in the Manor/Manor Park area, as my mum had done before me. It was a happy time, always a welcome and offer of a cuppa on a cold morning. People became my friends and I often accompanied them on outings, or did a quick perm of an evening when my work was done.

One lady always hid her keys for the doors, and immediately forgot where. Often I was hoisted up through her kitchen window or lent a ladder by the neighbours.

After a while I joined a Residential home and worked night shifts. Nights were very busy as chairs were washed, and the laundry and ironing continued all night long. When the hourly rounds were made you got a chance to chat to residents who were awake. One lady told me her father was posted to Hillsborough Barracks and she used to help exercise the horses, by riding one and leading two more up to Loxley and back. She also had photos of when she was a ballet dancer on stage in Paris, a wonderful lady!

I once baked an imaginary cake with a lady, she even sat and timed the cooking time. She was delighted when it was iced and handed round.

I have no fear of ending my days in one of these homes, compassion and care is there.

Alongside this job I did a few hours community care, which was a lot of travelling and strict clock watching, or the day would finish an hour later than it should.

One day I visited a lady for a one hour visit. I had to empty the bins and serve a meal. Whilst I was taking the rubbish out the door was closed behind me. When I knocked for entry, I was told she didn't know me. I finally had to go and phone the office to get the lady's daughter to get her mum to let me in for my coat and bag, and yes, it was snowing that day!

I've spent the last ten years running after school clubs. I passed my NVQ3 in Playwork at the age of 53, and really enjoyed my last years working with 4-11 year olds. They taught me how to ride a scooter and do tricks on it at speed - whoo!. They would ice 30 fairy cakes some days. As they said, after eating them, it was a good activity. Decorated ice cream cornets were also popular!

I think they organised me!

I'm now 64 and slowing down, a bit.

The Blood Transfusion Service is a vital aspect of the NHS, and this is where Christine Deakin spent most of her working life, which began in 1962. Hours were long, especially on the Mobile Units, while the premises used for some Donor Sessions were less than salubrious.

As in the previous account, sterilising needles and other equipment for re-use was a major and very uncomfortable part of the job, but it was the coming of AIDS and the use of disposable needles which brought great changes.

Christine Deakin – Blood Donor Service

My name is Christine Deakin and I was born in Woodseats Road in 1944.

I went to Woodseats I.J. School until I was eleven years of age, then went to Jordanthorpe School until I was 15. My dad was George Eric Hill Muxlow and my mum was called Emma. Dad worked for Laycock's Engineering company, his trade was a blacksmith, and my mum cleaned for the Midland Bank on Chesterfield Road.

My first job after leaving school in 1959 was working at the S&E (Sheffield & Ecclesall) Co-op on Archer Road. It was great for getting home - the job was errand girl and baking tin scrubber. This lasted for 12 months, then I got a job as confectioner. We were supplied with a white smock, which was cleaned by the Co-op, but the white apron I bought and had to take home to be washed.

In 1962 I left the S&E and applied for the National Blood Transfusion Service. I think I was successful due to my First Aid certificates, which I gained at the St. Johns Ambulance Brigade in my early teens. I had to attend H.Q. at Heavygate Road, Crookes, which closed in 1972, then moved to Longley Lane.

Uniform was essential - blue double breasted cotton dress, starched white collar and a starched white apron. The collars were so sharp that they cut into your collar-bone, so we put swabs under the collar to stop the rubbing. No shoe supply, no allowance. I was told that 'The best way to learn the job was to do it' after basic training.

I remember doing a blood session in Fargate, through a small door between Richards Shop and Marks & Spencers, down some steps into the basement. There were no windows, no emergency exit - rather unwelcoming to say we were trying to enrol blood donors - I nicknamed the place 'The Dungeon'.

I was paid on a weekly basis and my wage helped support the family between 1962-1969 as there were three brothers as well as me. Then in 1969 I married Roger.

There were two types of job - Depot work and travelling work.

When in Depot work, duties included cleaning and preparing equipment ready for sterilisation before going out on sessions, making up 'Give sets', 'Take sets' and 'Cell-con sets'. Needles were sharpened, then cleaned with fine twisted wire with a piece of string looped in the end, rinsed, twice with soapy water, twice with clear water, syringed with pure spirit, then stilletted. They were then put into sets and sterilised.

When working in the 'Wet Room' there were two of us with plastic Rain-Mates on our heads, a large full length cape which fastened at the back, and on our feet a pair of Universal Wellies. We stood in this trough with duck-boards and we had to jet wash all the rubber tubing to ensure no blood was left inside. The returned needles were soaked in peroxide before the cleaning process.

All these procedures were before AIDS came on the scene. Later we progressed onto plastic sets in bottles, then complete disposables including needles.

Mobile Assembly was where all the equipment used on sessions was assembled and checked ready for loading onto Mobiles.

Travelling Work i.e. Mobiles

Working hours were based on a 40 hour week, but this could be up to 60 hours on some weeks, with some days being 15 hours. Example - leave Sheffield 9.00 am, arrive Leicester 12 noon (don't forget - no motorways), then lunch until 1.00 pm. Setting up took until 2 pm then taking donations until 4.00 pm. Tea was taken until 5 pm. Further donations until 7.30 pm. With donations finished for that day, we packed up. This took until 8.30 pm, supper until 9 pm. Arriving back in Sheffield at midnight, all the girls had to be ferried home by minibus. These were basic times, but sessions usually over-ran.

Gazette Newsround

Sports stars give blood

THE Blood Transfusion Service called up some new blood from the area's sporting teams to promote their new sessions at the Forte Poste House Hotel on Manchester Road.

New Wednesday midfield star Ian Taylor is pictured here with boxer Johnny Nelson and Nurse Christine Deakin. They were joined by boxer Nas Hamed and his trainer Brendan Ingle and speedway riders Greg Bartlett and Nas Hamed.

The Division Street centre is closed for refurbishment until August 23, but sessions at the hotel run from 10am-6pm, Monday to Friday.

Blood stocks are still low and many regular donors miss sessions because of holidays and days out during the summer, said a spokesman for the donor centre.

Some of the venues used had little or no heating at all - very cold in winter.

When on sessions, jobs were allocated by the team leader. These jobs were, Haemoglobins, Bleed Beds, Bottling Table, Rest Beds.

Haemoglobin tests, taken from ear-lobes using about four lancets kept in a small container with cotton wool soaked in pure spirit. These lancets were used on all donors over and over again.

Bleed-beds, where blood was taken using rubber giving sets with a small piece of airway glass which had to be observed at all times to ensure no air bubbles were going up towards the donors arm, which could be fatal.

Bottling table, where all donations equipment was set up, then issued to bleed beds. On return after the donor had given blood, the needles were taken out of the bottles, the bottle tops then cleaned and viscapped. The needles were placed in kidney dishes with water in them, and these were then hand syringed through, wearing no gloves, then put in needle boxes to be returned to depot.

Rest beds, here dressings were applied and the donors rested, then they were sent for a drink and biscuits.

There were three very responsible positions in the blood donor sessions,

D.A. (Donor Attendant) - who wore a blue belt, looked after the blood donor plus other duties.

Senior Nurse - who wore a red belt, was in charge of training new D.A.'s in all aspects of the job, keeping progress charts for submission to management, and after D.A, training, making assessments of results in the absence of the team-leader. You were expected to run the sessions without extra pay.

Team Leader - who wore a black belt, was responsible for the operational side of the blood donor sessions i.e. allocation of jobs, ensuring clerical staff had all necessary forms, making sure drivers knew what was expected of them, liaising with the medical officer to ensure that girls on travelling work had transport home.

In the early days there was a lot of heavy equipment to be carried into sessions, all done by the nurses. Even iron beds had to be carried, then assembled, as well as trestle tables, pot boxes, H.B. boxes. We were tired before the sessions started!

In the thirty five years I worked for the N.B.T.S. I got promotion from D.A. to Senior Nurse to Team-Leader.

Looking back I think we were a little I regarding health and safety, but as I've said, there was no AIDS in those days. There was also no maternity pay and we had set holidays, but I gave priority to the nurses who had families. In the early days I was a union member with C.O.H.S.E., later to become UNISON.

My worst memories were working in the Wet Room, and while working on the Mobiles, having to put a white gown on and walk in front of the bus in a thick fog.

My best memory? – Too many to remember.

Anne began her working life like many other girls, as a shorthand typist, but her job as medical secretary to a highly eccentric hospital consultant, led her into another direction altogether – that of social work.

It would doubtless vex that peppery gentleman greatly to learn that it was his intense dislike of social workers which helped to add one more to their number!

For Anne, that formative experience with a difficult boss, led her into an immensely satisfying lifelong career.

Anne – Social Worker

I left school in 1961, aged 16, and at the end of the school year I moved from Sheffield to live in a small village on the outskirts of Bradford, as my father was due to start work in Leeds. I had little idea of what I would like to do job-wise, so enrolled on a secretarial course at Bradford Technical College. The course was for one year and included shorthand, typing, book-keeping and learning a foreign language (Spanish). At first I felt rather 'at sea' as most of the girls were very middle class and, I assumed, better educated than I. They had been to Grammar or private schools, whereas I had attended a Secondary Modern, having failed my eleven-plus. However, I soon settled in and made friends.

At the end of the year I applied for a job as shorthand typist at the college and was successful. I continued learning shorthand at night school until my speed was up to 120 wpm (words per minute). I worked in a typing pool with nine other girls. We were watched over by the typing pool supervisor, Mavis. Mavis distributed work to us and walked up and down, ensuring that we were getting on with it! We were not supposed to talk whilst working but my friend, who sat behind me, would make frequent quips or would whisper my name and, when I turned round, would be pulling a funny face. Consequently I would burst out laughing and Mavis would be down the office like a shot with a very disapproving expression. I still keep in touch with my friend and we have a laugh together as we reminisce about the 'good old days'.

One of the tasks assigned to me was to make tea for the college Principal twice a week. The college building was a converted chapel, so, to take the tea to his office I had to walk across what had been the balcony of the chapel. Science students were in the laboratory below and watching the girls was a pleasant distraction for them! One day I tripped, fell, and the tea tray went flying. The students looked up and had a good laugh. I was so embarrassed; I didn't stay to pick up the broken crockery!

After two years in the typing pool I decided to apply for a job in a smaller office, near to home, so I was appointed as shorthand typist at Cleckheaton Medical Centre. I thought I would be working for the medical officer but it was a very hierarchical set-up. The senior clerk took notes in shorthand from the medical officer. He then dictated the letters to me. He would look over my shoulder, checking my shorthand and correcting any wrong outlines. He was a perfectionist! As there was little correcting fluid available and he didn't like corrections to be apparent, I would throw away anything that wasn't perfect in the bin, and re-type the letter. However, that didn't suit him either. One day he picked the bin up in my office and said – "We can't afford to waste paper. You'll be sacked if you go on like this". After this conversation I hid any such mistakes by taking the paper home in my handbag and burning it! I stayed in this job for eighteen months, which, on looking back, was far too long.

I applied for the post of medical secretary at Leeds General Infirmary, where I was appointed to work for a paediatrician, Dr. B. I think Dr. B was about 60 years old, although it was hard to tell his age. He was quite an eccentric, with very strong opinions. He wore ancient suits, at least 30 years old. One day he asked if I thought his suit was old fashioned. I replied cautiously –"Well, it's very good quality". "Precisely what I think," said Dr. B, "I'm not wearing these drainpipes they all wear just to be in fashion". As I sat taking dictation I was fascinated as I tried to work out what he wore round his legs. I eventually realized they were suspenders, worn to stop his socks from wrinkling!

My secretarial duties included sitting in clinics where he saw patients, and then dictated notes to me. On initial visits the children had to hand in a urine sample. Dr. B would give the nurse a knowing look and say – "you know what to do with that", which meant she was to save it all in a large jar, which he then took home to throw on his compost heap.

Many years prior to my appointment, Dr. B and his colleague, Dr. D, had applied for the professorship attached to the paediatric consultant's post. Dr. D was successful, much to the disgust of Dr. B. I was told that since that time (20 years previously) they had not spoken to each other. As they had patients on the same ward, this created problems. They communicated through their registrars and secretaries and never undertook ward rounds at the same time.

One of Dr. B's pet hates was social workers, whom he described as interfering busy bodies. He wouldn't speak to them directly, either. If a family needed information about services available or help such as funding toward convalescence, Dr. B would ask me to make the necessary arrangements. I, in turn, would ring the social worker, who would advise me on how to do this. As my tasks in this direction extended, I began to realize that I found fulfilment in this role.

I attended a large church near the hospital – St. Georges' – where the crypt was used as a shelter for homeless men, providing them with food and a place to sleep. They also employed a full time social worker who recruited volunteers to visit families in need. I became a volunteer and visited a family for whom I had a great deal of admiration. They had very little money but heaps of optimism and Mrs. J told me of numerous occasions when she had been down to her last few pence with no hope in sight but 'the good Lord had blessed her' by sending help in one form or another to save the family from either eviction or starvation.

After working for Dr. B for two years and acting as a volunteer for a year, I decided that social work was the career I would like to pursue. My parents, by this time had moved to Cheshire and on one of my visits, my father pointed out a job in the local paper for a temporary post of social work assistant. I decided to apply. I was granted an interview but wasn't successful. The letter I received explained that although I had been a promising candidate, as I was single the panel did not want to put me in the position at the end of the year of being without an income. They had decided to appoint an applicant who was married, as she would be ensured an income to fall back on. I don't think equal opportunities existed at the time! However, the letter did go on to encourage me to apply for training as a social worker. Enclosed were application forms for a course in social work at Manchester University. At that time it was possible, from 23 years of age, to enter university as a mature student, provided one passed the entrance exam. So at 23 years of age I applied, and much to my surprise, passed the exam and the subsequent interview. I began social work training in September, 1968.

I had to ask Dr B for a reference. He hardly spoke to me thereafter. When I had been on the social work course for a few weeks my tutor asked me if I had seen Dr. B's reference. I explained that he wasn't the sort of person to divulge such information. She went on to say that he was partly responsible for my success. Apparently the letter stated, 'Anne....is a perfectly normal person and I cannot understand why she would want to work in such a stupid profession'. His letter didn't say anything more about me, but went on to expound his views on social work. Apparently the members of the interviewing panel decided that if I was patient and resilient enough to put up with him for two years, I'd probably have many of the attributes needed in social work.

Training

There were twenty students on the course, some of whom had quite a lot of experience and who had been seconded from their employment. I realised very quickly that although the course would be challenging and intensive, I had chosen a career in which I would feel fulfilled.

There were a number of residential as well as fieldwork placements, ranging in length from a few weeks to three months. One of my fieldwork placements was in the Social Services Department in Salford. As this was a long way from my home I decided to rent some accommodation there. I was managing on a student grant so could only afford to rent a small room in a large house. The room held the bare essentials, cooker, sink, small table, chair and a bed. I often felt nervous as approximately a dozen rooms were let out in the house. There would sometimes be the sound of thrown crockery, shouting and screams in the middle of the night, which wasn't conducive to a good nights' sleep. I was glad to get home at weekends even if only for a good nights' rest!

My office in Salford was only two streets away from the original Coronation Street. A lady came in each day to cook for us at lunchtime. The placement proved to be a maturing process for me in more ways than one, as my supervisor was murdered (not at work) a month after I arrived. The placement was for three months. There was no one to handle my supervisor's cases and some of her closest colleagues were both grief-stricken and in shock. I was allowed to take over most of her cases for the remaining two months and managed this with the minimum of supervision. It was valuable experience.

My final placement was in a residential home in Chester, which accommodated approximately twenty people with mental health problems. It was run by the Richmond Fellowship, a charity based in London which had houses throughout England, ranging in size from family sized homes which accommodated four to six people, some of whom would live there long-term, to very large houses where the emphasis was in trying to rehabilitate people back into their own communities.

A career in social work

I had remained in contact with a few of my fellow students, two of whom worked in Wrexham, in North Wales. Les (one of the students) encouraged me to apply for a vacancy that was to be advertised for a social worker in one of the children and families' teams. I began work in Wrexham in December, 1970, and spent two and a half years working hard, learning a lot and having some very happy times there.

The majority of my work involved offering support to families that, for a variety of reasons, were unable to cope. I also worked with a number of young people who were either living in Children's Homes or who were leaving care and attempting to gain some independence. Some of them went on to do well in a variety of ways but some young people had had such damaging experiences and chaotic lives that it affected their abilities and they remained unsettled and extremely vulnerable. The geographic area I covered included a huge housing estate, but also some rural communities and isolated farms. I would sometimes stop for a few minutes on my way back from such visits to take in the beautiful countryside surrounding me and to think through the situations I had encountered. This always helped me to get things back into perspective and was more beneficial than many a long discussion with my supervisor.

One of the families I visited consisted of five children cared for by their father because the mother had left home. They lived on a small-holding in a rural part of the County. The ages of the children ranged from five to thirteen. Local teachers and health workers were concerned at their somewhat dishevelled state and wondered if their father was able to cope. Sometimes they went off to school without a wash and in less than pristine clothes, but their dad made sure that they had all eaten something before setting out on the long walk to school. I thought he was managing incredibly well under the circumstances. Each child was designated a job to do before and after school.

The house was a tip and the amount of clothing to be washed was somewhat out of control, but when the father realised that the Department was there to support him rather than take his children from him, he agreed to have some help in the home. Within a short time the home helps (who at that time were allowed to clean and undertake household chores, unlike the home helps employed today) were able to work out a routine with the family.

The children returned home to a warm house every day and were able to sit down to a cooked meal a couple of times a week and the older children also began to learn how to cook a decent meal. One of the touching scenes I recall was that although the house, when I first visited, looked as if it needed a good clean, dad had handed over to the children two unused pig sties for them to use as a play area. They had cleaned these out, put cushions in them and their dad had put bits of carpet down and strung a hammock across one of the sties. The children spent hours playing and acting out their fantasies in there – it was truly their haven in the midst of chaos! The children would invite me into their 'den', where we would play and talk through their concerns. I think to have similar therapeutic sessions set up in a council building, with such facilities, would have cost a lot of money!

Emergency Duties

Today, there are teams appointed to cover 'out of hours' work of an emergency nature. For a number of years after my appointment, however, no such teams existed. So every six weeks a field worker would cover emergency duties for a week. This meant that at the end of a working day, including the weekend, you would be on call, usually with one other person, to cover any emergencies that were needing social work intervention in the area. This might include taking abandoned children into care, assessing problematic situations and taking action in areas involving children, the elderly and the mentally ill. One was pretty exhausted at the end of the week but it did help to build up a terrific camaraderie with other social workers, the police and hospital staff.

The move back to Sheffield

In 1973, due to my personal circumstances, it became important for me to find employment in Sheffield. I was sorry in many ways to be leaving Wrexham and still keep in touch with some of the friends I met there.

I began work in the Children and Families section of Sheffield Social Services Department and worked there for two years. I had gradually begun to realize that my niche lay in supporting families during a crisis and working with them over a longer term, rather than in short-term crisis intervention. When a newly created post was advertised, helping families to adjust after their child had been diagnosed with a severe disability, I applied. One of the challenges of the post was gaining acceptance from my colleagues in the medical profession, many of whom saw the appointment as an intrusion on their territory! I'm pleased to say that eventually, although this probably took about two years, they acknowledged that my role was useful. The final accolade was when I was asked by the original sceptics to give lectures to trainee midwives and doctors.

I provided counselling and support to parents and their children for periods ranging from a few months to a few years. I think the work proved particularly beneficial when I was asked to join a team headed by a Community Paediatrician whose role was to work as much in the community as in the hospital. I found the work enormously fulfilling but also emotionally draining at times, especially when children did not survive. I realised that after seven years in this post it was time to move on.

My new post was in a team established to provide short breaks for children with disabilities by placing them with volunteer carers who were assessed, trained and supported by workers in the team. I was appointed to the post in 1980 and became a member of a very small team consisting of a part-time manager, two field workers and a clerical assistant   I'm pleased to say the team gradually grew in size to consist of a full-time manager, five field workers and a full-time clerical assistant. At it's height, eighty carers were providing short breaks for approximately 160 children but, due to standards today requiring greater monitoring and also to budget constraints, I think there are now between fifty and sixty volunteer carers. One has to wonder sometimes whether there is now an over-emphasis on meeting and monitoring standards to the detriment of providing an adequate service for those in need.

The work offered great variety, as each worker was involved in the whole process of recruitment, training and support of the volunteers. The process was very similar to the one undertaken if applying to be full time foster carers to a child.

The work also entailed getting to know the families who were requesting a service and, hopefully, introducing them to a carer in whom they felt confident. This sometimes entailed children being placed on a waiting list for some time but when they were eventually introduced, both families and carers usually formed a bond, which they both found was very special, and where the children looked forward to visiting their 'new friend'. Many of the placements, once established, continued for many years, and some carers continued to work on a similar scheme, established for adults, which enabled the young person to carry on receiving short breaks on a similar basis.

I enjoyed every aspect of the work, which is probably why I continued in the same job for twenty four years! I'm thankful, however, that when I felt that many changes were established to satisfy bureaucrats rather than to improve the service, it was nearly time for me to retire. Over the years carers were asked to be subject to so many checks that they were sometimes seeing social workers as often as they were seeing the child placed with them! For the majority of my career on the Family Placement Scheme, I was in the office for 30% of the time and the remainder of my time was spent in work related directly to the placement of children. However, in the last two years, due to the expectation that social workers would undertake more administrative work on their computers, I was sometimes spending 60% of my time in the office, which I didn't think was making the best use of my time and experience! When I reached 60 I reduced my working week to three days and retired a year later.

Reflections

"I still feel thankful to Dr B, whose attitude to social workers led me into a career which I've found fulfilling, challenging and, on the whole, enjoyable. I hope that younger social workers or those moving into this field will find they are similarly fulfilled. My fear is, however, that in managing the amount of form filling and general administration which now has to be undertaken, many workers will find this detracts somewhat from the passion or vision that originally motivated them to train for this work."

Our contributors have frequently commented on changes they have noticed, good or bad, either in practice or attitudes. They can be summed up under the following headings,

Respect

"There was more respect in those days and less money" - Eleanor Hickinson

"I could hardly believe my ears when I heard a nurse calling a doctor by his first name!" - Ellen Davis

Cleanliness (in Hospitals)

"Cleanliness was drilled into us" – Carol Hill

"Those wards were clean" – Esmee Haywood

"I thought the ward did not look very clean and seemed shockingly untidy" - Ellen Davis (on a recent visit to a local hospital)

Health & Safety

"Nowadays they would have Health & Safety down on us like a ton of bricks" – Carol Hill

"Looking back, I think we were a little naïve regarding Health & Safety" – Christine Deakin

Friendliness

"There's more choice in nursing now, but hospitals are less friendly. You are a number these days, not a person" – Sylvia Graham

Bureaucracy

Anne (social worker) says – "For the majority of my career I was in the office 30% of the time" (the rest being given to clients) - " but in the last two years I was sometimes spending 60% of my time in the office"

Esme Haywood (nurse) simply states – "Too much time on the computer, too much paper work"

Staffing Levels

This, it seems, is a case of "everything changes, but nothing changes" as Esmee Haywood says – "We were short staffed all the time – right up to me retiring after 36 years – we were short staffed"

Present day hospital and care workers would probably say - "Hear, Hear" to that.

Alphabet and typeset

From drawing board to computer screen

Not so long ago, few people would have understood what was meant by fonts, point sizes, A4 sheets, justifying etc. These and many more expressions have become part of everyday jargon, familiar to anyone who has basic experience with home computers. We now have a generation of people who once spent many years learning to use skill and patience in order to produce various printed products. These same products can now be made to appear quickly at the click of a mouse.

"Having acquired the ability to hand draw lettering, it soon became apparent that technology was about to do away with the need for it".

Jack Morris, Sign Writer

"My first job was to paint the Red Cross symbol on ambulances"

One such person whose work was often on public view was **Jack Morris.** *As a signwriter, he learned skills which have now almost become extinct. This is how he started*

I left Burgoyne Road School in July 1944 at the age of 14. I had always been interested in Sign Writing and started work in early August with a small firm. This was a partnership called Walker and Senior limited. Mr Walker was the poster and showcard writer. The office and workshop were on the first floor above Cambridge Arcade, which used to run between Union Street and Pinstone Street. My dad went with me for the interview, which was a very brief affair. The hours were to be from 8.30 to 5.30 with half an hour for lunch and I would be paid 15 shillings per week. The first remark made to me when I started work was "Oh no, not another left-hander"! There was an older boy already working there, and he was also a left-hander. Whilst working we wore smocks and were in the habit of frequently wiping our hands down the front. Eventually these smocks were so stiff with paint that they would almost stand up in a corner by themselves when we took them off. My dad made me a special lunch box in which to carry my snap and I've still got it to this day.

Soon after I started, Mr Senior retired and left to run the tobacconist shop which was underneath the workshop, this was on the corner of Cambridge Arcade and Union Street. After a short while, he went to live down south intending to grow orchids as a pastime. His place in the business was taken by Mr Siddall. I learnt a lot from him.

Sign writing is a specialised trade and requires a long period of training and experience before becoming able to do the lettering. The style of training in my case was simply a matter of 'look and learn', in other words follow the boss and watch what he does. Because it was such a small firm, close contact with the boss was no problem and I had some excellent tutoring. The other boy had previously been to art school and had been trained professionally, but this was not necessarily any great help to him. Pictorial art is quite different from sign writing.

Mr Siddall was artistic however, and covered much of the outside work taking me with him. My first job was to paint the Red Cross symbol on ambulances at a firm called Holmes and Younie. This was a firm of vehicle body builders, and just after the war they were producing emergency ambulances. Mr Siddall would carefully outline the Red Cross symbol on the side of the ambulance and then it was my job to fill in the shape with red paint.

In addition to my normal working week I also attended night school on two evenings in order to complete a scholarship. This continued for four years. The course was not particularly helpful in my trade but I was keen to complete it because when I passed the exams, I was given a cheque for £8 per year.

As time progressed I worked on larger projects including lengthy names for shop fronts etc. It was customary for two people to work on the same sign at the same time but when both of us were left-handed, we sometimes got in each other's way. However, we always managed to dodge around each other and complete the work.

After four years, my career was interrupted by National Service and I was conscripted into the RAF. At that time, a national serviceman was required to serve 18 months. I was told to report to Padgate and very soon joined the camp band as a drummer. This turned out to be a good skive because when I was moved to Wilmslow for the eight weeks' basic training, I was able to miss out on much of the square-bashing and rifle drill. The downside of this was that when I was moved on to join the RAF Regiment, I had had no experience with weapons and had to start learning rifle drill etc from scratch. I then spent the next few months based at R.A.F. Catterick Camp which was conveniently near to the A1 trunk road, making it easy to hitch-hike home at every opportunity. This carried on until I was posted to Germany in time for the great Berlin airlift. At first we were stationed very close to the edge of the Russian Zone, but were soon moved further away to avoid any sort of confrontation with the Russians, who were always very suspicious of our activities. We eventually moved to Luneburg Heath, where we lived in relative luxury. Our billets had originally been built for the Luftwaffe. Whilst there I joined the station band still as a drummer and was often involved in various ceremonies and parades. This involved more blancoeing. Being part of the RAF Regiment, our duties were generally concerned with security and guards, but in addition, on No1 Armoured Car Squadron I often did sign writing jobs on camp and on vehicles.

I was demobbed at Easter 1950 and returned to my original employers. They were happy to have me back but in any case, the law demanded that they employed me for at least six months following the completion of my National Service. In the meantime whilst I had been away, a new man had joined the firm and believe it or not, he was also a left-hander.

By this time of course, I was quite experienced and was able to join in much bigger projects. These could include large signs on the sides of buildings or shop fronts and could involve working at heights outside. Ladder work was largely a hit-and-miss affair and it very often meant that two or three short ladders had to be spliced together with rope in order for us to reach high enough to do the work. Sometimes if we were working on a long sign, we would put up two ladders, one near each end of the wording and we would then use a seven inch batten between the two so that we could walk along it as the lettering progressed. This saved us having to repeatedly move the ladders along the length of wall. Looking back on this, it must have been extremely dangerous as the plank was springy and there were no safety barriers at all. At the time, we accepted it as normal practice. It would not be allowed these days.

Some of our work was done on vehicles for firms, most of which have now disappeared. These included Brooke Shaw's at 'Ford Corner', T C Harrison's, Swain and Bradshaw, and Kennings on Brown Street. We also did work for breweries such as Duncan Gilmour's and Tennant's. These signs were a familiar sight in and around Sheffield and involved putting gold leaf on to wood letters.

The wood letters would be sized at the end of the afternoon and left to get tacky overnight in the workshop, by which time they were just right for the application of the gold leaf next morning. The individual letters would then be mounted on frames to be attached to the outside walls of buildings. A typical sign like these could use up to 30 books of gold leaf.

Another skilled aspect of our work was putting gold lettering on to shop windows. This was done by first of all applying a paper pattern onto the outside of the window, then going inside and outlining the letters onto the glass with vegetable black. The inside of the glass was then applied with isinglass (gelatin), within the outlines, and was left to go tacky. Finally this was applied with gold leaf. After this, the gold was burnished and backed and varnished with a layer of Indian Red. This kind of work often meant that there would be tiny skewings of gold leaf left over. These were very carefully collected together, and when sufficient quantity had been collected, they were sold to the Sheffield Smelting Company Ltd for reprocessing.

By this time, I was earning about £4 per week, which was not tremendously generous, but my employers were extremely cute with money-saving tactics. For example when they produced posters for items such as cinemas and theatres, there would often be a narrow strip of paper left over. They would use these to carry messages such as "Welcome Home Albert" which people would buy and display outside their homes when a relative was returning from the forces. The firm would charge one and sixpence each for these strips of paper. One day, I was given the tram fare and told to deliver a wad of these posters to a shop on Infirmary Road. I carelessly left them on the tram when I got off. We never did find them again. We also wrote coffin plates. These were painted on cards (which were offcuts from larger posters) and sold for two and sixpence each.

After a while I was offered an extra £5 per week to go and work for another firm called Maurice Holmes. By this time, 'Letraset' was being used for a lot of the lettering, which cut out much of the original skill in outlining letters by hand. It was much quicker and more economical. Of course most of the outside signs still had to be designed by hand, for example, when we painted the Hovis sign on the side of their building in Rotherham, it was more than 100 ft above the ground.

The way this was done was first of all to obtain measurements of the building and then to design the letters on paper to a scale of one 12th full-size. We would then erect ladders and scaffolding and out line the letters on to the actual wall before painting them in.

Sometimes when we were sent out to work on a shop front for example, we would not have any ladders of our own. The boss simply told us to have a look around the area and see if we could borrow some Air Raid Warden's ladders. It was not uncommon for us to have to place ladders on uneven or sloping ground and many a time, a ladder would be placed on top of a beer crate or an old table to gain a bit of extra height. We would be working up the ladder without anyone on the bottom end to steady it.

Many of the signs which we painted up on buildings in town were very prominent in their time. For example, we did Walter Trickett's, John Walsh in Trippet Lane etc, but many of these have now gone since the properties have been demolished. Another sight, which was very common in Sheffield at the time was the 'King Coal' symbol on coal lorries, all painted by hand. In those days, the amount of work was enormous.

Eventually, I wanted to work on something different and found a job with the Recreation Department where I stayed for 17 years. This involved more variety and interest. I would work on projects like the Recreation Department float for the Lord Mayor's Parade and the Sheffield Show when I hand painted many of the signs and decorations which were involved in these occasions. We would spend up to 14 days creating a float for the Lord Mayor's Parade and very often this was done in the Pickmere Road Tram Depot or sometimes in the Tram Depot at Holme Lane. I progressed to using polystyrene sheet where I cut out profiles of animals and people before painting in the details. On one occasion I was asked by the BBC to provide some background scenery for a programme which was being made locally. I particularly remember one of my work mates who had lost a leg during the war, being able to run up and down ladders with the best of us. You would never guess that he had a false leg.

This was probably the most interesting stage of my career but then things like the signs for all the parks, the Lord Mayor's Show and other annual events began to lose general appeal and the work became less interesting. Consequently I opted for early retirement and finished full-time work 14 months early at the age of 64.

"The editor wanted his front-page altered immediately so that his story could be on the streets before anyone else had heard the news."

Publishing a newspaper was once an extremely labour intensive job involving many different people and a wide range of skills. Laying out a page of information today, follows pretty much the same pattern as it did half a century ago, but the method of going about it has changed considerably. One man who has experienced these changes as they happened is **Ken Nixon** *who worked on local newspapers. This is how we heard his story,*

Ken Nixon, compositor at work

Ken Nixon started work at William Townsend's in Eyre Street where he worked for seven years to become a compositor. This included two years away on National Service. At the end of this time he was married and living with his wife's parents but naturally, he and his wife wished to have a house of their own. The council house waiting list at the time was 12 years long and Kenneth decided it would be better to buy a house. In order it to manage this, he would need to be earning a better wage.

He saw a position advertised at the Sheffield Telegraph offices and moved there in 1953, when he was able to start saving towards a deposit. He knew of some new houses which were due to be built and having secured one of them with a deposit, he was able to watch its progress as it was built, finally moving in, in 1957.

As a newspaper compositor, it was necessary to work early evening shifts, starting at 6.50 pm and finishing at 2.50 am for five evenings per week. There was no shift on the Saturday because there were no Sunday editions to produce. A five night week was worked, having a night off on rota. The first night of the week was Sunday, so every six weeks, we had a three night break, Friday rota, Saturday, and the Sunday rota.

There were two union branches, known as chapels, one serving the evening shift and the other serving the day shift. The only occasion on which these two chapels could meet each other was the Thursday night prior to Good Friday because neither shift was required to produce a newspaper for the following day. Working permanently on the early evening shift precluded any social life outside of work. The only way out of this situation was first of all to become long established on the evening shift, then be in the right place and time when a member of the day shift either retired or died, and winning the vacancy.

Finishing work in the early hours of the morning could lead to some unusual encounters. On one occasion when walking alone in the dark along Chapel Walk, a voice suddenly shouted out "What time is it" making Kenneth almost jump out of his skin. It transpired that he had almost trodden on a tramp who had found a warm place to sleep in front of a shop basement window. In winter, he would often be the very first person to walk through virgin snow, and his were the only footprints through the centre of town for a while. As a joke, he would sometimes walk round in a large circle in the middle of the road in order to fool people who might see his tracks later on.

His journey home from the centre of town was by tramcar which took him to Wadsley Bridge, and he would often be the sole passenger aboard. On one of these journeys, as the tram went round a sharp bend at the bottom of Halifax Road he heard a loud bang. On looking round, he realized that the conductor had disappeared. He ran to the front of the tram and alerted the driver who immediately stopped. The pair of them ran back to find the conductor lying in the road. They helped the poor man back on to the tram and then had to scrabble around trying to recover all the money which had spilled from the conductor's leather pouch.

Kenneth's first job at the Telegraph was in the Adset department where his job was to make up display ads for companies such as Atkinsons and Cole Bros. This was done on a piecework basis and he could earn £14 per week if he managed the full bonus. This was in 1960 and was a relatively good rate of pay. The hot metal process was still in use at this time. Small ads covered the Births, Marriages and Deaths etc. columns of the adverts.

Having gained experience setting up pages of small ads Kenneth was then qualified to deal with the more demanding job where full pages of news were made up. This was very stressful, working against the clock to meet publication deadlines.

There was constant pressure to complete pages before the time deadline arrived. Once the page was complete, the set-up would be taken away and used to create a master plate in metal. Printed proofs would be run off this and sent back to the editor for his approval. Once approved, each plate would then be impressed so that it would fit on a cylinder ready to be used in the printing process. Sometimes, if a late news item came in, there would be last minute alterations to a page already completed.

Hold the front page

On one occasion having finished work at ten minutes to three in the morning and having gone home to bed, Kenneth was woken up at 4.00 am by a loud hammering on the front door. He looked out of his bedroom window to see a Star van driver who was shouting to him to come back to work immediately. He quickly dressed and sped back to work in the van to find that news had just come in of an incident on the Woodhead Pass. A local M.P. had apparently driven off the road and been killed. The editor wanted his front-page altered immediately so that his story could be on the streets before anyone else had heard the news. Of course, Kenneth was not the only member of staff involved in this special edition, it was a team effort. The newspaper was produced on time, but then an argument commenced when the staff requested overtime rate for working out of their normal hours. The management argued that only normal hourly rate should be paid because it was still the same shift which was working. A similar occasion arose when newspapers announcing the death of President Kennedy were out on the streets within a very short time of the news reaching this country.

The chapels (the print union branches) were very active and could be very supportive to individuals. On one occasion a dishevelled man, apparently down-and-out, was noticed to be frequently hanging about in the street outside the Telegraph Offices. He turned out to be a former employee who was very much down on his luck. Members of the union took pity on him and helped to find him a job on the evening shift and helped to restore his self-respect.

Occasionally if a dispute arose with the employers, workers would be advised to stop work. They had an expression for this, the expression was 'Pull the handles in' and this was the sign to down tools and walk out.

The hot metal system

The process at this time was using the hot metal system. This meant working on a 'stone' a large metal slab where pieces of news, previously prepared and passed to him, would be arranged to make up a complete page. He would work to a grid plan on the page, using news items cut to fit into the space allocated to it. These items were cut using a steel rule and a surgical scalpel. He would leave space for headlines to be added later, which were put together by another worker.

Linotype would be assembled by an operator who would type in the news and the machine would line up the stories in blocks. These blocks would be passed on to the 'Random' desk for stories to be collated. Each part of the story would carry the same headline and would be numbered to show in which order it should appear. When the stories were correlated, proofs would be taken on the press and a messenger would take these and put them on a spike to be collected by the sub editor for his approval. When these proofs were finally approved, they would be passed on to the plate to be set up in columns on the pages.

Small gaps would be filled with 'fillers', these were short, undated stories which were kept in reserve on a side galley. Examples of these fillers might be items of undated news, or film and book reviews.

Book publishers would often send a copy of a newly published book to the newspaper in order to have a literary correspondent review it. Once the book had been read it would be put on one side virtually brand new. Eventually, there would be an accumulation of such books and these would be occasionally sold off, with the proceeds given to charity. Through working on the newspaper, Kenneth would have early notice of any good books which were about to be published, and this gave him the opportunity to go along to the public library and order a copy well in advance.

When the production method was modernized and hot metal production methods finished, there was no interruption to production due to the changeover. The new method of working happened between shifts. Work was no longer carried out on the 'Stone' and a drawing board was used instead, and about this time measurements became metric. Despite metrication, the age old method of measuring in 'Point sizes' still prevails.

Each compositor would sit at his own drawing board which would have a page number displayed on top. This meant that messengers delivering items of news would know which board to leave it on. The system now, was for a typesetter to turn a story into a series of short blocks, which were then fed into a machine, and which in turn reproduced them in the form of punched tape. The punched tape produced by the machine was then transferred to a second machine, which would translate the story back into print to be reproduced on 'bromides', i.e. a photographic process involving wet development. The bromides, initially damp, had to be dried out before being delivered to the appropriate board.

The messengers who delivered the stories were often young and inexperienced boys and this was one way for them to learn their way around the building. There was one occasion where an elderly man was employed in the Editorial Dept. and who was always getting lost in the building. One day, he asked someone where the canteen was when he was due for a break. Although he didn't realise it, it was just in the next room, but he was given directions which took him up several floors, then across the width of the building, and back down a different set of stairs to finish up almost in the same place he had started from.

The next technological development was when the drawing board pasting system moved on from punched tape to computer screen. At first this method still produced bromides. Eventually the system was improved further until the whole process of compositing was carried out on computer screen.

Unfortunately, these improvements on the technological side led to fewer stages in the production chain and, to a consequent reduction in staff since fewer people were involved in the process. One thing which did not change was the pressure under which compositors had to work, meeting very tight deadlines and subjecting operators to considerable and constant stress. Kenneth would complete a shift, go home in the middle of the night, and would lie in bed with his head still buzzing with the activity of the previous few hours. He took the opportunity to take voluntary redundancy in 1987 and so left the company.

The Sheffield Telegraph ceased daily production after approximately 130 years, using the hot metal system, and restarted after a time as a weekly paper.

Kenneth had contributed into a company pension scheme all of his working life and was able to accept a lump sum when finishing work. However, he was not allowed to draw a pension at that stage since he did not qualify immediately on grounds of age. On enquiring, he discovered that his eventual pension would not be as high as he might have expected.

As an ex employee, he was eligible to attend the annual Christmas dinner but for years, he never felt inclined to do this. One day, he happened to meet at an old colleague who persuaded him to attend the next one. As it happened this was the only one Kenneth attended, because new owners took over the company and put a stop to all Christmas dinners.

A tradition was observed every New Year's Eve. It was called 'Banging in **the New Year'**. On the stroke of midnight, everyone picked up something to beat, buckets etc., it created a heck of a din!

"Having acquired the ability to hand draw lettering, it soon became apparent that technology was about to do away with the need for it".

Another man who knows what it is like to spend many neck-aching hours poring over a drawing board is **Jeffrey Nettleship.** *He learned the art of producing printed matter by what now seems to be very primitive methods, but kept up to date with new processes throughout a long career in the industry. He reminds us how much harder it would have been to produce this book twenty years ago. This is his story,*

Having been born in 1939, I started work as an apprentice commercial artist in 1956. I spent the whole of my working life in the area of industrial publicity up to retirement in 1998, and the production of commercial print was a daily aspect of my working life.

To this day, (May 2007), I remain the only person I have ever come across to have had the job title of 'Apprentice Commercial Artist'. The term of 'Graphic Designer' was certainly not then in common use and possibly not even in existence in the 1950s. Most young people entering commercial art studios were known as trainees or junior artists. I was originally employed in the publicity department of an engineering company in Sheffield that took on school leavers each year as apprentices to learn various engineering crafts and draughtsmanship, so I became their first 'apprentice' Commercial Artist.

As with so many other trades and professions, it is computers that have had the biggest impact on changing practices during my working lifetime but I find it difficult to think of any other areas of work where the introduction of computers has had more profound effects than in creating print. In 1956, it was utterly inconceivable that I could sit in my own home and create an article such as this, correcting typing errors, changing at will type sizes, fonts, styles, bold, italic, colours and overall layouts, in seconds! just by tapping a few keys.

When I started my training, it was not uncommon for lettering to be hand drawn. My tutor, a highly talented member of the Royal Academy who had served in the Artists' Rifles during the First World War, told me that I could consider myself a lettering artist when I could put the whole of the Lord's Prayer on an area the size of a silver threepenny piece, (less than one square centimetre), using a fine sable brush. I was not only successful in achieving this but did it several times with serif style letters and without the aid of a magnifying glass. I should perhaps add, that the only time this was of practical value to me, was proving I could do it for a bet whilst serving as a national serviceman some years later!

Having acquired the ability to hand draw lettering, it soon became apparent that technology was about to do away with the need for it. 'Letraset' had just been invented. It cut down the time needed to create customised typography tremendously-but it still wasn't the 'rub-down' sort you can buy in any stationery store today. It was a wet transfer system, requiring each character to be individually cut from its backing sheet with a scalpel, still attached to a layer of thin and gummed paper. This would then be placed face down on the underside of a wet screen mesh stretched over a wooden frame. Once the gummed paper had become well soaked, it was slid sideways, leaving the character on the screen. The screen was then flipped over, blotted from above to remove excess moisture, and then used to position the character over the artwork before pressing it down into place. If the letter wasn't positioned perfectly, you had a few seconds to slide it into place, using a brush while the gum was still moist, before blotting the artwork dry. It was very easy to break-up the character during the process and you then had to scrape it away and replace it, but this was still quicker than hand drawing.

'Instant' Letraset (the dry kind you just to rub down into place) came into being a year or two later.

During the 1950s and 60s, letterpress printing was still more common than lithography and was generally considered to give a superior printed image, whereas today litho is the most preferred print method, employing photo images on smooth-surfaced flexible plates. Letterpress is the system that uses a raised surface for type and drawings or photographs. The raised surfaces are inked, using a roller, and the paper placed on the wet ink. A dry roller applied from above transfers the ink to the paper to create the desired image. As a print process, it is little different in principle from the movable type created by the Chinese in the 11th century and very similar to the process developed in Europe in the 15th century by Johanne Gutenberg.

As an apprentice, I attended evening classes and learned to hand set type for letterpress printing. Holding a 'setting stick' in the left hand, individual characters were selected with the right hand from a large wooden tray, (the type case), divided into small compartments, each containing only 'a' or 'b' or '?' etc. The individual characters were placed in the setting stick to give one line of (adjustable width) text. Each line was then transferred on to a flat surface within an adjustable frame, called a 'forme' to create a column of type. Small wedges, known as quoins were used to lock the type into the forme before it was transferred to the printing press. Anyone who was careless in locking up his forme, risked hours of painstaking setting ending up on the floor in a useless heap of bits of metal.

It was at this stage that you could 'proof' the type, (print it) so that it could be read properly for the first time and detect any setting errors, no such thing as a spell checker!

Bear in mind that each variation of every type face required a different type case. In every size you could have normal/light/extra bold, plus upper and lower cases, and all of these in italic also. Conventionally, sizes ranged from 6 point up to 72 point, (25 mm) in one point increments, so for a popular typeface you could have as many as two 224 type cases-a whole lot of metal!

The smallest sizes-if I remember correctly, called 'Ruby' and 'Pearl'-were 4 and 5 point. Larger sizes, for headlines or posters, were known as display type, sometimes made of hardwood rather than metal. Remember this next time you use your mouse to swipe the text on your computer screen to change the size or style in an instant.

If your print job involved a lot of text, you would probably order it from a typesetting service rather than your printer. At best, it would be a few days before you received a proof to check for errors and then another wait before checking the corrections had been done correctly.

Now you have your text. It's probably what was known as a galley proof. That means that it's been set up in the size of type and line width that you specified using a hit and miss formula that told you what depth it should make. It was hit or miss because different typefaces, give different depths-plus there was the matter of the horizontal space between each line, known as leading- (pronounced ledding). Bearing in mind that we are now dealing with solid metal, if the type has made an inch (25 mm) more in depth than your formula suggested, you have very few opportunities for adjustment.

Resetting in type one size smaller, would probably give the best end result but would entail going through the whole setting/proofing process from scratch and double your typesetting costs. The same would apply if you changed to another type face. You could try replacing the leading between the lines with narrower pieces of spacing material-provided that you had not specified 'set solid' originally-leaving you with no leading at all to adjust. You could accept that it was just one of those things and let the extra inch of text run over on to the following page – (assuming there was a following page).

If your job was for lithographic reproduction, (i.e. you were preparing artwork to be photographed with text stuck in place), you had the chance to set work with your trusty scalpel, cutting the thin slivers of paper from between each line of your paper proof and even between words in order to squeeze the text into the available space -satisfying from the designers point of view but very time consuming. It could take a couple of hours to do this with a full column of text on an A4 sized page. Today, the problem would be resolved in seconds by sweeping the cursor across your screen and either changing the type face or reducing the size by an imperceptibly small fraction of the original size.

Moving from type to the reproduction of photographs and drawings, computers have again revolutionised the amount of time needed to retouch, resize and generally rearrange images. With inexpensive graphics software today, a photograph can be retouched, deliberately distorted, masked or morphed by any amateur remotely interested in playing around with images on a pc. As a young artist, I spent hours carefully cutting masks round the complex images of engineering items before using an airbrush to smooth out imperfections or remove unwanted backgrounds, (incidentally, whilst there were electric pumps to provide compressed air for the airbrush, my mentor used a foot pump to pressure his tank and, as his apprentice, I was the one who did the footwork to maintain the pressure).

A trained artist will always be able to create a desired image on paper using traditional skills and materials but an experienced Mac operator today can transform an image in so many ways in a tiny fraction of the time we would have taken 50 years ago.

Even the simplest possible graphic, drawing a straight line, is so much easier today. With a line drawing tool and your computer, it takes seconds to create a line, make it longer or shorter, thicken it, bend it, or colour it.

In my day, to draw a line, you sat before a drawing board and started by using a tee square, (plus a set square if the line was vertical), to draw a light pencil line or fix two points on your artwork. You then loaded a Ruling Pen with Indian ink from a brush and used a bevelled straight edge to draw the line between the two points. If your hand wasn't absolutely steady, or there was a hair on the paper, or a touch of grease from a fingerprint, or the pen clogged and didn't deliver the ink evenly, you didn't get your perfect line. You were then reduced to scraping off the ink with a scalpel or alternatively, trying to clean it up by waiting for the ink to dry, cleaning out the pen, reloading it with opaque white paint and tidying up the outer edges, all with the possibility of the repair work going just as wrong as the original line!

Take another simple shape, -an ellipse. With a computer, you select your tool, drag it over the screen with your mouse and create any shape from a circle to an elongated cigar. Then, if you don't like, it you can stretch or squeeze it at will until you're happy with it. Again it's done in seconds.

Pre computers, (if you were lucky) you had a set of plastic stencils with a range of different oval-shapes, one of which was just what you wanted. Chances were however, that you didn't have either the right shape or the right dimensions for your needs. This left you with three possibilities. The first was to draw your ellipse free hand –not an easy task, even with a skilled and steady hand. Secondly you could go to your collection of French Curves, spend a few minutes finding part of a curve which would give you a quarter of the desired shape, mark the start and finish points on the curve and then draw the image in four quarters by reversing and inverting the curve to give top left/top right/bottom left/bottom right/top. Thirdly, you could put two pins inside the widest part of the desired shape. Next, tie thread loosely to the pins, leaving enough slack to allow your pencil to reach the widest part of the required ellipse when the thread is stretched in a straight line. Keeping even tension on the thread, move your pencil tip up and across the paper until it is drawn back down outside the second pin, thus creating half of your ellipse. If this has produced a shape that will automatically give you the desired dimension-great!- repeat the drawings motion for the other half. If not, back to the drawing board, it's a trial-and-error method.

I'll finish on two aspects of print that haven't been changed by computers

The first is the introduction of the A and B paper sizes. Everyone knows what you mean by a sheet of A4 today but it meant nothing to me back in 1956. I think it was the late sixties before A sizes came into fashion. Prior to that, there was a wide range of odd paper sizes to be had. The nearest to A4 was probably Quarto, (10 inches by eight inches) and Foolscap, (13 inches by eight inches, and so named because back in antiquity it had a jester's cap for its watermark). Most office filing cabinets up to the seventies were a couple of inches wider than those of today, because they had to fit foolscap sheets.

American Foolscap was half an inch wider than the British size and there were lots of larger sizes for commercial print with names like Imperial, Double Elephant, Crown and Double Crown. The use of A and B paper and envelope sizes has certainly made life much simpler for the print buyer.

The last point is design itself. Computers are invaluable for assisting designers in all spheres of activity to develop ideas but it is the human aspect of design that creates what is aesthetically pleasing. A computer alone is no more of a guarantee that you will become a great graphics or bridge designer, than the best camera in the world will make you the world's best photographer.

Another man whose work was equally exacting is **Cecil Higgins, stained glass designer.** *In his case, computers have still not completely taken over and probably never will. Although computers can help with new designs, the practical side of Cecil's craft still employs very ancient skills and methods to this day.* ***He tells us a most incredible story here,***

I was born 3rd August 1912 in the small village of Gleadless near Sheffield, then part of the West Riding of Yorkshire, Education Authority – Wakefield, and educated at Gleadless Council School.

In 1926 I won a four year free scholarship to Sheffield School of Art in Arundel Street (destroyed in the Blitz of World War 2). That year, (1926) there were four students – two girls and two boys, all from Sheffield. At the end of your four years came the Board Examination of Drawing and the Board Examination of Painting for the Royal College of Art in London from which you could get your A.R.C.A., letters which my father wished me to achieve.

However, a local firm of Stained Glass Manufacturers, namely – Robertson & Russell Limited, "Ionic Studio" of 43, Carver Street, Sheffield, contacted the principal of the School of Art for any student interested in stained glass designing, and that really appealed to me, so I put my name on the list and was sent with two other male students for the interview by the Artistic Director, Mr. G. Hammond Steel.

We had to take samples of our art work which he carefully perused in private, and I was the one he said would suit him. So off I went and told the Principal at the School of Art, who asked me if I had my father's consent to apply for this post because I was a Bound Scholarship Student for four years and was only in my second year. But I so wanted the job that I said "Yes" which put me in trouble at home, with my father saying - " Well, you have made your bed, you can now lie on it".

I served a long and testing apprenticeship under a very strict teacher, and often I wished I'd stayed at the Art School because Mr. Steel said I must continue three nights a week from 6 p.m. – 9 p.m. at the School of Art until I was 21 years of age and he asked for regular reports on my work and attendance.

Unfortunately 1926 was the year of the General Strike so there was no public transport and very few people had cars so I had to walk from Gleadless every morning, and back again at 4 p.m. on two days, and at 9pm. when I left the Art School on three days, which made matters worse.

Strict discipline at the firm and reports from the Art School and I now had a local girl friend (Winifred Pashley) and we were hoping to marry. All these factors made me take life more seriously. Mr.

Steel (who I had to address as 'Sir'), and who once, caught me in a rage, kicking his brown felt hat about the studio, said – "If I didn't think you had it in you to do this job I'd kick you into Carver Street now", nevertheless, he saw the difference in me now and we became reconciled to each other much quicker than I ever thought possible at the time.

G. Hammond Steel was well known as an artist over a very wide area and consequently he was commissioned by Cambridge Tutorial Press to illustrate three books – 'A History of England', 'Poems and Ballads' and a medical book, but I can't remember the title now. He said this would take too much time from his painting but if I would help him we would go 50/50 with the proceeds, so as I was hoping to marry I knew the extra money would be very welcome. But then, the clients knew Mr Steel's work, but nothing about mine, so they demanded a specimen before they would give him the commission. I promptly submitted one, which they quickly approved and we were sent manuscripts of all the three books with the places clearly marked "illustration wanted here". We worked together and completed everything to their satisfaction.

Mr Steel was meticulously clean, both in his person and also in his work and insisted on the same with me and the studio and equipment also. I was pleased to comply with him on both matters so much so that I even wanted to dress and write like him.

Winifred Pashley and I were married Easter Saturday 1937, then came the Munich Crisis of 1938 and then while working in the studio I heard the newsboys running up Division Street shouting – "Germany invades Poland –it's war", (September 1939) and this of course changed everything.

Into the studio came the Finance Director (Mr Alfred Coplestone) who had suffered for his conscience in the 'Great War' and he said he could have me made exempt from military service since I was doing work for the City Architects Department converting large basements in the city into Public Air Raid Shelters, but I had heard (on the radio) what Hitler said he would do to England when he got here, and I said I was going to go if called – this was September 1939.

Almost immediately the Provost of Sheffield Cathedral, Alfred Charles Eustace Jarvis, phoned the company about the removal of their stained glass – also from churches in the Sheffield Diocese, and he was closely followed by Canon Bradley of St Marie's, Norfolk Row (now the Roman Catholic Cathedral), and other non-conformist churches in the city.

I was 28 years of age now and in sole charge of this operation, and expecting to be called up in 1940 for army service after Dunkirk, so there was little time for all this work, and the question was where to store it all. The firm got in touch with the manager of Nunnery Colliery at Handsworth, who offered us a working that was subject to flooding, but the flood water would be kept at a safe level by pumping. All this of course was at owners' risk.

Next I had to make sketches of every window I considered should be removed and the remainder to be boarded up with 1" thick timber, inside and outside, and the cavities outside and inside filled with sand forming a cushion against expected bomb blast. The new stained glass by Christopher Webb of St. Albans was removed by his own men and stored by him down South. Copies of my sketches were printed in triplicate and were kept by the Company and also by the clergy of each church from where windows had been removed. The third copy was put in a cylindrical steel container with a water-tight screw cap, and was placed in the crates with the windows. These sketches gave the subject matter and inscriptions, also the precise location of the window and name of the church from which it was taken.

I spent the next six years in the army. Sadly, Robertson & Russell Ltd in Carver Street was burned to the ground before I went into the army (but not by enemy action), so all our records were lost. So far as I could discover, the stained glass in the colliery had been under flood water for a considerable time, because when I went back in 1946 I found no trace of the crates or water-tight containers, because the working had been flooded for a long time. The crates had rotted and the stained glass had disintegrated and settled down into the mud and after pumping the water away they shovelled the lot up and brought it to the pit-top for my collection.

It was a complete jumble, a jigsaw puzzle of glass.

This was a nightmarish situation which was only going to get worse, because not one of the churches, including the Cathedral and St. Marie's, could produce their copies of the sketches, so it was entirely up to my memory, interest and knowledge of the job, if this whole matter was not to become a disastrous expense. I was the only person in the company who knew what had been done, so I had to give the retiring directors, who were all leaving the company, my solemn word that I would remain with the company under it's new owners until I had seen all the stained glass put back in its' rightful place.

For 18 months I worked from 6 a.m. to 11 p.m. most days and this cost me dearly in health. I was under a specialist for nervous and mental troubles for a long time before I changed jobs. The war and it's subsequent problems put an end to my work of designing, painting and firing of stained glass windows, but I was commissioned to design two fairly large stained glass windows for Scotland Street Methodist Church in memory of two well-known families there. Sadly when the place was closed they were not removed and consequently vandals smashed them out altogether. Other windows I designed were,

- A small window at St. Mary's Bolsterstone to the memory of Blanche Swinburne.
- A window in Killamarsh Methodist Church to the memory of a local miner.
- One in Gleadless Methodist Church donated by Mr Cyril Plant.
- A small window in St. Bartholomew's Church, New Whittington, to Peter Nunney aged 20 years, lost at sea during the Second World War.

- A Coronation window at St. Wilfrid's, Moor End, near Thorne.

- Before the war I also designed a window for the Black Swan Inn, Snig Hill, of Dick Turpin's famous ride to York, but this, along with the old building, was completely destroyed in the Sheffield Blitz.

- A depiction in stained glass of York Minster from the city walls, for the staircase window of a house in Grove Street, Retford.

When I left Robertson & Russell I became Chief Draughtsman and designer for Woollen & Co. Ltd., I believe Sheffield's oldest established sign firm, established 1883. Woollens have been very generous to me and I've been very happy to work for them. I retired when I was 72 years of age and have been back several times since to do various clay modelling work for the company. I modelled, in clay, a large mural for the new extension behind the old Duffield Hall near Derby, the headquarters of the Derbyshire Building Society, showing places of historical and architectural interest in the county of Derbyshire, also several heraldic coats of arms for different Authorities and various Company Trade Marks.

Now at 94 years of age I still visit them just to keep contact.

Library work in the 'Swinging Sixties'

Looking back from the 21st Century

Sheffield was the first town in Yorkshire to establish a public library service, back in 1856. It was located in Surrey Street, though not in the present building, and between 1870 and 1905 six branch libraries were built. Between the two world wars the present Central Library and several more branch libraries were opened, and a further expansion was marked by a real building boom in the 1960's, aimed at serving the new housing estates.

In the sixties reading was a highly popular form of entertainment, education and information, with television still not widely used, no computers and the majority of the population living on very modest incomes. Public libraries were an unlimited source of free books and the Sheffield Library System was regarded within the profession as one of the best in the country.

The result of this was that libraries were very busy places with high staffing levels to accommodate the considerable manual labour required. There were no computers and most clerical work involved handwriting or bashing away on an old manual typewriter, plus lots of filing. There was little need to publicise reading as a good thing, because most people knew it was. Now our libraries have Reader Development Officers or Reading Champions, whose job it is to make reading as attractive as possible, since books now have to compete with a great variety of media for peoples' attention.

Our libraries are now highly computerised, a far cry from the early 1960's, when those whose memories are recorded here started work. Other changes include attitudes to rules and discipline, bullying, health & safety issues, and working conditions in general. Although these stories relate specifically to public libraries, anyone who worked in clerical or public service departments during the 1950's and 60's will find much to identify with.

Irene Davy writes about the rather unusual way she got her first job, and her early experience of work.

On leaving school in 1961, at age 16, I had only two ambitions. One was never to study or take an exam again, and the other, to join the Civil Service. I am delighted to say that neither ambition was fulfilled.

During our last term at school we were all sent to be interviewed by a Careers Officer, filled in forms and answered questions. I stated my wishes, and as a result got an interview for the Civil Service, and was accepted, subject to getting the required GCE O-Level Grades.

I left school, and during the course of that summer of waiting, I was astonished to receive a letter from the City Librarian, saying he understood I was interested in library work, and inviting me to attend an interview. As I had no intention of taking the job, and only went at my mother's urging, I was extremely relaxed, and it went well. The interview was conducted by one man, in an office on the top floor of the Central Library at about 5.30 p.m. – unthinkable now, due to complex modern employment laws and the fear of abuse or accusations of the same.

The exam results came and were duly sent off to both prospective employers. The Library Service responded immediately with a start date, and the rest, as they say, is history. At the end of the first day I returned home ecstatic, and when, at the end of a month, the Civil Service were still sending me forms to fill in, I told them I was no longer interested. So, without ever having applied for a single job, I had two interviews and could take my pick.

By the end of the first year, I was so sure that I wanted a career in library work, that I began studying part-time at day-release courses, to become a chartered librarian. End of ambition number two! After several years of study I qualified, and later, in my forties, took a year's unpaid leave and did an MA Course at

Sheffield University. Finally, at the age of 60, I retired after a varied and interesting career, which spanned 44 years. I still feel grateful to that wise Careers Officer who knew better than myself what job would suit me.

"We had the best collection of books on steel-making in the whole of Sheffield."

In 1961 Sheffield City Libraries had over 20 branches, in addition to the Central Library, and I was assured that they always tried to place new people near their home. It was therefore, quite a surprise to find I was to begin my working life at Attercliffe, almost as far away as possible from my home at Meersbrook. Despite the promise received at my interview, I never did work less than two bus-rides from home.

My mother was frantic at the thought of her 16 year-old daughter going to such a terrible place. She had never been there, but she knew it was 'The East End'- full of steelworks and slum dwellings, with a reputation for roughness. Mum knitted several pastel-coloured twin-sets for me, which soon took on a dingy hue because of the polluted air, so after a few months I gave in and bought some skirts and tops in dark colours.

I loved it from the start, the job, the neighbourhood and the people. Although we were poor, I had never seen such extreme poverty in my life, yet people were so cheerful and never whinged. Women in particular often looked years older than they were, due usually to too much childbearing and the endless struggle with poverty and grime. Sometimes when filling in cards to join the library, women would mistakenly put their date of birth, which was only really needed for under 18's. I would be shocked to see that someone I thought about 50 or 60 years of age was in fact only thirty.

The library was a fine old building on Leeds Road, next to the swimming baths, and opposite Brown Bayley's steelworks, which loomed over us like a great black cliff, shutting out the sunlight completely from our windows. Their apprentices used to come over in groups to learn how to use our resources for their studies, as we had the best collection of books on steel-making in the whole of Sheffield.

Reading was a very popular hobby, so big queues would develop in both the adult and children's libraries. Despite the fact that tempers sometimes flared, usually in disputes over fines or damaged books, I never heard the sort of obscene language so common today. The children were a lively lot, and some of them spent most of their spare time in the Junior Library, in the role of 'helpers'.

Attercliffe was the last district in Sheffield to have milk delivered by horse and cart (owned by the Co-Op), and it was the job of the juniors to go out and buy our daily requirements, but the horse was a creature of routine, and would only stop at it's regular locations. The result was, that if we missed it at one 'stop', we had to run after it and buy our milk literally 'on the hoof'. When the horse finally retired, it merited a picture and article in the local papers.

My salary, paid monthly, was £6.50 a week, £1 more than the Civil Service, and I thought it was a fortune. When I got my first months' wages of about £24 I just didn't know how to spend it. The one thing I'd always wanted and been denied by my parents was a coconut (I was a girl of simple tastes!), so I went out to the greengrocer on Attercliffe Common and bought one, to the amazement of my colleagues. It turned out a great disappointment, requiring my father to use an axe to break it open, and neither the coconut nor the milk resembled the contents of Bounty Bars as I'd expected.

Our salaries were paid by cheque, and the cheques for all the staff were sent out to the library each month. I, at 16, was given the lot and despatched to the Midland Bank up Attercliffe Road to get them cashed, fetching them back in a carrier bag. It never entered anyone's head that either I might steal from them, or be in danger myself of being mugged and robbed – I never was.

The cleaners were paid weekly in cash, and every Friday we juniors took it in turns to collect the packets from the Central

Library, along with clean hand and tea towels for the week ahead.

Holiday allowance was ten days per year, which as we worked a five day week, gave us just two weeks annual holiday, plus Bank Holidays.

Our hours of work were not standard office hours, as we worked every Saturday 9-5 and had Thursdays off. Opening hours were long. Reference libraries stayed open till 9 pm four days a week, and lending libraries till 8 pm four days a week. This entailed each person working till 8 pm two nights per week, one of these being a 'long day', 9 am-8 pm and the other 1-8 pm. It was almost impossible to get a Saturday off as this was the busiest day of the week, and I sometimes finished up so exhausted that I had to cry off the usual Saturday night dance with my friends. You were on your feet all day, with continual queues. At small libraries young women were expected to work at nights alone, which is certainly not the case today.

At Attercliffe Library we worked slightly different times from all the others, on the two weekdays we did office hours, due to a transport problem. At 5 pm prompt, the offices of all the big steelworks further up the Common emptied, and the staff boarded buses for town, which were so packed there was no chance of us getting on them. The solution was for us to work from 8.45 am till 4.45 pm and get on a bus before the great exodus.

More than forty years after they first worked together, **Isobel Stonecliffe, Janet Smith, Irene Davy, Jane Beresford and Beryl O'Brien** *met up for a grand reminiscence session, read on....*

"When we started work in the early sixties, every desk in each library had three inkpots for blue, red and black indelible ink, and all our writing was done with steel-nibbed pens in wooden holders - no such luxury as fountain pens, and the very idea of biros was anathema. They were much too easy."

"If anyone found that rare thing, a good, smooth nib that was not scratchy, they would keep it to themselves."

Staffing - the workforce in the sixties was totally different from what it is today. The mainly female staff were primarily young, as girls left work either when they married or when expecting their first child. The man in charge of Personnel reckoned to get on average seven years work from female staff, i.e. from their being 16 to 23 years old. Only those who remained unmarried, and the men, went on to senior posts. There were no part-timers until the early 1970's, few married women and also no ethnic minorities, as indeed, there were very few in the general population. Because we all started work when we left school and were of a similar age, we usually related well together, and lifelong friendships resulted.

Health and Safety issues - these were not matters anyone gave much thought to. In addition to sending young female staff out to collect large sums of cash, we had to do something called '**Call-booking'.** This involved visiting the homes of people whose library books were long overdue, in order to collect them. It was something that young junior staff did quite alone, and at times involved one in strange situations, but we never came to any harm. Irene reckoned she once walked five miles round Attercliffe in one afternoon, and came back staggering under the weight of several bags of books. She actually enjoyed the chance of an outing and the detective work involved in tracking people down, but most girls disliked it, and the job is now done, if at all, by security staff employed for the purpose.

Lifting - we carried enormous piles of books around in our arms, whereas now they have trolleys – no one thought of possible injuries.

Dealing with discarded books was another unpleasant task, as it had to be done in the cellar. One sat there for a whole afternoon, packing dirty old books into coarse hemp sacks, and fastening them at the top with string, ready to be taken away for salvage. As the cellar was cold, damp and dirty, it would certainly not now be considered a suitable working environment.

Moving Around - another facet of library work in those days was that we only ever worked one or two years at any given library, and would be transferred at short notice to another branch.

Training - this was very much a 'sitting with Nellie' approach. You were taught to do each task by watching a more experienced person, and your work was checked and returned to you to re-do if any mistakes had been made. The librarian at Attercliffe, Dennis Lynch, was a great boss, and took time to talk to staff about the more professional aspects of the job, and how to handle difficult customers, at which he was adept. His saying was 'Remember that the customer must always be allowed to think they are right, even if they are wrong'.

New staff spent the first weeks practising writing and printing neatly with steel nib pens and ink, usually by a girl one or two years older than yourself, who was known as a 'Senior Junior'. Some were very strict, for instance one would be told scornfully – "Any fool can stick labels in crooked. We stick them in straight"- as the said label was ripped out.

Open Evening - Every Autumn the new intake of staff was invited to an Open Evening at the Central Library, and our parents were invited too. After refreshments were served, and introductory speeches made, we were shown a film, which was the pride of the Service, and used for many years for publicity purposes. The film was called 'Books in Hand', with a commentary by Alvar Liddell, a famous BBC radio commentator, and showed the full range of services on offer. We were then taken round the building, shown all the different departments, and the underground stacks and storerooms. This practice continued on into the early 70's, and Irene remembers taking a new young assistant and her parents to such an evening. Her very strict father asked –" How is she doing?" When told that his daughter was one of the best assistants she'd ever had, his reply was a dubious - "Well, she seems to be enjoying herself too much in my opinion". Who can imagine such a thing happening today?

There was a six months probationary period, and then at the end of the first year we were given the choice of going to day release and night school to study for the First Professional Examination, which would enable all who wished to take further exams and so become Chartered Librarians. There was no pressure to do this, and many people took that first exam to improve their knowledge and skills, but chose not to go further. Also there was a system to train those who wanted to specialise in running children's libraries. They were 'apprenticed' to assist a more experienced librarian, and learnt all about children's literature and how to run craft and story sessions. No CRB (police record) checks needed!

In those days it was possible to study to become qualified and chartered whilst working full-time. Then the fashion changed and people had to go to college for two years, and later still, to university for a first degree and then do one years' Masters Degree. Now the wheel seems to be turning full circle, since there are many ways of qualifying, and full-time courses are not always necessary.

Rules and Discipline - strict rules governed the life of both staff and customers, and for the most part were accepted by both. The 'Swinging Sixties' did not swing much in our workplaces! Life at work was so much more formal than it is today. Take the use of Christian names. Although we used these in the privacy of the staffroom (though not even then to older, more senior members of staff), in front of the customers we addressed each other as Miss, Mr or Mrs so-and-so. Irene remembers - "The thrill, when I first started work, at 16, of being called 'Miss Davy'. What a change from school – it made me feel so grown-up!"

There was a dress code – no trousers for women and definitely no bare legs. No matter how hot the weather, you wore nylons or tights. Male staff wore jackets, collars and ties, though few went to the extent of one older senior librarian who wore bespoke suits, stiff white detached collar with studs, and brought a starched white table napkin to work every day for lunchtime.

Customers too laboured under a galaxy of rules and regulations, and the long waiting lists for popular new books, whereas now they are more demanding. It's a case of – "I want it now".

"When I joined the library recently after years of working away from Sheffield, I was amazed to discover that I could return my books to any library in the city, not just the one I'd borrowed them from, and that if I merely mentioned that I'd be on holiday when my books were due back, they would offer to extend the loan period". In the sixties we were much stricter - I guess we had a captive audience.

One thing that has become tougher over the years is the business of joining the library, which used to involve filling in a simple form. Sadly in our seemingly less honest world, it is necessary to provide several proofs of identity and address. There is also the matter of staff name badges, which must now be worn, but were unheard of back then.

Children, now so welcome in libraries from the earliest age, were expected to be seen and not heard. Isobel recalls her (male) boss emerging from his office and saying to a customer – "Is that your child, Madam? Kindly keep it under control".

Censorship was routinely practised back in the sixties, but is non-existent now. Certain books were kept 'under the counter' and represented on the shelves by wooden blocks with the author and title printed on them. It took a very brave customer indeed to come to the counter with one of these, which would be exchanged for the book.

The kind of books kept under the counter were anything about sex or childbirth, explicit novels such as 'Lady Chatterley's Lover', and art or medical books with nude pictures in. Beryl relates the story of one older lady librarian who insisted her staff made little paper bikinis with which to cover pictures of naked ladies on book jackets.

Among some librarians at that time there was also a sort of intellectual snobbery about certain books such as Enid Blyton's children's books, Mills & Boon romances and Westerns (much beloved of elderly gentlemen). These were not bought at all for a while, but common sense and public demand soon brought them back to the shelves.

The whole could be summed up by saying that years ago we saw ourselves as the custodians of books and the arbiters of rules, whereas now libraries try to give a totally customer-focused service.

Technology - from steel nibs to computers

When we started work in the early sixties, every desk in each library had three inkpots for blue, red and black indelible ink, and all our writing was done with steel-nibbed pens in wooden holders - no such luxury as fountain pens, and the very idea of biros was anathema. They were much too easy.

New staff had to learn to print neatly, as all the readers' tickets, labels for books, catalogue cards and ledgers for statistics, cash and stamps were hand written and must be legible. Practice made perfect, and any work found, on checking, to be less than perfect had to done over again.

Every Friday came the terrible job of **'doing the inks',** which fell to the lot of the junior staff, in turns. All 15 inkpots had to be collected up, washed out in the sink and re-filled, and while the red and blue inks were relatively easy to deal with, the black ink was not called indelible for nothing. It was a nightmare to soak and scrape these pots free of their sticky black gunge. Finally all the blotters were replenished with fresh paper and the pens with new nibs, though if anyone found that rare thing, a good, smooth nib that was not scratchy, they would keep it to themselves and hide it.

Even worse than the inks, was the weekly cleaning and **replenishing of the glue-pots.** Glue was needed for sticking in labels and repairing books, and had to be made up in basins from packets of powder. There were two kinds, L.A.P. Hotwater Paste and L.A.P. Coldwater Paste, both equally tricky, and Irene says – "My efforts were always disastrous. Bitter were the complaints of the other juniors as they tried to use pots of lumpy gunge so thick the brush stood up in them, or at the other extreme, paste as thin as water".

The only equipment we had that could even vaguely be described as technological was a typewriter and a telephone. Although the old Victorian buildings were on two floors, they had only one telephone, in the ground floor office, with no extensions. Staff were faced with a dilemma every time the phone rang and there were queues at the counter.

Should we abandon the counter and leave people standing to answer the phone? This did not go down well with the customers, so our boss ruled that we serve the people in front of us and ignore the phone, as they were probably sitting in an office somewhere and would ring back. For many years afterwards all the branch libraries had only one phone, and they were not much used in those early years. The Central Library had a small switchboard in the Admin office operated by a blind ex-serviceman. As for the typewriter, it was a heavy old manual affair, which sat in the office and was hardly ever used.

No-one working today in high-tech libraries packed with computers could imagine the labour-intensive routines we followed forty years ago, or the strict discipline we submitted to, but they were very happy times.

There was a lighter side to our work. In some respects there was more freedom than today, when a corporate image is seen as necessary. Back then, each Branch Librarian had total responsibility for his or her own library, from buying books to sorting out repairs, and as there were quite a few eccentric characters in the library service of those days, each place had a different atmosphere. Some librarians had favourite customers who they let off paying fines, while others tended to choose more of their own favourite sort of books, so that one library might abound in flower-arranging books, and another in football.

Children's Librarians also were free to select books, liaise with local schools, and to run story-times, craft sessions and any other activities that took their fancy. They and their trainee were often pretty-well independent of the adult department of their library.

There was also a monthly free film show for the children, and this was a major event, requiring considerable policing. The kids would start to queue up outside long before opening time, and fights sometimes broke out among the queue. The operative would arrive with a huge old projector and large reels of film prior to the show, and we set up long wooden benches for the audience.

The benches were a bit rickety and occasionally collapsed, tumbling a whole row of children onto the floor. The films were old and dire, but tremendously popular, due to the lack of other entertainment and/or lack of cash.

"At Attercliffe Library the big event of the year was the pantomime, which was put on for the children's families. We had to make all the costumes from crepe paper, as parents could not afford to buy material. The staff room was turned into a dressing room, and I helped with the dressing. Never shall I forget the night I sent a small girl on stage, in a pretty pink fairy frock, wings and wand – and hefty snow boots! "

The latest 'entertainment ' for adults was the Listening Group, which was a music appreciation session (classical, of course), which met monthly at branch libraries. A large record player and speakers would be delivered to the library in question, and either the librarian or a member of the group would present a programme of their own favourites. It was a very sedate affair, with great discussions about the new invention – Hi-fi. It now seems incredible that people would go out on a cold winter's night to listen to records in a library, but for some years they were very popular, and at least one librarian met his future wife at a Listening Group.

Some things were much more relaxed years ago. Smoking in the staff room was common, and is forbidden now. Jane recalls a lady who worked in a back-room department at the Central

Library wearing a print overall fastened at the back, a turban, and always with a fag in the corner of her mouth.

Each branch library had a cooker so that staff on 'long days' (9 am to 8 pm), could have hot meals.

"I recall one Shrove Tuesday when we made and tossed pancakes, one of which hit the ceiling"

"At one library we cooked a full Christmas dinner in the staff room and invited the library van-man to take a long lunch break from his delivery round and join us".

Many large organisations had social clubs back in the sixties, and the library service was no exception.

In the 1960's Sheffield Libraries had a lively social club, run by some dedicated, hard-working members of staff. It was known as SPLSA (pronounced Spelsa), which stood for Sheffield Public Libraries Staff Association. We each paid a modest subscription, which paid for extras on the dining tables in the Central Library staff quarters, and for food and drink at the parties, of which there were many.

Various trips were planned, at extra cost. These included a day at Stratford on Avon with a matinee at the Royal Shakespeare Theatre, a tour round the Wedgewood factory and a private evening visit to the library at Chatsworth House, which is normally closed to the public. More seriously there were also visits to new and exciting library developments such as the British Library at Boston Spa.

But it is the parties that stand out in our memories, and it was a case of 'any excuse for a party', and not just the usual retirement 'do's'. Food and wine were there in abundance. Contrary to the popular media depiction of librarians, we were a lively lot who enjoyed a few drinks, or more. The weekend schools put on by our local professional association were renowned for the 'extra-curricular activities', and we younger ones would wait with eager anticipation to hear the latest 'goings-on' from these conferences.

I believe that Askham Bryan College actually banned the librarians from holding conferences there after a particularly riotous and boozy weekend.

The one that Irene always remembers was on the night the news came through of President Kennedy's assassination. The party was actually an American Night, because two of our staff had been on the very first study tour of libraries in the U.S.A. and wanted to show their slides and tell us all about it. She relates –

I had gone upstairs to get changed for the party, and when I came down, I found my parents looking at an empty T.V. screen and some solemn music playing. "What's wrong with the tele?" - I asked, and was told – "President Kennedy has been killed". The newsflash had been brief, so we immediately assumed that the Russians must have done it. The idea that this wildly popular man might have been killed by one of his own people never entered our heads.

When I got to the staff room at the Central Library, I found all ready for the party, but one of those who had so recently been in the States, was crouching by the side of our ancient bakelite radio in tears, trying to hear the latest news. The windows were open, so we could hear the bells of St Marie's Church on Norfolk Row (later the Roman Catholic Cathedral) tolling mournfully. The party continued, but in subdued fashion, and the slides we saw of the States, and in particular of the White House, now had a deep poignancy. They say everyone alive at that time can remember where they were on that day. It would be hard ever to forget the SPLSA American Night.

Greenhill Library, which was opened in February 1963, marked the start of the boom period in library building. In fact, it was one of two libraries opened by the Lord Mayor on the same day, the other being at Hemsworth. Although Greenhill is still going strong, Hemsworth fell victim to the spending cuts of the late 20th century, and was closed down despite spirited opposition from local people and librarians. Here is a personal account from those heady days of expansion.

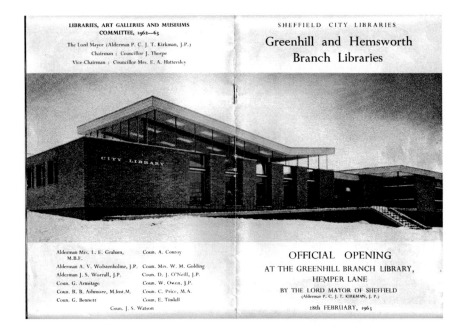

LIBRARIES, ART GALLERIES AND MUSEUMS
COMMITTEE, 1962—63

The Lord Mayor (Alderman P. C. J. T. Kirkman, J.P.)
Chairman : Councillor J. Thorpe
Vice-Chairman : Councillor Mrs. E. A. Hattersley

SHEFFIELD CITY LIBRARIES

Greenhill and Hemsworth
Branch Libraries

Alderman Mrs. L. E. Graham,   Coun. A. Conroy
M.B.E.
Alderman A. V. Wolstenholme, J.P.   Coun. Mrs. W. M. Golding
Alderman J. S. Worrall, J.P.   Coun. D. J. O'Neill, J.P.
Coun. G. Armitage   Coun. W. Owen, J.P.
Coun. R. B. Ashmore, M.Inst.M.   Coun. C. Price, M.A.
Coun. G. Bennett   Coun. E. Tindall
Coun. J. S. Watson

OFFICIAL OPENING

AT THE GREENHILL BRANCH LIBRARY,
HEMPER LANE

BY THE LORD MAYOR OF SHEFFIELD
(Alderman P. C. J. T. KIRKMAN, J. P.)

28th FEBRUARY, 1963

Opening of Greenhill Library

In September 1962, aged 17, I was given the exciting opportunity of joining the staff of the new Greenhill Library, then being built on Hemper Lane.

Thousands of new books had been purchased and needed processing from scratch – a very labour-intensive job. Every book needed a plastic jacket cut and fitted to size, and catalogue cards and labels neatly printed with pen and ink. This task took the five permanent staff, supplemented by temporary help from other libraries, nearly three months to complete.

The building was not yet ready for occupation, so we were located in a backroom at Highfield Library, and as the work was rather tedious and repetitive, and we were out of sight and hearing of the public, we brought in a record-player and our favourite discs, discussed every subject under the sun, and generally had a lot of fun. In fact, we bonded together so well that we still meet up over forty years later.

The library was due to open at the end of January, and before Christmas we had accomplished the task of moving all the bookstock in, though it was stored in the stacks at the back rather than the public part of the library, which was still not complete. On Christmas day disaster struck – the boiler blew up, and the resulting smoke and water damage put the official opening back another month.

Technically the building was uninhabitable, but being young and enthusiastic, we volunteered to work there without any heat, during what has become the legendary bad winter of 1963. It snowed heavily on Boxing Day and there was still snow on the ground when the library opened at the end of February. Our offer was accepted, on condition that each person only worked there for one or two days per week, and we were given special permission to wear trousers – an immense and unheard-of privilege!

The day would begin with me walking half an hour through thick snow to the bus, then another half hour from Meadowhead through the old village to the library. I shall never forget the beauty of the huge icicles which hung from the roofs of every house I passed.

In order to keep warm, we dressed in many layers of thick clothing, worked very hard, and constantly used the cooker in the staff kitchen to produce hot drinks, soup, toast and jacket potatoes, the whole supplemented by a substantial lunch from the chippie in the village.

We enjoyed ourselves hugely, and were immensely proud when, at the end of February, the Lord Mayor came and officially opened the library, which was so popular that queues of new customers formed outside the library day after day.

The reward for our efforts was a promise not to transfer any of us to another library for the first two years, since we got on so well. This was quite unusual in Sheffield Libraries at that time, and a real privilege. The promise was kept, but precisely at the end of two years, I was moved elsewhere.

To celebrate the fortieth anniversary of it's opening, Greenhill Library got a makeover, and some of the original staff went back to take a look.

The original solid oak Ercol furniture had been replaced by cheerful items from Ikea, but we found that the staff quarters were unchanged, and the current staff were astonished at the mayhem created by we fifty-sixty-something ladies as we re-lived the days when we were young and daft.

This last story illustrates in a nutshell some of the changes since the 1960's and is told by one who prefers to remain anonymous!

I started work in the early 1960's at a busy suburban branch library with a staff of 12, which included a children's librarian and her trainee. Ten years later I left to start a family, and three babies and twelve years later I returned to the library service. The changes were very apparent!

One of the first things I noticed was the use of Christian names, including the City Librarian – what a contrast with the formal Mr and Miss of my first bosses. Gone were the somewhat unpleasant jobs to be regularly performed – washing inkwells, filling sacks with old books in a cold cellar after covering ourselves in an oversized overall, and a half hour weekly dust of the book stock.

Some incidents stand out particularly in my memory which would almost certainly be seen today as totally unacceptable. Each week a member of staff had to take a bus ride carrying a small leather case containing dirty towels which were exchanged for clean ones at the Central Library. The day dawned when I was allowed to do this for the first time on my own, and as I left the library I was called back by the librarian, who informed me that the typewriter needed taking to be repaired. I was handed an extremely large, heavy old-fashioned machine (no slim laptops in those days) and struggled almost to the end of a very long drive to reach the bus stop, close to tears, before being called back and told it was a joke!

On another occasion I was instructed to turn down every tenth book in the library for stock taking, only to be informed after a morning's work that this too was a joke and I would now have to turn them back. Very embarrassing for a somewhat naïve seventeen year old, was to be pushed forward to serve any young male borrower who entered the library, always accompanied by somewhat suggestive remarks.

How many members of staff today would happily take the monthly pay cheques of the entire staff to the bank a good fifteen minutes walk away, cash them and return through a not very salubrious area carrying hundreds of pounds?

I discovered that the whole atmosphere of a working library had changed. Staff question everything now. We used to be told that from the following Monday we had been transferred to a different library, with no consideration as to travelling time or distance. It would be interesting to see the reaction this would cause today! Times certainly do change, and I think most would agree that what amounted to bullying of staff is unacceptable, but gone also to a great extent is respect for authority. What will the workplace be like in the future I wonder?

Lord Mayor and Christine Pontin at Greenhill Library

Job interviews

Anyone who has changed jobs many times during their working life will tell you that interviews can vary tremendously in style. It may be on a one to one basis or involve sitting before a panel of two or three people. The interviewer might be an expert in the particular job being applied for, or might be someone from the personnel department with only vague knowledge of technical processes. This usually depends on the level and status of the vacancy.

John Nettleship *tells of two very different interviews which he experienced many years apart. The second of these took place at the age of 36, having spent the previous four years as a Training Instructor at Laycock Engineering Limited. He writes,*

I was approached by the Chief Training Officer of a large group training organisation who was looking for an assistant. He had secretly observed my performance on a course which I had attended some months previously and decided that I was the one suited to fill his vacancy. He offered a much better salary plus many extra perks including a company car, but warned me that there would be a very rigorous interview to endure. I was tempted by his offer and agreed to attend the interview. To call it 'rigorous' was putting it mildly. I was shown into a room to find a panel of twenty people looking at me. The panel was arranged in a semi circle and I was invited to sit on a lone chair placed at the focus of their attention. It felt like the loneliest place in the world. Random questions began coming from all different directions for what felt like hours, but was probably about twenty minutes. I came through it successfully and was offered the position, but it was not an experience I would like to repeat again. I mention this occasion because it is in complete contrast to the interview I attended when I applied for my first 'proper' job on leaving school.

I left the Sheffield Central Technical School in July 1951, at the age of 16. It seemed logical to look for a job in the engineering

John Nettleship

industry. I spotted an advert in the Sheffield Star in which the University of Sheffield was looking for an apprentice mechanic. I liked the sound of it and sent in what must have sounded like a very naïve and schoolboyish letter of application. I received a very prompt reply on impressive looking headed notepaper, from Professor Tuplin in the School of Applied Mechanics and which invited me to an interview. I almost decided not to go ahead with it because people like 'professors' had never featured in my life before, and also, the word 'school' in the title was enough to put me off. It was only my parents who encouraged me to give it a go and find out more about it.

I went along on a Saturday morning at the appointed time and arrived at the grand entrance to the university on Mappin Street. There, I was confronted by an impressive looking uniformed porter who said "The likes of you are not permitted to use this door". I explained that I had an appointment with Professor Tuplin and was directed round to the back of the building where I found myself in a maze of narrow back streets off Portobello. These little streets were full of small back to back houses, most of which were empty and boarded up. There were gaps where some of the houses had been demolished and prefabricated huts had been erected in the spaces. I discovered later that Professor Tuplin was in charge of a brand new department which he was setting up and which would specialise in a particular branch of engineering. His office was temporarily housed in one of the prefab huts. A secretary showed me into his office where he was sitting behind a huge desk, on which there were piles of papers and assorted mechanical gadgets.

Professor Tuplin turned out to be a very friendly and approachable man and soon calmed my nerves. He asked me a few basic questions and then said he would like me to meet his chief technician, Ted Hill. He led me to the door and directed me along the street to another prefabricated hut and told me to go straight inside. This second hut appeared to be deserted but the door was open direct onto the pavement and I was able to peer inside. It gave me the impression it was some sort of laboratory. I ventured inside the door and then realised there was a man in the far corner sitting at a bench. He appeared to be studying the contents of a large glass beaker which was being heated over a Bunsen Burner. Having done some chemistry at school, I assumed that he was carrying out some sort of experiment, and I hesitated not wanting to disturb his concentration. I coughed and shuffled my feet then asked him if he was Mr Hill?

"Come in lad, I was expecting you". He pointed to a high stool near the bench "Sit yourself down".

By this time, the contents of his beaker had come up to the boil.

"Fancy a drink of tea lad?" he said.

"Er yes please, sir".

"Forget the 'sir', my name's Ted".

Ted opened a drawer in the side of the bench and took out a packet of tea. He poured a small pile of it into the palm of his hand and tipped it into the madly bubbling beaker.

"We'll just give that a few minutes to mash," he said, then straightaway, "I understand you went to the Technical School, so you'll know something about tools and machines then".

Before I could reply, he took a small steel ball and a micrometer out of his smock pocket and pushed them along the bench towards me.

"Tell me the size of that ball to the nearest thousandth of an inch", he said.

He was obviously impressed when I had no problem in providing the answer.

He then pointed to the end of the bench where there was a pile of smaller glass beakers upside down on a draining board and asked me to pass him a couple of them. He then put on a pair of welder's gloves so that he could pick up the beaker of boiling tea, and then poured some into the two smaller beakers. Next from his drawer, he produced a bag of sugar and a tin of condensed milk which he used to complete the brew. Finally, he completed the ritual by taking a six inch steel rule from his top pocket and stirring the brew commenting "Careful now, it'll be too hot just yet".

He then began to ask me questions about my general background and interests and particularly about practical subjects covered at school. I was beginning to feel more relaxed and was finding that Ted was easy to talk to when suddenly, in mid sentence, he stopped talking. He held up a finger. "Shush, listen, I think they're coming. Quick, follow me". With that, he was off his stool and dashing away towards West Street.

I hadn't a clue what it was all about but thought I had better do as I was told. We ran about five hundred yards up to the main road where a large crowd was gathered. It then dawned on me that the annual Student Rag Parade was due to come past. Ted spent the next ten minutes dropping coins into tins being rattled by oddly dressed people. I spent the same time dodging the tins because I only had two pence in my pocket and that was for my bus fare home. As the tail end of the procession disappeared along West Street, Ted turned to me saying "Come on lad, we've got some unfinished business to attend to and besides, our tea's getting cold".

Arriving back at the hut, I realised that we had left the place deserted and the door wide open, but that was not uncommon in those days. Once back inside, we sipped our tea as we walked around the workshop area, whilst Ted asked me questions about technical matters. We stopped in front of a small lathe and I hoped Ted was going to let me have a go on it, but instead, he began pointing to different parts, asking me to name them. I was beginning to feel at home in this place and it never occurred to me that I might not get the job.

Eventually Ted looked at me and said, "You sound like the sort of young feller we could use around here, when can you start?"

I could not have been more excited. I worked in that department for fifteen years interrupted only by two years of National Service, and loved every minute of it.

Preparing for interview is a subject for discussion all on its own. Most people who left school in the 1940s, 50s even 60s had little or no careers guidance. If they were given any at all, it would often come from a teacher who had been given the task as an extra duty, and one for which they were not necessarily qualified. Sometimes, the potential school leaver would simply be advised to "Make sure your shoes are polished and your tie is on straight. Oh! and remember to say 'Sir' when you apply for a job".

"My dad went with me for the interview, which was a very brief affair."

At that time, most people when asked for a copy of their Curriculum Vitae, would just say that they had not done Latin at school. In later years it has become fashionable to coach people on how to approach interviews. You can be taught how to write letters, fill in forms, adopt the right attitude, how to dress, how to research the post being applied for etc. Many of the older generation have to smile at all this, having spent a lifetime moving from one job to another, often without any formal interview at all.

Twenty first century work

"Sheffield has gone through an extraordinary period of change since the 1940s, to what? We're not sure yet."

More and more people work in offices, in call centres, at computers. They work for branches of the civil service that were moved to Sheffield during the 80s. They come to Sheffield as students, and stay to work here. They leave Sheffield to work in other countries in the European Union. Many more continue to study after leaving school than did forty or fifty years ago.

Four very different young people, all of them tell cheerful stories full of optimism. The jobs they describe make a contrast to the rest of the stories in this book, stories that chronicle an extraordinary change in the nature of employment in Sheffield and South Yorkshire. A contrast indeed with Syd Morton's words, "With the uniform of a pair of wooden clogs, and a sweat towel, I was ready to face the future in steel."

Anita Guy *started work in 1988, these extracts from her story gives a picture of many young people's working life nowadays,*

I was born in North London in 1972, but as a child I always dreamt of travelling round the world. I guess I must have had over 100 different jobs, both in Britain and abroad, and I'm only 35 now. Some of my family thought I was crazy, but my mother encouraged me.

My first job at 16 years of age was at Wimpey's, then I went to college and worked part-time at Sainsbury's, then Littlewood's at Marble Arch. I studied Social Care at college, and my first job when I left in 1991 was with a Care Agency linked with Camden Council. I worked with children as a teacher's assistant and in care homes for the elderly. I enjoyed the kids, and to some extent the old people, but it was very hard work in those homes, which were always short-staffed and relied largely on agencies.

After travelling and some office jobs, Anita tried a hospital job.

The HSDU takes care of hospital equipment, including theatre gowns, ensuring everything is clean and sterile. I didn't realise how important it was until I began. You wore gloves, black enclosed shoes, a gown and net to cover your hair, and if you moved from one room to another, even if you just went to the toilet, you had to take everything off and put it in a bin, then put a new set to put on when you came back, and there were certain special soaps for hand washing.

In a way it was a bit like working in a factory, with staff at different tables doing different tasks, e.g. folding gowns. There was only one right way to do everything. If you got it wrong you had to re-do it. Gowns were folded in a particular way, and operating equipment was put together in a certain way. We worked to targets and it was really tough. You couldn't talk to each other, because you had to concentrate on what you were doing, so it was quite stressful and pressurised. It was interesting, but could really affect your health and there was a high turnover of staff. The pay scales were also weird, going from trainee to technician and then supervisor. In a way it was the same as sales. There were no subsidised meals and the hours were unsocial. There were three shifts, 7-2, 2-9 and 6-11, and these were rotated. You were on your feet all the time and the floor was hard. Because of not being able to talk, and also because of the commuting, there was no social life among the staff. We went for breaks at different times and I would feel bored being alone there. I would have liked to go on, but it was tiring and stressful so I only stuck it for two weeks.

I later had a job in market research, doing interviews over the phone, but it was only seasonal, so I got another job in Tunbridge Wells, with a health insurance company. The pay and benefits were good, likewise the hours and social life, and I am still in touch with some of the other staff. The prospects for promotion were also good, and in six months I was moved up, being amongst the top salespeople, but I came into conflict with another employee who tried to cause problems for me, probably because I was doing so well. He tried to push me down, so I asked for someone else to monitor my calls. They agreed with me, but did little about it.

It is a very big company, with branches all over the British Isles, and about 2,000 employees. I became more conscious here of being one of an ethnic minority. Despite the huge workforce, there were only about ten black or Asian staff, they never stayed long and there was no policy of actively recruiting from minority groups. My training group were a very mixed bunch. I was black, another girl Asian, and there was a gay guy and a couple of Australians, and all of us had strong sales backgrounds, so why didn't they stay?

Some people said they were scared of me at first, but why should they be when they didn't know me? I was probably employed because I have a good clear voice, but I was aware that people were wary of me. They judged me without knowing me. They were very set in their ways, and rather cliquey – if your face didn't fit, you were excluded. I guess they stereotyped people. Of course it was a very posh area, a bit snobbish, and very few black people lived nearby. This probably contributed to my becoming bored with the job, so I decided to go travelling again.

After travelling and working in Manchester, Anita started work in a call centre in Sheffield,

One of the worst places I worked at was a call-centre. Our department was customer service, but it was the very opposite of that. I was shocked during training by the attitude of the experienced staff who were really rude to the customers and sometimes put the phone down on them. I believed customer service meant providing a high service to a customer, but they didn't care, even if the people on the phone were in tears about their faulty washing machines or whatever. The attitude was – 'It's not our problem'. The turnover of staff was enormous. Of the 15 people in my training group, only one was left 12 months later.

I am now working and training at Sheffield Live Community Radio Station, presenting programmes and producing, and learning the technical side. It is a great opportunity, totally different from what I'd done before. It has been fun, and although I didn't know a soul when I first came to Sheffield, I have made friends.

My hours are variable. It was full-time at first, but now I do shows on Tuesdays and act as duty manager in the studio at weekends. In the New Year I shall do more producing, which will involve more time input. So my working life has moved from retail to care work to sales to hospital work and now media. Rather than say, sales, which I know I can do easily, I prefer to do something new and challenging, that I've never done before. Maybe I'll settle down one day, but not yet.

In comparing living in Sheffield to living in the South, I would say that people here have more time to talk to each other on a daily basis, i.e. on the street or in a shop. The pace of life is slower here than in the South, but having said that, the city of Manchester is fast becoming like the South, with the rush and busyness of London.

Work, study, and travel in England and Europe

'A' has also worked in all kinds of jobs, "on building sites 'firelining' (plasterboard and Rockwool), £25 a day, hard work", often studying at the same time. His studies took him to Spain where he worked to pay for his studies. Later he found work in Italy, "Then I moved to Milan. I was working three jobs", and back in Sheffield, at a call centre, as Anita did.

In 1982 I started work aged 16 in a fish and chip shop in Rotherham, working 40 hours a week for £1 per hour whilst studying physics, maths and art A levels. Chips were 18p a bag.

I did a computer operator course at Dinnington College at 17 and was paid £30 a week on placement at CDS in Sheffield - data processing for Curry's accounts. My managers were all excited about buying BT shares and the computers had big black TV screens with flickery green typing. The data was stored on big magnetic tapes a foot in diameter, hard discs as big as a car tyre with a disc drive as big as a washing machine with other data stored on cardboard punch cards. There was a pool of 30 women typists with typewriters and carbon paper.

On a daytrip to London I got a job at Macdonald´s, Victoria branch and moved down. I moved back after four months.

In 1984 I got on the Community Program Government Scheme three days a week digging, cutting grass etc. in church yards. Then I did a bit of paving, and landscaping and painting and studied computer aided design (City and Guilds) at night school.

Off I went again on my bike to London. I worked in the stores and packing at a Rolls Royce factory, then moved to the night shift as a machinist in the blade shop making turbine blades for inside the engines. I didn´t like the nightshift so I quit and stayed in North London working as a draughtsman (on a drawing board) at a marble factory, doing site visits to James Bond type houses in Mayfair and Kensington.

Back home to Rotherham for a couple of years as I had missed my friends. I started playing the trumpet, and got temporary jobs – the more temporary the better –often the companies' own permanent staff used to treat the temps badly. Then, driving cars, working part time, through a very respectable car auction. I was the first one to of the drivers to get the sack after nearly a year (I was also the only one who was declaring my earnings to the dole office – no coincidence there!)

The next day I got a job as a removal man earning £3.50 an hour, and enjoyed the hard work for a year, but eventually went back to college and studied Philosophy (Access course at Rotherham College) then found an European Union course: PETRA 2 for ´non university´ young people to learn Spanish and live and work in Spain. I was told I was lucky to have got on the course but then found that I was the only ´non university´ person on the course. There were a few Hooray Henrys who dined out on Daddy´s credit card all the time – I had saved the money for expenses working in a dog biscuit factory. I also worked as a waiter, cook and barman in Jerez and Valencia.

When I returned to Rotherham after the work placement I spent a while painting and decorating, factory work again and then on building sites ´firelining´ (plasterboard and Rockwool), £25 a day, hard work.

I decided to go to university and started Philosophy at Sheffield University, changed my degree to Philosophy and Spanish in year 2 and left for my 3rd year ´ERASMUS´ in Malaga. After a year I spoke Spanish well.

Then I moved to Milan. I was working three jobs; getting up at 4.00 am to open up the breakfast restaurant at a Japanese hotel, serving English breakfast to French pilots who all spoke to me in Spanish for some reason. Then at 8.30 I finished my shift and set off by car to teach English in an Italian secondary school for a few hours. The kids were really nice and the teachers didn´t mind them smoking – as long as they did it at the end of the corridor - how strange (when I was at school if they caught you doing that they were allowed to beat you with a stick).

After my morning job I journeyed back into Milan, had a bite to eat and in the afternoon taught businessmen, bank managers and councillors using the Westminster School´s own method.

I then got a fulltime job as a team leader at the Fiat Alfa Romeo call centre, which was a great experience. I met loads of people (women mainly) from all over the world. There was a team for every European language and a team for Brazil - the nights out were great. At work the bosses were all young and self important – they were allowed to smoke but no one else was. There was a huge canteen for the Alfa factory workers and the call centre staff got subsidised food – a three course Italian meal, for 17 pence, with wine or beer if you wanted, for another 17 pence. I made friends with the Sicilian and Calabrian chefs and they let me have an evening meal as well.

The down side really was that I had to spend all day on the phone with English people complaining, shouting or threatening me down the phone, usually about their broken Fiat. But I felt I was missing something. I was driving out at 8:00 am every morning to get to the call centre. So I took on private students, public relations and translation work, which was hectic. I was running a small ebusiness as a translator and getting to know the Italian tax system and the frustration of dealing with Italian bureaucracy.

I returned to the UK in 2001, I had skills now – I spoke Italian and Spanish fluently and got a job for a couple of years at the William Hill call centre for Internet enquiries as a multi lingual customer services adviser.

I found a Latin American group to play with, in the year before my next job in the offices of a factory in Sheffield as a multi lingual sales consultant – I did the job for a year and was laid off, but the trumpet playing was earning me a few pounds a week and the guys in the band were good friends by now so I could take my time to look for something else.

Julian *says "education really wasn't suited to me", and he hoped to get a first job as an apprentice. Like many of his generation he now works in an office.*

The civil servant

I'm not entirely sure where I should start, so I'll do what I do best and begin right at the very start and present a brief background of myself and my growing up. My name is Julian Paul Batty and I was born in Sheffield, in the snow of the 10th of January 1977 to my parents Charles Jeffrey and Jean Batty. I've been told of many things about my childhood, of which I actually recall little.

The first sketchy memories I can recall of my educational life were attending playschool as it was affectionately referred to. We were all subjected to activities such as cake decorating, painting for the under 5's and some sort of pasta gluing activity which I'm still not entirely sure holds any relevance for the big wide world. I met a number of what have later turned out to be good friends there, which undoubtedly I will know for the rest of mine or indeed their lives.

A little later in life I was introduced into the educational system proper! I was enrolled into Holmesfield Infant School and started out in my educational life. We undertook such things as basic reading and writing, playing Army at break times and running around in our underpants under the prescribed auspices of P.E., something that I would suggest does not go on in today's day and age.

Upon reaching the age to move on to my next level of learning I was transferred to Northfield Junior School. This move was particularly convenient for me being that the school was located just at the end of the road where I lived. Even at my then estimated height of three foot nothing, the daily trip took just minutes. I attended this school for four full years and despite being one of the few kids who were advanced to the 4th year of learning 12 months earlier than usual, I do seem to remember regularly being punished on varying occasions for differing types of mischief. My long term dread of the arrival of each parents' evening did initiate around this time.

And so, four years down the line, yet again another school change. This time, I prepared to take 'Big School' on and all the pros and mostly cons that go with it. The school I was enrolled into this time was Gladys Buxton Senior School. I have no idea who Gladys Buxton is, however I assume she must have been or have done something unique or important enough to have the local school named after her. This was the first time I experienced being a part of several classes with varying friends in each one, depending on different options selected for the educational subject, which we had previously chosen. I attended Gladys Buxton School for just two years before everyone was shipped out to join a larger school in the area named Gosforth Senior School. This school was much further away from home, so much so that I was required to get a flippin bus there and back daily.

Eventually I arrived at the age whereby the rest of my educational life would be in preparation for my final GCSE exams. I started attending Henry Fanshawe School. You may now know this as the

Dronfield School on the corner of the bottom of Green Lane and Chesterfield Road. I was taking a variety of different subjects and I hoped to be able to attain a reasonable level of knowledge and a reasonable final exam result for each, with the minimum of effort. If I'm being blatantly honest, and at this stage I already knew this, education really wasn't suited to me. I never shirked attending any classes however, nor did I waive the mind numbingly dull requirement of completing my homework to an acceptable level, (well a level which was deemed acceptable to me).

I did enjoy attending school, mainly to see friends, play football at break and dinner times and attempt to make each lesson entertaining or more accurately less dull, as I reasonably could.

I suppose my first experience of paid employment was when I took the standard teenage boys' task of delivering early morning newspapers from the local paper shop before school. I didn't particularly mind the task, but I've never been good at rising from bed in a morning. I delivered these newspapers around the village seven days weekly, pedalling my bike along whilst trying to out fox any domestic dogs awaiting my arrival through their front gate, and facing all kinds of weather notoriously common for the North end of England! My normal delivery route between Monday and Saturday paid me the princely sum of around £3.50 per week and then in addition I did a separate round on Sunday morning, which again paid me roughly the same (flippin newspaper bag was heavier tho!).

During my time at Henry Fanshawe School I was required to undertake a period of Work Experience. We were given the option of which employment sector we wished to experience. I plumped for an IT based company, loosely based upon the fact that I enjoyed playing computer games with friends and writing basic programmes for my Commodore Amiga. I was allocated a place with a good friend of mine at a company based in Bolsover, Chesterfield. The name of the company escapes me now, but doing an entire day's work quickly hit me hard! I obviously use the term 'work' loosely as my friend and I were probably no more than

14 years old at the time, but still, entering simple data onto a PC for hours on end did take its toll. I did, unfortunately in hindsight, find the placement very repetitive and uninspiring, so much so that based on that 'experience' I binned the thought of that particular long term occupational plan.

My second dabble in the big wide world of employment was when I was taken on by a local members' club to assist with the bar work. I was initially responsible for collecting and washing glasses, keeping customers' tables clear and clean and generally being the bosses' and committee members' working slave. In return, I did receive a reasonable amount of cash for the chore of working there (well more than the paper round paid me). I suppose all things considered it was worth it. I worked there with a number of friends, many of which I still keep in touch with. After a few years I was promoted to bar work, serving of customers and working the till. This promotion came with another appropriate wage increase, which was mildly appreciated. All in all, I enjoyed my time there and it was another feather in my employment cap.

Due to the disappointment I felt in the previous IT based work experience, I was offered the opportunity to undertake a further stint of work experience. This time I was offered a week long placement in the, now late, Lunn Poly organisation. The branch for which I would work was on Pinstone Street, across from the Peace Gardens in the centre of Sheffield. This week's experience was better. I started out undertaking basic roles such as filling the shelves with brochures and opening post, to being responsible later in the week for approaching customers and attempting to point them in the correct direction in relation to their holiday needs. I found the confidence to communicate with customers over the telephone. This I'm sure now doesn't sound too exciting, however, it would have been the first time I had ever spoken in a business like manner.

So after that brief stint, back to school it was for me, back to the early start of the paper round and back to the late finishes from working in the bar and welcome back to playing football three times daily! Within about a year, I was submitting my final pieces of coursework and preparing for my exams towards my GCSE grades. It was a difficult and stressful period as my folks were always drilling into me the importance of gaining good school grades as they would be a very important ingredient towards the mould which the rest of my life would fit. I was realistically happy with the grades I attained, I did especially well in both English and Maths, two subjects for which my folks were keen on me achieving a good grade.

Finishing school, I had to decide what would be best for my future. I had already decided that traditional education itself didn't really suit me and therefore I applied for a number of advertised youth trainee or apprentice style jobs. One in particular was back at Lunn Poly where I'd enjoyed my work experience period and another for a YTS place at a business travel company by the name of Wagonlit Travel. At the instruction of my mother, I had also applied for a place at Chesterfield College on their Business and Leisure Management course. I had not received any contact from either of the posts for which I applied by the time the course was due to commence, and so, I made my way over to the college to start the training course, which honestly, I didn't really want to do.

After about two weeks, I was asked to attend a formal interview at Wagonlit Travel. I prepared as best as I could, got myself all togged up, and for some reason, which I'm still not sure of today, I was strongly encouraged to sport this 'Pontins' style blue blazer with brass buttons over my shirt and tie. I looked hideous, but was reassured by my parents that such a look was what would be expected at a job interview, I grudgingly agreed to wear it. Just a few days later I received a phone call explaining that I was the successful applicant of the recruitment and was invited to start in my new job the following Monday.

I was elated! I was soon to be earning the sum of £29 per week, this of course would be in addition to the money, which I received for my paper round and that from working in the Club. I had never felt so wealthy!

In the summer of 1997, I applied for, and was successfully appointed as an Administrative Assistant in the Department for Education and Employment. Initially I worked for the Policy Team within the Careers and Development Directorate. My main duties were tasks such as taking meeting minutes, ensuring information was circulated around team management, in addition to basic tasks such as the ordering of stationery and photocopying documents in preparation for meetings and presentations.

I was keen to progress my career within the Department and fairly quickly exchanged my role for a post on the Careers Information Team. My primary duty was gathering careers advice and information from a number of sources and collating the documentation. I drafted pieces of work in preparation for entry into the Occupations 1998 publication and collated many sources of additional centres or points for further advice for differing occupational choices. For my work and efforts on this project I gained a credit in the final published draft as a writer / researcher.

Within the year I successfully gained promotion to the Administrative Officer grade and was posted into the Overseas Labour Service of the time. My primary role was to assess and consider Work Permit applications for overseas nationals to work in the UK in either the sporting or the entertainments field. I particularly enjoyed this role and travelled frequently with colleagues to meet with the governing bodies in various employment fields. As I am a football fan in my spare time, I felt particularly privileged when dealing with applications for high profile players and clubs. Occasionally I was required to meet up with football club officials such as managers and coaches to discuss the finer details of particular applications. I especially enjoyed this requirement of my role and still today maintain that such duties were the most enjoyable and satisfying of my working life.

After eight years, I was promoted to the role of Executive Officer. I was posted to manage a small team which dealt with applications for overseas nationals to continue and extend their permissions to stay and continue their working life in the UK. I am happy in my current role and continue to be positive about working within the organisation. I do have aspirations to continue to widen my horizons and hope to continue up the ladder of the organisation.

So far that is me. I'm still in the occupation most recently explained and am very happy being there. I'm sure given time many things will change, both in myself, and also internally and externally in the job. I do hope that I can continue in my quest to continue positively in my career and maybe one day a further book like this one may be released whereby, if you've enjoyed my story so far, you may be able to read how I've got on from now (wow! to read such an article now, for me, would be a great advantage). I hope you enjoyed reading this, I personally have enjoyed writing it.

Sheffield has not only been a great manufacturing city, it has also been a university city. The University of Sheffield was founded in 1905, by the amalgamation of three colleges in 1897, the School of Medicine (founded 1828), Firth College (1879), and the Sheffield Technical School (1884). Sheffield City Polytechnic became Sheffield Hallam University in 1992, and now the two universities teach 40-50 thousand students, and are among the top three employers in the city, with the National Health Service and the City Council. Students contribute much to the life of the city.

Generations of students began their careers here, and many of them liked the city so well that they remained here permanently.

'S.PO', a newly qualified doctor, tells us how she found herself following in her father's footsteps.

Medical training

My home is in Bedford but my mother was brought up in Sheffield and my grandparents still live here. My dad came to Sheffield University as a student, which is how he and my mother met. Dad is a doctor and mum a school nurse. Although I toyed with one or two other career options, I really always wanted to be a doctor. I chose Sheffield University because of having family here and knowing the city centre and the Peak District so well.

When I left school I did a gap year. For eight months I worked as a Health Care Assistant in a hospital in Bedford, doing basic patient care such as washing, dressing, and giving meals and hot drinks. I was on the Bank, covering for sickness, so worked on both medical and surgical wards. It was very satisfying work and useful to me now, because it helped me to relate to patients.

Later on in my gap year I spent six weeks in Borneo at an Orang-utan Rehabilitation Centre, doing construction and conservation work. We lived in a camp in the rain forest and washed in the river.

I've now been in Sheffield for six years. When I first came I lived in student accommodation in Broomhill, but now I share a house at Crookes with two others. I really like Crookes. When we lived at Broomhill we used to walk to the Bolehills on Sundays. We called it 'the end of the world' because of the view.

I qualified this summer and am now doing my F1 (Foundation1) year, which used to be called House Officer Year. The course lasted five years, initially with lectures and basics, then going on the wards, with placements in Worksop, Chesterfield and Barnsley. Talking to my dad, I realise how different the training and the job is now, from how it was in his day. I even had the chance to spend nine weeks in Vietnam, with some time in a hospital in a rural town and some time in the big Infectious Diseases Hospital in Ho Chi Minh City.

We are taught much more about communication skills to enable us to relate better to patients, who are far more informed than they used to be, and have often got information off the Internet and have many questions. Also there is much more paper work, and lots of form-filling. Every interaction we have with a patient has to be documented – "if it's not written down, it didn't happen".

We should work a 56 hour week according to the European Time Directive, but at present it is more than that. The Directive states that by April 2009, the working week should be reduced to 48 hours, but I don't see how we are going to manage that with present staffing levels. For me an ordinary day is 8 am to 4 pm, plus on-call cover one day a week, with every third weekend doing three 12 hour days.

I expected the work to be hard and a bit scary, and sometimes it is, but it's much better than when my dad started out. He had to handle so many situations alone, whereas we get lots of support. I've never been left alone to look after a ward at night. There are always some Senior House Officers or Registrars around, and a Consultant at the end of a phone.

This time next year I'll be applying for jobs. I'd prefer to stay in the North, but that may not be possible. There are doctors two years above me who are out of work. Every year 250 medics graduate from Sheffield, and 7,000 nationally. A team normally consists of one consultant, two registrars, two senior house officers and two first year house officers. Lots of house officers are needed, but fewer registrars and even fewer consultants, so the higher up the pyramid structure you go, the fewer jobs there are. I'm not sure what the future holds for me. I'll probably become a G.P., but I'd also like to work abroad for a while.

Patients nowadays have higher expectations than they used to. They know what service they should be getting and can vocalise it, and they look up stuff about their conditions on the internet. A while back a patient was really rude to me, which I found very upsetting, but recently when he was re-admitted, he apologised. The vast majority of patients are lovely, and that's what I like most about the job – talking to people.

Final words

What have we lost? What have we gained?

Days gone by

"My dad believed quality was everything, we'd try to better our craft whenever possible."

"- making the pewter blanks into beautiful pewter mugs."

"We were not well off – as children, my brother Jack and I had to stand at the table for meals, because we only had two chairs."

"I remember when my dad was on night turn he would take me with him to work, where I would stay, and sleep for the night in his cabin until morning."

"In the 1940's and 1950's if you were on the early turn before 6 am you would get a caller-up tapping on the bedroom window until you answered the caller."

"Just before we left school at 14, we were asked what we wanted to do. I desperately wanted to be a children's nurse, but I would have been the only girl in the class to say that, so I said the same as all the other girls, shop work, which is what I did."

"There were only three types of jobs for lads in our area at that time, the pits, the steel industry or the railways. I didn't want to go down the pit, and I'd always liked trains, being a keen trainspotter as a kid, so railways it was."

"Ladder work was largely a hit-and-miss affair and it very often meant that two or three short ladders had to be spliced together with rope in order for us to reach high enough to do the work."

"If anyone found that rare thing, a good, smooth nib that was not scratchy, they would keep it to themselves."

"The only equipment we had that could even vaguely be described as technological was a typewriter and a telephone."

"Serious minded men, with years of experience in their trades."

"It is difficult to believe now, looking back, that there was no single

person in charge. A woman in the warehouse (senior in work years) saw to the general routine."

"At that time in Sheffield 20,000 men would go fishing every Sunday."

"While you're talking to the gaffer you're not earning."

"The biggest crime was to cancel a passenger train."

"I thought this job was a 'fill-in' whilst I got a lorry driver's job. Little did I know I would be driving buses for 37 years."

"It now seems incredible that people would go out on a cold winter's night to listen to records in a library,"

"If we knew someone important was coming we made the beds, got everything perfect and told the patients - 'Don't move until Matron's been'. Most patients knew how terrified we were of Matron and did as we asked."

"If you wanted to get married, you had to ask matron's permission, and you had to leave nursing."

"There was more respect in those days, and less money."

"One manager called the workers greedy, but I said - "If it weren't for us, you wouldn't have a job"."

"I wouldn't want my daughter to be doing what I did, but in those days I just accepted it."

"Sometimes we couldn't breathe, sometimes we couldn't see. I hate anything that isn't right and I'm glad it's closed now. In this day and age people won't work like that, and I'm glad they don't."

"We had to work wearing our coats, hats and scarves, but it was fun. It was like home from home. Conditions were bad, but the atmosphere and the workmates were lovely."

"My dad made me a special lunch box in which to carry my snap and I've still got it to this day."

The end of a way of life

"As I look round at our Brightside and Tinsley deserts of land which were teeming with steel shops, it can be very depressing. When you enter the public houses in these areas there's photos and memorabilia on the walls showing what the steel shops used to be like."

"There were some men still working at the coal face at the age of 65."

"We only worked for six months after the strike."

"There was a general air in the department that if too much technical information was given to someone, then their own jobs could be at risk because from time to time during the five years, some mechanics were 'laid off' when there was insufficient work around."

"Privatisation –this brought the biggest change of all and had the biggest impact on our jobs and lives."

"Unfortunately, it was necessary for us to disclose our manufacturing secrets to these companies, who were previously our competitors, in order to ensure they achieved the quality levels we had developed and achieved in the UK over the last 110 years."

"The big closures of the Thatcher era caused many redundancies and men who were out of work would take anything. They would advertise for an apprentice and a skilled man, such as a toolmaker, would apply – it was heart-breaking."

"We were called into the office, asked to sign a piece of paper, and asked to leave the premises within the hour. I felt like a condemned man."

"The day I finished work we went on holiday, but it was odd to think – 'I've no job to go back to".

"When every day is a Sunday the time takes some filling-in."

And these days

"In 1956, it was utterly inconceivable that I could sit in my own home and create an article such as this, correcting typing errors, changing at will type sizes, *fonts,* <u>styles</u>, **bold**, *italic, colours and*

overall layouts,

in seconds!

just by tapping a few keys."

"Nurses are hard working. They've got a lot to put up with - the doctors to put up with, the relatives to put with - and now all the changes ever since the 1980's. Too much time on the computer, too much paper work."

"It is very hard work in those homes, which are always short-staffed and rely largely on agencies."

"When I was at the pit, I worked such long hours that I hardly saw my older children, and often rarely saw daylight, but with the youngest I could spend much more time. I remember when my eldest son told me he was getting married, I had no idea he'd even got a girl-friend."

"I discovered that the whole atmosphere of a working library had changed. We used to be told that from the following Monday we had been transferred to a different library, with no consideration as to travelling time or distance. It would be interesting to see the reaction this would cause today! Times certainly do change, and I think most would agree that what amounted to bullying of staff is unacceptable, but gone also to a great extent is respect for authority. What will the workplace be like in the future I wonder?"

"In my opinion South Yorkshire has changed for the better. Since the pits and steel works closed, families in general enjoy improved health, and also other improvements from looking at life from a different point of view. Once, young people were brought up to follow the same jobs as their dads and mums, but now they can go to college and learn different trades and professions. The younger generation are doing things their parents never dreamed

of, whereas if the pits were still open, they'd have gone into them."

Over his working life, Ken Hawley has always made a point of looking out for and collecting, unusual tools. This interest has resulted in what is possibly the most comprehensive collection of tools in the country.

"I've got a talent for silver work, so I've carried on. I've always said, these hands are mine".

"As with so many trades and professions, it is computers that have had the biggest impact on changing work practices during my lifetime."

As we wrote in the introduction,

"Sheffield, has gone through an extraordinary period of change since the 1940s, from being a major world centre of cutlery and hand tool manufacture, a city where thousands of men and women, many of them highly skilled, if without paper qualifications, were employed by the steel and heavy engineering industry, to what? We're not sure yet."

Sources of information

For most of the background information we used

'A History of Sheffield', by David Hey (1998)

'The History of the City of Sheffield, 1843-1993' (1993)

Also
'A Guide to the Industrial History of South Yorkshire', editor Derek Bayliss (1995)

'Sheffield Parks and Gardens' by Douglas Hindmarch (2005)

'Remember Sheffield in the fifties and sixties' by David Richardson (2002)

'Council house building in Sheffield, 1919-1970'. by Simon Ogden. Thesis in Sheffield Local Studies Library

'The South Yorkshire Coalfield, a history and development' by Alan Hill (2001)

'Behind the counter, shop lives from market stall to supermarket.' Pamela Horn (2006)

'Home from home, British Pakistanis in Mirpur' by Irna Imran and Tim Smith (1997)

Tinsley cooling towers erected 1938
demolished 2008

Glossary

Annealing   heat treatment of steel to soften it, by heating and cooling slowly.

Backer   operator who receives material which has been passed through a rolling mill. He returns it to the roller if more rolling is required.

Beck iron   a beak shaped tool, also the pointed end of an anvil, used for bending metal.

Bellows   A leather construction, which can be compressed, which forces the air within through a metal tube (a twyer or tueiron) into a forge or blacksmith's hearth.

Blank   a stamping of metal requiring further work to finish.

Bosh   a container of fluid, ie water, oil or similar. Used for quenching a heated item for rapid cooling, this is re ferred often referred to as hardening or tempering.

Bull week   the week prior to a recognised holiday when workers would work at maximum production to receive maximum money.

Burnish   a smooth steel tool used with much pressure, by hand, to bring a high polish to an item, which then resists corrosion.

Calender   machine in which cloth or paper is pressed by rollers to glaze or smooth it.

Capstan lathe   a machine for shaping revolving metal into a required shape with a series of pre-set cutting tools.

Chamfer   a bevel or angle.

Cogging   using a power hammer to form a required shape. Forging or rolling steel.

Cross roll   a method of extending width of metal sideways, for forming extra width for spoon bowls.

Cuckoos   work rejected, and sent back to be put right.

Datal   a person paid by the hour/day/week, as against piecework (paid by the item). Also a slang expression for someone slow or dilatory.

Donkey stone   a fairly soft fawn coloured stone, used for decorating steps and window sills of houses. Sometimes whitening was used instead.

Drawing   reducing the diameter of steel wire or rod by forcing through steel dies.

Fash   a rough edge produced during manufacture of an article.

Fashing   removal of this unwanted protrusion

Fettling   cleaning metal castings with a pneumatic chisel.

The Finishing of metal

1. Grinding, first process in the finishing and polishing of a metal piece. Gritstone or sandstone grinding wheels were used until they were replaced by synthetic abrasives (carborundum) in the 1920s. (grinder)
2. Glazing, the next process, using a wooden wheel covered in leather or hide, dressed with glue and emery. (glazer)
3. Buffing, following process, polishing the metal further using a wooden wheel, and a hide surface dressed with buffing sand (pumice). (buffer)
4. Polishing, Final process, using cloth dollies, and polishing compound.
   A dolly being a number of calico discs clamped together and revolving on a spindle.

Firth Staybrite a patented form of stainless steel, an alloy with nickel chrome, which lacks cutting properties.

Fly a hand operated machine, sited on a bench, used for cutting, punching and bending small items.

Gaffer foreman, manager, supervisor, or often the boss.

Ganister/ gannister a mixture of grit or hard sandstone and fireclay found with some coal seams, eg at Parkwood Springs, used for making crucible pots and furnace linings.

Gross 144 items.

High speed steel a steel alloy containing cobalt, capable of cutting and drilling other materials at high speed, without losing its hardness or temper, used for making tools.

Linishing a method of finishing a metal piece by applying it to a (linen) belt covered in abrasive material.

Little mester a self employed craftsman.

Milling machine a machine for shaping a piece of metal by using revolving cutters.

Pickle to immerse metal items in strong acids to remove oxides, and scale.

Pyrometer an instrument for measuring very high temperatures, eg in a furnace.

Sheffield type press a machine, with a flywheel approx 4-5 feet in diameter, driven by a motor and a heavy 5-6 inch width belt. Rotary motion is converted to reciprocal motion to press metal into a required shape, using steel dies.

Shot blasting using a violent blast of air to force shot or sand onto a material to remove oxide, paint to produce a better finished surface.

Special steels   steel alloys used in the tool and aero industry, also stainless steel.

Stamping   shaping metal with a heavy hammer, free falling, but raised by a power driven belt and pulley. (hammer driver)

Tapping   pouring molten steel or iron from a furnace.

Teemer   a man who pours molten metal from a crucible or a ladle into a mould allowing it to cool into a permanent shape.

Tup   striking head (steel block), part of a steam or belt driven hammer, raised high, then released onto a piece of metal to be formed into a special shape. Similar to a drop stamp.